From ...
To: Doll Hospital
Naples
28 Oct 2021

OSPEDALE DELLE BAMBOLE · NAPOLI · DAL 1895

i

ACKNOWLEDGEMENTS

A special thanks to Alessandra de Tilla for jump starting my writing career after a seven-year hiatus. Through her unwavering support and encouragement, I was reintroduced to my love for the written word.

Ben Cox, the first reader of the initial chapters of this manuscript. Thank you for seeing the merit in it long before I did.

Patrice Gaines. For nearly thirty years, she believed in this story. Thank you for believing in me and this project for so many years.

The Children of My Knee

The Children of My Knee

A Memoir by Len Cooper

www.lencooper.eu
ISBN: 1542740770
ISBN-13: 9781542740777

Contents

INTRODUCTION

CHAPTER 1... IN MY FATHER'S HOUSE 1

CHAPTER 2... RESPECTFULLY DISRESPECTED 7

CHAPTER 3... THE FARM 13

CHAPTER 4... IRRELEVANCY 23

CHAPTER 5...HOPE AGAINST HOPE 55

CHAPTER 6... FROM BLACK TO WHITE 57

CHAPTER 7... WHAT ABOUT YOUR FRIENDS 63

CHAPTER 8... A LEAP FROM DEAR'S FAITH 69

CHAPTER 9... THE POOL 76

CHAPTER 10... THE SINS OF MY FATHER'S 88

CHAPTER 11... SAY GOOD-BYE TO LOVE 92

CHAPTER 12...THIS IS NOT MY HOME 186

CHAPTER 13... HOW LOVELY IS THY DWELLING PLACE 195

CHAPTER 14... LIFELINES 202

CHAPTER 15... MY LAST GASP 207

CHAPTER 16... ASKED AND ANSWERED 214

CHAPTER 17... JERUSALEM 217

CHAPTER 18... THE YMCA 224

CHAPTER 19... THE WASHINGTON POST TO JERUSALEM 227

CHAPTER 20... MARRIAGE AND THE FAMILY 319

CHAPTER 21... DEATH AND DYING 346

CHAPTER 22... THE SECRET 378

CHAPTER 23... O' BLESS ME FATHER 382

EPILOGUE... Page 388

Dedicated to my parents Annie Marie Walker
and Archie Lee Cooper.
Through difficult times, together they
taught me the true meaning of forgiveness
redemption.

Some of the names are changed in this memoir

Introduction

The title "The Children of My Knee" is derived from the term "knee baby," which was used primarily by blacks in the Old South in reference to the next to the youngest child.

I am not the knee baby in my family. I am the youngest child of three brothers close in age. But I suppose in many respects my life has been a reflection of the role cast upon the knee baby, a life that's conflicted and filled with contradictions, a sense of feeling you never quite fit in.

My mother often talked about how the day she first brought me home from the hospital. Alfred, my middle brother, had a difficult time adjusting to a less prominent place in her life. His days of suckling came to a rapid conclusion upon my arrival once his place in my mother's arms was to be shared or reserved primarily for me. Alfred became the knee baby, longing for days gone by, relegated to hanging on to my mother's knee, begging for lost attention, attention that was reserved for me, the newborn.

Yet this was early in life and perhaps the only time I felt special. Even as I wrote this book, I went to sleep one night and had a dream (or experience—because it appeared so real) that my relationship with God is like that of a knee baby. I express anger, loathing, and yes, even contempt for Him and still I have made nearly 50 trips to Jerusalem, hanging around the foot of the throne of God.

CHAPTER 1: IN MY FATHER'S HOUSE

Sunday, September 15, 1963. I remember it clearly, though more than 50 years have passed. The cool of the Birmingham morning was slowly surrendering to the scorching heat. The trees and high grass were loaded with cicadas, katydids and locusts. Their cacophony of sounds competed with the faint chimes playing "Just as I Am" from the church in the distance: *Just as I am, Lord, Just as I am.*

Church was a respite from all of the commotion going on around us. Leaders of the civil rights movement instructed all Negroes to stop shopping at the stores in downtown Birmingham and people complied. Some folks said business downtown was so slow now that you could see grass growing between the cracks in the sidewalk.

I stood by the ripped screen door, waiting to go to Sunday school at New Salem Baptist Church with my two older brothers. I was 10 years old. In the front bedroom Daddy was laying on the quilt made by hand a long time ago by my grandmother Muh, friends in the neighborhood, and Dear, which is the name my older brother gave my mother when he was three years old. Dad was watching one of those Sunday morning religious television shows he hated and taking an occasional drag off an unfiltered Camel cigarette. Sometimes he let me roll those cigarettes. I loved the smell of the tobacco as I licked the thin, white paper to seal the job after returning the excess tobacco back to the colorful tin can.

"Those preachers with their prayer cloths, healing potions and highfalutin talk are nothing more than charlatans and thieves," Dad said.

Dear cringed. Not only was she a Christian but she was also a devoted church worker, one of the stalwarts in the choir. Whenever the doors of the church were open, Dear was there. When the choir director asked her to lead a song at the 11 o'clock service, she displayed mild displeasure, but everyone knew how important the choir singing and this brief moment in the limelight were to her.

1

"Don't talk like that in front of the boys!" Dear said to my father. "You ought to know better. The Lord don't like ugly."

For Daddy, those religious TV shows were strictly entertainment and nothing more.

"Tell that to those lying ass, thieving preachers," he said, taking another puff off his roll-your-own before sending a wobbly smoke ring into the stuffy Alabama air.

"Damn preachers' hair all slicked back with Murray's pomade, heads so full of grease it's a wonder they don't slip and slide right off the pulpit and break their necks."

I wanted to laugh but I knew better. With my brothers scurrying around trying to get dressed in their Sunday church clothes, this was not the time to upset Dear. The men in my church wore denim overalls and blue jeans, but Dear insisted we look our best in God's presence. My older brothers, Archie Lee, Jr. and Alfred Lloyd, were already dressed for church and decided to go on without me because I was making them late. My shoes weren't quite dry, my hair wasn't combed and my face still had to be greased down with Vaseline.

Dear went back to the kitchen to check on my shoes. Her tall and slender frame stretched over the porcelain counter as she tried to wash the black Griffin shoe polish along with the sole and heel dressing stains from her hands. Occasionally, she checked the remaining pair of not quite dry leather shoes as she hummed the gospel tune she had been rehearsing for days. Meanwhile, Dear also watched the blue flame lap at the old pressing comb with the burnt handle, which rested atop one of the two working burners on the stove.

When the hot iron was heated enough, Dear slid it through her shoulder length, black hair, which sizzled as clusters of smoke floated toward the ceiling. The smoldering Dixie Peach pressing oil filled the house with a familiar smell. Every Sunday Dear went through her hair ritual, which took what seemed like hours. Once she had her hair fixed just the way she wanted it, she slapped one of her two cheap wigs on. Dear's long beautiful, black hair was much nicer than any old fake hairpiece. I often told her how pretty her natural hair was. But the compliment would have meant a lot more coming from Daddy, who only had nice things to say to Dear on rare occasions or after he thought we children were in bed asleep.

I continued waiting by the screen door, trying to blend in with the dark wire mesh and not be noticed by Daddy or Dear. Sundays were serious and no time to laugh at Dad's bad mouthing of God's servants. But our house had a lot in common with other houses on Sunday: the women did, children were made to do, and the men watched the doing.

My brothers decided to go on without me and I was late for Sunday school. The walk to our church was a short one. I dilly-dallied, fascinated with the bumblebees dancing and darting about the yellow and white honeysuckle bushes. It was a sweet, sweet Birmingham morning -until Dear's voice cut through my lackadaisical mood and stung me.

"If you don't get away from there, it's going to be too wet to plow!" This was Dear's way of saying that the tears I would shed after a good whipping would soak the earth.

At that very moment a huge noise cracked the air. It sounded like a thousand locomotives crashing. The earth shook. I turned toward the house. I saw terror on Dear's face as she peered through the window. Her words froze in her mouth. I stumbled, falling and crying, away from the sound, back toward the house. I fell into the screen door, ran past Daddy, stopping only after I reached Dear's arms.

"I ain't never heard no noise like that before," Dear said, pulling me closer to her.

Dad, startled, ran out the door cursing, seething with anger. I thought he was mad because the noise kept him from watching his Sunday morning TV shows. Then I heard him spit out Martin Luther King's name, as if it was a bad taste in his mouth. "I'll bet a dime to a bucket of bullshit that Wallace or Bull Connor is behind this," he grumbled. "Where in the hell is that *King* now?"

Dear nodded in agreement. Ever since those civil rights people came to town and she lost her job as a cleaning woman, Dear had few favorable comments about King and his ideas of equality. It seemed King frightened everyone with his talk of freedom. Dear said all King's speeches did was get her and some of our neighbors fired by the white people they worked for.

"Those are just words," Daddy said. "If they don't mean shit to white people, you know damn well they don't mean nothing for us. All that niggah is doing is stirring up trouble and causin' decent people to lose they jobs and what little credit they got. When white folks start kicking our ass, where he gon be? I'll tell you. Somewhere away from here marchin' or makin' one of those damn speeches."

.

"I'm gonna go see what the hell happened," Daddy said, his voice quivering. "Ya'll stay here and don't open the damn door for nobody." He slammed the door behind him. "Nobody, damn it!"

Dear rocked me in her arms. "Everything is going to be alright after while," she said. "Everything gonna be alright after while."

She said this over and over so many times I had to look at her mouth to see if she was singing or talking.

Minutes ticked by. We couldn't tell if the loud noise came from down the street, downtown, or from across town. Some of the men from our street congregated in front of our house. Some of them were Dad's drinking partners. They seemed to agree that the sound was definitely an explosion, maybe a bomb. But no one could figure out where the sound had come from.

We listened for clues, for screaming sirens, police cars or ambulances. There was nothing. Dear turned up the sound on the radio she played softly each Sunday morning. At first it was the usual gospel music but then we heard the announcer say: "The 16th Street Baptist Church has been bombed."

As a child I thought: How could that be? The church was where God lived. No one in his right mind would blow up God's house.

Then we heard: "From the WJLD news desk, this just in. Four little girls are believed to be dead, killed while attending Sunday school at the 16th Street Baptist Church."

I tried to imagine this. In my mind, I figured out they were probably girls about my age. I imagined four small bloody, twisted bodies lying lifeless under piles of brick and mortar.

Tears streamed down Dear's face. I wiped some of them away with my small hands. But I was scared. My jaws locked, my stomach quaked and my chest felt as if it was going to cave in. Little lines of sweat trickled down my face. "Maybe they are coming for us next," I thought.

About this time Daddy stomped through the house, waving his shotgun and screaming, "The bastards ought to be killed, and they'll wind up going free!" He said he heard someone say, "Dr. King shares the blame for those four girls' deaths."

Before the day was over we heard more about what had happened. At 10:22 a.m., a bomb exploded in the downstairs basement where Sunday school was held. My friends Anna Iris and Alfred Knight were injured in the blast, but not severely. Both came to school the following day wearing white bandages on their arms and legs. Addie Mae Collins, Denise McNair, Cynthia Wesley and Carol Robertson were the four little girls who died, crushed to death by a hatred that had suffocated Birmingham for as long as my young mind could remember. We had come to accept that this was the way life was in the South.

But now four dead girls did what thousands of us living children had been unable to do. Their killings captured the attention of the world, which seemed astounded that anyone could hate black skin so intensely that they would blow up children.

The message scheduled to be heard at church that morning was "The Love that Forgives."

Although one senseless act of violence catapulted my hometown and the plight of blacks in Birmingham to the front pages of major news organizations all across the world, the local newspapers did not mention the bombing nor the four tender lives lost under walls of brick rubble. The lack of newspaper print did not make a difference in my life. I knew what happened and I would never forget, which meant in some way that morning would never end for me. I was a child who before that day could not fathom such hatred. Yet that one morning made me a prisoner of fear because it showed me that white people could kill me when and wherever they wanted to. They could pluck me right out of the hand of God Almighty at any time.

I pressed my head deeper into Dear's bosom and heard her heart beating, hard.

After Sunday, September 15, 1963, it seemed to me that whites outside of Birmingham were more sympathetic to the cause of civil rights and less vicious toward black people. There was also for a while a noticeable decrease in bombings in black neighborhoods throughout the city.

Looking back today, I see a collage of fear. A 10-year-old boy resting his forehead against the frame of that screen door, my mother Dear behind me, the woman who loved me dearly but could not always protect me from my father's wrath. In front of me, I see the winds and hell of racial alienation. There was no refuge for me, no place to hide.

Years later, I wonder if my search for a home for my heart was fed significantly by this hatred in Alabama and that unbelievably cruel Sunday. One day I would flee from my native town only to find that a change in physical location offered limited reprieve for such a deep aching of the soul. Every heart longs for a place to feel safe, a land where it can be loved and nurtured. My heart began to long for this even before my mind could comprehend the nagging, haunting hurt.

CHAPTER 2: RESPECTFULLY DISRESPECTED

In the heat of the civil rights struggle there were constant reminders of who was in charge. We saw Gov. George C. Wallace's grimacing face on posters throughout the littered landscape of the neighborhood. When Martin Luther King, Jr. came to town I held him in greater contempt because he was black like me and should have been more respectful of whites - or at least careful. Black people around me said that King and Wallace were two of a kind because whenever they were involved in anything that had to do with colored folk, Negroes ended up being fired, imprisoned, or dead.

King frightened people, both black and white, with his rhetoric of freedom, equality and inclusion. These words were hollow and meaningless when pertaining to blacks in Birmingham. Besides, we were already free as long as we didn't make trouble for white folk and stayed to our own. What I witnessed was Negroes worrying that King's presence would trigger whites to use even greater violence against us.

Dear and Daddy were neither Uncle Toms nor handkerchief heads, who kissed up to white folk for special favors. They, like many other people, shackled their lives to what they saw as reality. White people ran the world, hired people for jobs, and made and enforced the laws. They owned the land for the most part, and the factories and stores.

"Calling them names and out of their names isn't gonna change nothing," said Dear, who was angry with Dr. King for publicly criticizing white people. "That Negro is old enough to know better," she said.

Born Annie Marie Walker in Cuba, Ala., near the Mississippi state line, Dear had lived in Alabama all of her life and knew the restrictions the Jim Crow laws placed upon her. Although her grandfather, Professor Henry James Walker, was the first Negro to own a cotton gin in the state and prospered as a landowner, most of his sons and daughters refused to tie their lives to the soil; refused to plow, plant and reap what they considered to be the bitter harvest of Negroes on their own land. So eventually, most of the land fell out of their hands.

Was it stolen? Taken for taxes? Given away? Sold? No one in the family seems to know.

Dear's father, Samuel Walker-Daddy-Yo" to us -- left the farm and headed for the big city of Birmingham with his wife and baby Annie Marie, seeking new opportunities.

In the 1930s, Birmingham was a booming town. The steel mills were going up; it was a railroad center and a man could earn a living. Of course, black men were given the dirtiest and lowliest paid jobs in the mills, but at least they had jobs. By 1950, the median income for blacks in Birmingham was the third highest in the nation, falling behind Atlanta and Washington, D.C. Black businesses were being started and prospering. Most notably in Birmingham were those of A. G. Gaston, whose banking and insurance payroll exceeded one million dollars at the time of the bombing. Daddy-Yo was a successful contractor and Dear grew up in comfortable circumstances-until she married Daddy.

Daddy-Yo hated Archie Lee Cooper. He thought this tall, chocolate-colored, bean pole-of-a-"niggah" ruined his daughter. Dear got pregnant before "jumping the broom." Daddy, of course, did the right thing and married Dear. In spite of marriage, Daddy-Yo never forgave Dear or Daddy, so neither of them ever shared his riches.

Daddy-Yo didn't believe in accumulating debts. Every two or three years he bought a brand new Mercury and truck, paying cash for both. He invited his grand boys over and spread scores of hundred dollar bills on the floor for them to play in. But if his daughter needed money for rent or the children, he made it clear she was not to come to him.

Dear didn't complain. She loved her husband and with him struggled to provide for their three sons -Archie Lee Cooper, Jr., Alfred Lloyd Cooper and me, Leonard Lanier Cooper. I've never understood why I was named after a famous southern white poet, Sidney Lanier, or for that matter why my brother was named after the British poet Alfred Lord Tennyson. Dear changed the middle name for religious reasons, because she thought it would be sacrilegious to spell it the Biblical way, as Tennyson did. The irony of these names is that as far as I can tell there was never poetry in Dear's life; a life restrained by racism, poverty and the abuse of a drunken husband.

Dear and Daddy slept in a large bed in the living room. My oldest brother slept in the bed in our shared bedroom, my middle brother slept on the mattress, while I slept on a pallet. In time, I shared a mattress on the floor with my middle brother. For those two rooms, my parents paid $22 a month. Sometimes, Dear and Daddy didn't have the money and were late paying the rent. On those occasions, our landlord Mr. Spanno, a stout, ruddy Italian, came by to collect. If our door was unlocked, he'd walk right in shouting at the top of his lungs, "Marie, where is my money!"

Apparently, Mr. Spanno never heard the reverend's sermons on patience and benevolence or maybe his Italian Catholic church didn't hold the word of God in such lofty esteem. Mr. Spanno also owned the neighborhood grocery store where we sometimes got provisions on credit. It got so hot in his little dingy store that the penny suckers melted and fused together right in the glass case. Mr. Spanno put chunks of the broken cluster of sweets along with the cardboard sticks in a small brown paper bag and sold it for a nickel, right next to the two-for-a-penny butter cookies.

Dear sent me to Mr. Spanno's store when the rent was overdue and when food was getting low. I entered his shop with a few coins in hand and Dear's excuses for not having the rent money resting on my lips.

Mr. Spanno didn't bother to say hello. "Tell your momma and daddy I want my money the first of every month. Not the second or the third, but the first. I don't want to have to go looking for them. Now you run along and tell your momma what I said."

I can't recall which was more humiliating, Mr. Spanno embarrassing me in front of our neighbors or his showing up in our house to collect his money. We had become accustomed to living with this kind of disrespect and it seemed natural as air.

Even Daddy-Yo, a well off -if not wealthy-contractor, could not escape the chilly winds of the southern way of life.

Every Christmas, Arnold Drennen, a prominent attorney in Birmingham, paid Daddy-Yo a visit. Respectfully, we all called him "Lawyer Drennen" and Daddy-Yo, who described him to us as "a friend of the family," called his close friend "Sir." Daddy-Yo trusted Lawyer Drennen, yet I found it strange that I was taught a white man could never have a Negro for a close acquaintance.

Muh spent half the day cleaning when the Drennens planned to stop by. She never bothered with putting a tree up at Christmas. In the living room window she strung large multi-color lights in the shape of a tree. In all the windows facing the street she had fancy white plastic candelabras with blue flickering lights. The entire house radiated with the smell of oranges, grapefruits and assorted nuts. Hung on the mantle were three red and white stockings for me and my brothers. One year I made Dear and Muh's gifts in art class at school. I covered an apple with clove spice and placed it in a nylon mesh bag, which made the kitchen smell sweet and fresh. Muh and Dear loved it.

Everything in Muh's and Daddy-Yo's house was special. Daddy-Yo and a friend built the brick house from the foundation to the roof. The entire house had sparkling hardwood floors that Muh cleaned and shined every week. Our house had fragments of mix-matched crumbling linoleum. Muh's living room furniture included a white French provincial sofa and chair covered with plastic, all bought at Haverty's, the most prestigious furniture store in Birmingham in the 60's and a store that advertised home furnishings from Europe. In addition to his house, Daddy-
Yo also owned three tenant houses with two renters in each house. Lawyer Drennen and his family always stopped by on the way home from Christmas shopping, long before the streetlights came on. Every year he greeted Daddy-Yo the same way. "Hey there Sam boy, good to see ya."

"Come on in, make yourself at home," Daddy-Yo replied.

I thought that maybe the lawyer was fond of Daddy-Yo's money and didn't particularly care for him. I witnessed the same exchange every year.

"We can't stay; we just wanted to stop by and drop a few things off for you and your family," the lawyer said.

Mrs. Drennen always seemed nervous and said little, if anything. She and the son stood by the door, as if poised for a quick exit.

"We got some chitlins, maws, tongue, feet, pig tails and mountain oysters (hog testicles) for y'all," Mr. Drennen said.

"We sho' do appreciate it, sir," Daddy-Yo said, as he took the huge bag and handed it to Muh.

"My people won't eat this kind of stuff and it's a shame for it to have to go to waste. I knew you all like this sort of thing so we just drove over to drop it off."

With that, Mr. Drennen and his silent wife and son left.

Daddy-Yo owned a 300-acre farm 31 miles from his house, where he grew corn, beans and cotton and had cattle and more than 60 hogs. He sold the lawyer the pigs he slaughtered every winter. At any time Daddy-Yo could have had the finest portion of the shank or the parts that repulsed the lawyer and his family. Nonetheless, smiling, always smiling, Daddy-Yo graciously accepted his porcine gifts along with five dollars for each of his grand boys.

All of the adults seemed oblivious of the effect this exchange was having on us children. After all, the adults had layers of mangled thinking that needed to be straightened out before they could even understand how sick this relationship between these two men was. And it would take years, history and laws to assist and often force men to look at the wrongs they were committing. I am not convinced that even today most men understand the horrific ripple effect of what were seen as ordinary-even viewed as kind-exchanges. So no one paid any attention to me or my brothers, witnesses to this white man's diminishing of the patriarch of our family year after year.

I can tell you, though, as the man who grew from that little boy who stood at the door and watched Daddy-Yo accept, smiling, what the white man did not want, there is hell to pay for such witnessing. Each year I became more and more certain that one day I would escape Birmingham and never return. I didn't know how or where I would go. But I did know the ground I was birthed on would swallow my spirit if I did not flee as fast as any runaway.

CHAPTER 3: THE FARM

My grandfather believed the only way for Negroes to survive the harsh yoke of Jim Crow was for them to develop strong moral character and adhere to "strict discipline" when it came to work. Daddy-Yo's strict discipline was usually defined through long hours of picking cotton, chopping cotton, slopping hogs and stripping cane, working us until we literally dropped. Fevers, headaches, cuts and bruises couldn't save us from those endless hours, toiling in those dusty fields or slaving on one of Daddy-Yo's many construction work sites.

One time Daddy-Yo and his crew tore the roof off a dilapidated house that needed replacing. It was my job to load the scrap wood on to the back of his red and gray flatbed Ford truck. I was in the seventh grade. The splintery wood was riddled with wire and protruding, bent, rusty nails. Grandfather knew the hidden dangers in the heap but never expressed any particular interest for our safety or wellbeing. I was used to having wasp and bee stings, scrapes and even having wooden splinters embedded an inch into my flesh. Some of the injuries I endured as a child would probably have brought tears from the eyes of the toughest jocks in school. I barely winced at any pain until that day when I was given the task of loading Grandfather's truck.

I had hardly begun loading the truck when I felt the point of a sharp nail boring through the sole of my right sneaker. At the time, all of my weight was shifted to my right leg, which caused the nail to penetrate that much deeper.

"Owwwweeeee!" I yelped, as Daddy-Yo and one of the workers emerged from the vacant house to see what all the commotion was about.

I lay on the ground. The worker looked down at my foot, which was connected to a 2"-by-4" block of wood by a single nail. He scowled as he shook his head, and then turned to return to the house.

Daddy-Yo tried to pull out the board with his hands. I didn't cry until I saw him remove his silver hammer with the black rubber grip from the loop in his overhauls. Daddy-Yo braced one end of the board against his foot and in one monster strike of the block with the hammer, my foot was free.

Later, my grandfather said the nail had bored nearly two inches into my foot.

At the time, he demanded, "Boy, stand up!" He yanked me to my feet by the collar of my shirt. "Walk over there and back."

I hopped two or three steps on my good foot with the injured foot twisted over to the side.

"Skillet, don't make me tell you again!" Daddy-Yo hollered. He called me by this nickname throughout his life. I once asked him why and he said, "When your momma brought you home from the hospital, you looked like a big piece of black coal wrapped in a blanket. The only thing I knew that was as dark as coal was an old black skillet, so I decided to call you "Skillet.'"

After the nail accident, it would have been nice for my grandfather to have shown a little concern for me. This wasn't Daddy-Yo's way. There was no consoling, no doctor's visits, just a stern gaze of disappointment.

"Hush that crying boy before I give you something to cry about," he yelled. "Now git back to work!"

There were times when not even the prospect of going to church on Sunday offered my brothers and I a reprieve from work. Daddy-Yo had no use for churches, preachers or their misguided rituals. Those sandy burrows and terraces in the land were his only focus. When I was nine, my brothers and I worked the fields in the unrelenting Alabama heat, the dust and the flies.

We spent many grueling mornings and exhausting evenings picking cotton and working on Daddy-Yo's farm. Old folk call this working from "kin see to can't see," which translates into working from sun up to sundown. We learned to hate that farm, although it provided fresh fruits, vegetables, meats, honey and some recreation. The price for such luxuries was much too high for young boys who preferred spending time playing ball or catching crayfish in the neighborhood creek. To this day, my oldest brother says the farm and Daddy-Yo robbed us of our childhood.

During the summer months, Daddy-Yo got us up at the crack of dawn while the dew was still fresh on the tall grass. The three of us piled on the back of his opened flatbed truck. Daddy-Yo drove in excess of 80 miles per hour on the mountainous highway. His Blount County farm was far from our home. In the dead of winter we assisted granddaddy in slaughtering the livestock. If he had too many male pigs, we wrestled them down to the ground, sliced the testicles out with a sharp knife and poured motor oil over the wound. We were too young to have any regard for the pigs. We did as told and we knew that people paid top dollar for "mountain oysters."

When the day was done, we strolled through the pasture, collecting dried cow manure in huge burlap bags. People in town and in the rural country made what they called "miniweed tea" from the dried dung. This concoction was used to treat severe colds and flu. Once we made a delivery to a home where a man was so sick he could hardly hold his balance as he bent over clutching his chest while coughing violently, the congestion rumbling in his throat. He could not wait for his wife to make the tea. He yanked the bag from our hands, reached in and started chomping down on one of the dried chips. My brothers and I gazed at one another in total disbelief.

We were subjected to all kinds of home remedies, ranging from fighting a cough by sucking on a wad of Vicks VapoRub or, believe it or not, by tying a key around your neck and letting it hang down your back to stop a nosebleed.

On one of those rare occasions when all three of us were in the cab of the truck, my middle brother and I fought over who would change the gears as Daddy-Yo drove.

"Sit back and shut up!" Daddy-Yo warned.

We continued our arguing.

"I told you to sit back and shut up!" Daddy-Yo yelled one more time.

My brother and I were too involved in our screaming and jostling to pay any attention to our granddaddy. When we finally arrived at the farm, Daddy-Yo hopped out the truck and picked up an old piece of garden hose he found lying beneath the back porch. He took out his pocketknife, the one he used to clean orange pulp from his dentures, and cut the hose in one 10-foot strip and doubled it end to end. By this time my brother and I were silent and watching.

"Take off your shirt," he ordered, staring at me. "Go over there and stand against that oak tree and hug it. I'm gonna give you one lick and I'm gonna give Alfred one. I told you to sit back and shut up."

I didn't think much of this because I was accustomed to whippings.

Alfred taunted me by bugging his eyes and lifted his eyebrows up and down from afar as I buried my face in the coarse tree bark.

"Shut your eyes," Daddy-Yo ordered.

I knew at this point to hesitate in complying with his command would only make matters worse. Now Muh and Archie had joined Alfred in looking. No one said a word.

Suddenly the hose crashed across my back. My back felt like it had exploded. My skin was a melting inferno. I slid down the tree to my knees.

Daddy-Yo stood over me. I still faced the tree on my knees I tasted bark in my mouth and tried to spit it out.

"I dare you to move. I don't want to hear a whimper or a cry," Daddy-Yo said.

Alfred saw the two, one-inch wide welts stretching the width of my back like two serpents burrowing beneath my skin. He tore towards the woods, not to return until after dark. Meanwhile, Muh managed to calm Daddy-Yo, sparing Alfred his punishment. I wasn't angry about Muh's intersession. Archie and I were always protective of our middle brother. He was viewed by us as the most fragile of the three of us. I was happy he had been spared. And I knew that Muh had no choice but to go along with Daddy-Yo. That is the way it was. I could not imagine her doing otherwise.

I was mad at Daddy-Yo, but I was always mad at him. He was a ruthless, hateful, brutal man, and my disgust and love for him seemed to coexist for years until his death.

My brothers and I wanted to experience those long, fun-filled days of summer we heard other kids talk about. But every day during the summer months and weekends while school was not in session we were shackled to Daddy-Yo's land. There was never a discussion of pay or special consideration for our labor during all of those years. Occasionally, he gave us a 32-cents check he received in the mail from his bank. He promised that the land would someday be ours-and we believed him. But that never happened. Instead, when he died the land was surrendered to strangers and to his mistress.

Before that day came, I occasionally reminded Daddy-Yo, "Mr. Lincoln freed the slaves more than a hundred years ago. We are not slaves."

"Mr. Lincoln ain't freed no slaves," my grandfather snarled. "Lincoln didn't free no Negroes then and for sure colored folk in Sumter County were still slaves when I was a young man down there in the '40s," he growled.

Both of my grandparents often spoke of seeing Negro children suddenly appear in some white folks' yards, chained by the neck to a post or tree like a wild animal. They remained there for a few days, then disappeared. In a month or so a different child appeared in the same yard. Muh and Daddy-Yo suspected the children were taken to the Delta and sold to one of the larger landowners. My grandfather usually told us these stories as we sat in the searing heat of the Alabama summer sun, transfixed while eating watermelons, with names types like Congo, Rattle Snake and Charleston Gray. All the while Daddy-Yo recounted these stories, he stroked that gold watch that once belonged to his daddy. He mesmerized us with tales of how white folk stole black children off the streets of Alabama and took them to plantations as far away as the Mississippi Delta; how black people were held in bondage way after slavery was supposed to be over. Our eyes dared not stray from Daddy's mouth as we dug the red fleshy fruit out of the green striped watermelon rind with our wounded hands. We spat out the melon seeds as our parched, cracked lips sipped the sweet lemonade from dented tin cups. The tales left me terrified, wondering if those white men might someday come for me.

All my life I have lived with tales of slavery, especially while tending to Daddy-Yo's 360-acre farm. The tales led beyond the Emancipation Proclamation through the early 1950s. We loved and hated these stories of black men being stolen from the streets of Alabama. When Daddy-Yo started telling us these tales he was a young grandfather. The civil unrest going on in Birmingham at the time served as a backdrop for his stories and he spoke passionately about friends stolen away while walking to church, school or along some dusty Alabama road, never to return. Years later as a broken, older man, and just before his death in 1990, Daddy-Yo wept with each word of these stories as if ghosts had returned from the past to feast on his soul. None of us knew at the time that Daddy-Yo's tales of 20th century slavery would leave an indelible impression on me and that someday I'd go to southwest Alabama in search of the truth for myself.

As Daddy-Yo's reverberant voice echoed inside my head, I remembered the laughter, the sorrow, the pain, just as I remembered how it was to pick cotton; the spiny points on the cotton buds ripping our cuticles and making our fingers bleed. Then, in-between picking season, all signs of this particular torture disappeared. Once the skin toughened, the pain left our hands just as the stains of crusty, brown, dried blood wore off of the snowy white fibrous mound.

Today, the scars have faded from my adult hands. But the demons of the past revisit me as they did my fathers and grandfathers. Over the years I found myself telling these stories passed on to me to my children, as I stroke the same timepiece Daddy-Yo used to gingerly finger. I remembered word for word one particular story of the enormous hardships endured by one of Daddy-Yo's close friends.

It seems that in 1918, when Daddy-Yo was nearly seven years old, he and three of his friends were playing along a dirt road in the community of Tip Top near Morning Star Baptist Church. Daddy-Yo, the Strait brothers and Cleveland all lived in York, Alabama in Sumter County. They were on their way to visit Lily Mae Cooper, a tall, stately girl with flowing, black hair who lived nearby.

Most of the Negroes who lived in this rural part of southwest Alabama earned their living as sharecroppers. On that fateful summer morning, the boys were playing, as seven year-old boys do, when a brand new 1918 automobile pulled up beside them, followed by a huge cloud of dust. Two well-dressed white men sat in the front seat.

"Hey ya'll lit'il niggra boys, have ya'll ever seen the likens of such a beautiful machine?" The man on the passenger's side said.

"I can't reckon we have, suh," Daddy-Yo replied, removing his cap and lowering his eyes.

It was considered a sign of disrespect for blacks to make direct eye contact with whites. Blacks were thrown in jail and fined $25 in parts of the south for "reckless eyeballing," which meant they made eye contact with a white woman. This unwritten law was reserved mostly for black men and black women who were considered obstinate.

It wasn't often coloreds of any age got a chance to see a real car up close. The boys stood around the new vehicle gawking and awestruck in disbelief. One man got out of the car and offered them the chance of a lifetime.

"I'll tell you boys what. How about hoppin' in for a ride down to York. We'll be back before you know it."

It was unheard of for poor Negro boys to get a chance to ride in such elegance. They were more accustomed to traveling on splintery cross boards on the back of old rickety wagons. The boys were more than willing and eager to pile into the black leather rear seat.

Daddy-Yo reminded them where and who they were. "Coloreds don't ride in the buggy with whites, but we sho' do appreciate yo offer and we're much obliged," he said.

The men continued trying to lure the boys into the car.

"We sho' do appreciate it suh', but I reckon we'd better be headed on back to the house now," said Daddy-Yo.

Suddenly, in anger the driver forced the parking brake forward and jumped from the car cursing and swearing.

"Goddammit! Just grab them niggahs and let's get the hell out of here!" he screamed.

The four broke towards the wooded area along the roadside as fast as their legs would carry them. Several shots cracked the air as Daddy-Yo ran through the briar-filled thicket to the creek. He didn't stop running until he was on the front porch of his house. Daddy-Yo waited for a few minutes, hoping the others would soon join him. They never did.

He told his father, Professor Henry James Walker, what had happened. Within a few minutes, more than a dozen men on mules and wobbly old, field wagons traversed a familiar trail, searching for the three stolen Negro children. This time was no different from the countless times before. The fragile peace southern Negroes scarcely knew was once again broken. The Strait boys and Cleveland were gone without a trace.

Eventually, things returned to normal. And for the next 20 years, the memory of the three was relegated to stories of caution and fear told to little Negro children who strayed too far beyond the watchful eye of their Mamas and Daddies. The parents of the three missing boys never stopped lamenting over their loss, according to Daddy-Yo. Every day for weeks Cleveland's daddy stared down that long dusty highway past Morning Star Baptist, hoping that the road that took his boy away might somehow bring him back. The old man's prayers went unanswered.

Some years later when Daddy-Yo was in his late twenties he went to visit his father, the professor, at the house where he had come of age. Daddy-Yo was now living in Mississippi about 30 miles away. The two men were sitting on the front porch of the homestead when they saw a dirty, rundown, derelict family emerging from the back of a delivery truck, stopped along the side of the dirt road. The man in the group looked familiar, and as he walked closer they realized it was one of the three boys who had been abducted more than two decades before.

"When Cleveland saw us, it took more than an hour to settle him down," Daddy-Yo told us. "He looked at me and looked at Poppa and there come another big cry. We had to try to git him pacified. There were two or three children standing out there not far from him. He started asking about his daddy. Poppa stopped him and told him the old man died earlier that year. Folk said you could hear him screaming clear across the back holler to the next road, more than a mile away. I walked up to him and put both hands on his shoulders. I still couldn't believe it was him," Daddy-Yo said.

The scruffy, aged man told Daddy-Yo and Great Granddaddy that he and the others were taken to the Mississippi Delta region in the far west part of the state. He was held for all those years and forced to work as a slave on a plantation. He had no knowledge of what happened to the other boys. The area where he was forced to work was surrounded by two rivers and protected by armed guards, barbed wire and dogs. Cleveland told them that one day he and his wife were at the commissary when a white trucker expressed concern about the ill-treatment he received from the overseer. Apparently, the trucker had had business at the plantation on other occasions. He told Cleveland he would come back to the commissary later that night and for him to hide in back of the truck. The driver instructed them not to bring any of their belongings. A single knock on the side of the truck meant it was time to go. The driver said if they were stopped and searched for any reason, he would swear they were runaways.

That night, the truck left with the family in the cargo bay, frightened and suspicious of the sound of every passing motorist, thinking it could be a Mississippi State Trooper or a plantation owner coming after them. For hours they were locked in the back of the hot steamy truck without food or drink. The driver dared not stop until they had crossed the state line just outside of Meridian, Mississippi and gone into Alabama. The trucker took the family to York and let them out on the roadside—and never looked back. They never saw or heard from him again.

The last I heard, Cleveland was residing in a rural community about 35 miles south of Birmingham. During the summers for much of his life, he spent the day peddling fruits and vegetables. In the winter, he provided for himself and his wife by selling scrap metal to the local junkyard.

As a child listening to my grandfather's stories, I cried silently out of fear for myself. As a man, the fear surrendered to sorrow for the plight of innocent people I never met.

In high school I took issue with students and instructors who considered President Lincoln the ultimate emancipator of Negro people. My flesh cringed whenever slavery was considered to be an atrocity lost in the distant past. I knew a truth that I shared with very few other people on this earth, one of the few truths I got from my grandfather. No one else was interested in the ranting of an aging Negro man like Daddy-Yo, especially when it contradicted what most considered a sacred historical fact. Years later, after Daddy-Yo's death, I gave a voice to the history of those held as slaves even after the official ending of slavery, a history generally overlooked, by writing my grandfather's story for The Washington Post.

CHAPTER 4: IRRELEVANCY

In my early childhood, Dear left our apartment nearly every morning and took two buses "over the mountain" to the white neighborhood where she cleaned floors, toilets and children whose names I knew from her stories; I'm sure they didn't know mine. When crossing the threshold to our apartment, family and guests alike were greeted by the unmistakable stench of poverty; the smell of decaying linoleum and roach spray mixed with strong disinfectant. It dawns upon me now, those children Dear took care of may not have even known Dear's name. For certain, they didn't know her surname since they weren't obliged to address her by it. Of course, they never really REALLY knew her.

Because Dear had to leave us to care for white children, my oldest brother, then eight years old, cleaned, fed and dressed us for school. I was left at home alone for a few hours in the morning because my schooling didn't start until noon. Archie rushed home in the middle of the day from school, then walked me back to Finley Avenue Elementary. After classes, the three of us walked home together. But no matter how tired Dear was in the evenings, she always made certain our shoes were polished and shined for the next day and appeared to do it lovingly, not begrudgingly.

Dear was one of hundreds of black women in Birmingham who huddled on the street corners in frigid weather, blazing heat or pouring rain, waiting for the No. 11 bus to carry them far from the neatness of home to clean someone else's residence. Sometimes my brothers and I got up in the darkness with Dear to escort her to the bus stops. We often lingered to watch the sparks shoot from atop the electrical bus, lighting up the sky in every direction as it sputtered away. Dear said when black passengers overcrowded the rear of the bus-the only place they could sit or stand-the driver put some of them off and wouldn't refund their fare. While Dear was making sure those white children were well-fed and clean before going to school, God looked out for my brother who, in turn, cared for us. At the end of the day Dear dragged in, exhausted. Black women who were fortunate enough to get a ride home from their white employers when it was late always rode in the back seat of the car. A basket of clothes or a dog usually rode up front. Dear arrived home with intriguing stories and nice hand-me-down clothes. We were glad to get those clothes and strutted around our friends as if to say: "Our white people got better clothes than your white people." We tried to outdo our playmates and they tried to outdo us by telling tales of the big houses and fine things within them that our parents were privileged to clean. In retrospect, I know now that the white homes were really quite ordinary, made resplendent at the time only in comparison to our own. Dear and others like her worked for the marginal businessmen, civil servants and used car dealers. Was life better for those black domestics who worked for the landed gentry or the southern Aristocrats? For those domestics who wore starched uniforms and had been "in the family for years"? I think not. Does it really matter whether one is humiliated at the hands of soi-disant "Masters" or want-to-be "Overseers"?

Dear held very few aspirations or expectations regarding the civil rights movement. At first, Dear and Dad showed little excitement at the prospect of having black physicians working alongside white doctors or the possibility that whatever white folk had we would be entitled to also. But many in our neighborhood did discuss of the possibility that one day a black man would actually drive the garbage truck instead of just hanging on the back, running to keep up with the white driver, who seemed to always drive too fast.

We lived on a dead end street and all the garbage truck drivers refused to service our area, which meant they would have had to deviate from their regular route. On Thursday mornings, my brothers and I had to get up extra early to take the trash a block away for pick-up. Sometimes that truck, leaking its smelly payload up one street and down the other, came early. The black workers hanging on the back saw me running and holding on dearly to one handle of the metal can and my brother with the other. The driver saw us, too. But he still sped away.

The landfill was an unwanted gift from the city of Birmingham to my all-black neighborhood. When we walked down the street and smelled rotten garbage, the sulfur dioxide emitted from the foundries and the slaughterhouse, we were reminded of who was in charge here. To the white population, we were just niggers who did not deserve better.

Months after President Johnson signed the Civil Rights Bill into law in 1964, the rumor rolled through our neighborhood that finally, there was going to be a Negro garbage truck driver. Dear got us out of bed one morning in hopes of catching what she called "a glimpse of history." The sun was barely peeking through the smoky morning haze over the eastern horizon. I was surprised to see so many other people lined up along the streets and sitting on their porches waiting to see this man who was our very own celebrity of sorts. My brother and I struggled down the alleyway to the next street to take our can. We were just returning to retrieve my grandmother's trash when suddenly instead of the garbage truck making its quick left turn, it came up the hill, straight towards us. The men jumped off, throwing and catching the cans in mid-air. This was the first time the trash truck had rolled onto our dead end street. And then, there he was. Bigger than life. A black man driving the garbage truck! My brother and I gawked, nearly forgetting the can we were carrying. This one moment, a flash in time, was the talk of the school as well as worthy of mention during the Sunday service. And because of what I witnessed that morning, I knew without a doubt what I wanted to be when I grew up.

Maybe to some white boy, aspiring to be a trash truck driver wasn't much of a dream. But it was clear to me even then that Dear, Daddy, Daddy-Yo and all other black people only existed for the benefit of white people. We were born to work for them, amuse them, and when necessary to be ridiculed and punished by them. There was nothing in my childhood to say otherwise. I was separated from white children in school by the State of Alabama, and I used textbooks after these children finished with using them in their classrooms. Unlike the hand-me-down clothes Dear brought home from her jobs, the books were torn and tattered.

One fall morning in 1964, Mrs. Brunt, my fourth and fifth grade library teacher, announced, "Today we will receive new textbooks from Martin Elementary." Mrs. Brunt was a tall, lanky, fair-skinned disciplinarian.

Martin was the white school near us. In truth, the books weren't really new, but they were new to us. We were bursting with excitement about the delivery. Mrs. Brunt had to calm us every few minutes. It had been weeks since school started and the teachers relied on grossly outdated books from previous school years.

Finally, word came for Mrs. Brunt to send five able-bodied boys to the office to pick up the boxes of books. I was one of the five chosen to go. I was proud. As she passed the readers out to the first person in each row, Mrs. Brunt gave stern instructions not to open the books until each student had one. The books were worn and tattered but still better than no books at all.

"Will you please turn to the first page and print your name in pencil at the top left corner of the page," Mrs. Brunt commanded.

Everyone opened their books quickly. But some of us were stunned by what we saw. Scribbled all over some of the pages in big letters were words like "NIGGER!" "BURHEAD!" and "SAMBO!" And there were also drawings of Negroes in blackface with gigantic lips. We stared at the pages as if they were like apparitions from the grave, serving as a reminder that we might have somewhat new books but nothing was ever really going to change for us. The excitement and squirming was replaced with a soft murmur of disappointment. Mrs. Brunt didn't say anything about the hurtful words and drawings. She barely paused before requesting, "Get out your erasers and clean off those pages."

And so it became an annual ritual for us to spend one recess in September making a futile attempt to erase those hateful reminders of our existence on the lower rung of Jim Crow. I can't recall this happening in previous years, but Mrs. Brunt must have come to expect those degrading images and words because each September she had us rub those pages as hard as we could for 30 minutes. Regardless, before they disappeared or faded, those words impacted us. We could not erase the emptiness and pain caused by the racist words left by students who disrespected our very lives. I was embarrassed and ashamed to use the books, but I did. And while I cringed each time I saw the faded but still present hateful words, my teachers seemed so pleased that we had books at all.

Around this same time, some of us were given one of those experimental standardized psychological or aptitude tests that I also grew to despise. One of the pages had a drawing of a girl with traditional European features and the other a girl with stereotypical African features. The question under the drawings asked, "Which girl is prettier?" I always selected the answer I believed was correct: The white girl.

I had few if any positive recollections to build upon in my interactions with white people. As children, we never played together. After school my friends and I met in Melville Courts, the neighborhood that surrounded our block. We played tackle football on a field that covered several neighbors' yards. We filled an old pint size milk carton with gravel and used it for a ball. I knew without a doubt that someday I would be catching long passes from Johnny Unitas of the Baltimore Colts. At least even I, a black boy in the South, was allowed childish dreams, as long as I didn't tell a white person about them.

Often in the midst of our game, Sgt. Jack of Car 49 of the Birmingham Police Department rolled up and slid to a screeching halt. Sgt. Jack was the meanest, biggest, most intimidating white man I had ever seen. When he pulled up, the game froze. He swung those tree trunk legs out of the car with his eyes fixed on us all the time, as if to dare one of us to move.

"Come heah you li'l ole black ass niggahs!" he yelled. We ran as fast as we could over to the car, careful not to make direct eye contact with him.
"Come here and let me rub them naps and burrs. Might bring me a li'l better luck," he said, frantically stroking and gripping our heads. He raked his hands through our hair until tears came to our eyes and still we didn't dare move. Even though we were children, his actions stripped us of our dignity one painful nap at a time and he enjoyed it.

The nappier your hair, the more shame you felt because Sgt. Jack saved the loudest ridicule for those boys. Even today I can clearly hear his haunting laughter in my memory.

"L'il nigga, you done cut my hand with them burrs," he said, laughing, holding one skinny, crying boy. "Boy, I should whup your little black ass for trapping my hand in your head," he said to another he grabbed, laughing loud the whole time.

Some years later, after my friends and I were high school juniors or seniors, we decided it was time for the Birmingham police officer to pay for his hateful actions, for filling our childhood with fear and humiliation. One afternoon, Sgt. Jack, a fat, graying man by this time, was making his routine patrol of the neighborhood and as he turned the corner, we hurled bricks and stones at him as if all hell had broken loose.

The message was clear: The little nigga boys in my neighborhood were growing less fearful of him.

We never saw him again. Although Car 49 still patrols my old neighborhood to this day, Sgt. Jack was eventually replaced with a black policeman.

It astounds me the way in which Jim Crow touched every single area of black life in Birmingham when I was growing up. Blacks were not even allowed to buy new Cadillacs or any other car whites considered too luxurious for a Negro. Daddy once told me a story about a Negro who was employed by U.S. Steel. He said that the man worked for years, saving money from two jobs to buy a brand new Buick. When the man purchased the car, he decided to drive to work. Upon driving into the foundry parking lot, he was met by the foreman. The foreman inquired if the car belonged to the man. The man proudly answered, "Yes." The foreman said, "If a nigger can afford an automobile like that, he don't need to be working here," then he fired the man on the spot.

Daddy had his own brushes with the Birmingham Police. He told me that he was downtown waiting for the No. 18 Fountain Heights bus when suddenly a police car rushed up and stopped. Daddy said the police jumped out with billy clubs. They grabbed a young black male and wrestled him into the back seat of the patrol car. As the man was being forced into the car, he yelled, "Why are y'all taking me! What about him?" He pointed toward my father who was just standing waiting for the bus. The police once again emerged from the car, cuffed my father and carted him off to jail for a couple of days.

Some of the rules of racism were just plain stupid even to a child, like the one that said Negroes couldn't look at naked white mannequins. I discovered this rule when I was 10 years old and my mother yanked me from in front of the Pizit Department Store window because the employee was changing the clothes on the cold, heartless white mannequins that were indeed like many of the white people we encountered. But even at 10, I knew that this was a rule a black boy or a black man had to obey or he could get in to serious trouble.

That same year, my cousin who was also 10 years old was at the lake looking for tadpoles with his younger brother when a white man wandered by and without provocation grabbed my cousin and threw him in the lake. The younger brother ran home to get help. But by the time his father arrived, it was too late. My cousin was dead. Dear told me the man who drowned him was questioned and released.

Dear and Daddy tried to keep us children away from white people. They certainly didn't want us marching around town calling white people names and talking about black people running things. It wasn't even a dream to Daddy and Dear, just foolishness. "Bullshit," Daddy called it. After Dear lost her job as a cleaning lady because of all that civil rights mess, she got a job with a ladies' clothing store. Her wages increased. We moved to a larger place. That was the point-to keep bettering yourself to survive. You couldn't do that if Mr. Spanno put us out in the cold. You couldn't do that without accepting the leftovers from the white people for whom you worked. Dear and Daddy understood all of this. They bowed and scraped for white people every day. Their children were fed and clothed, their house clean, and they got along well with everybody until that slick talking preacher from Atlanta came to Birmingham talking about freedom. He got Dear freed all right, freed from her job.

One of the things I didn't understand then, and find hard to understand now, is why Dear didn't take us and run from Daddy. When the bombs, fires and taunts from white people came, I could always find solace in Dear's arms, or listen to her words of comfort: "Don't worry, honey. God will take care of us." God and Dear took care of me, but who took care of her? Certainly not Daddy or Daddy-Yo.

I can't remember a time when Daddy didn't beat Dear. Each time he hit her and made her cry, my world turned upside down. He cursed her and his maligning words sliced through me before piercing her heart. I am pained even now, remembering.

Dear protests Dad's accusations. "That's just that cheap liquor talking, Archie."

A vicious slap. "Don't talk back to me, bitch." A pause. Then, "Motherfucker!"

Dear screams, "Don't Archie! Please!"

A punch to the stomach. A moan.

"Whore," he yells, standing an inch from her face "Don't tell me what to do, this is my gotdamn house!"

He slaps her. "Bitch!" He screams more and issues a secession of slaps until I can tell he is tired and the pace slows. Finally, exhausted he sits on the edge of the bed and falls across it, and almost immediately is asleep, fully dressed.

A couple of times following a beating, as Daddy drifted deeper into a drunken slumber, Dear stood over him swirling a pot filled with boiling grits or black-eyed peas. But she couldn't bring herself to pour it on him.

Neither my prayers nor Dear's were answered. We asked for different things: She wanted the beatings to stop; I wanted her to stop living with Daddy. He overheard me once tell her this. Instead of coming to terms with what was bothering his youngest son, he took his belt off and beat me from my hiding place under the coffee table, as I tried to get away. Large whelps rose on my body, bruising me for days. And long after those bruises have faded, I am left with a scarred soul and horrific memories.

Dear often comforted me and told me stories of how kind and gentle my father was before the war. She believed he would someday be that man again. "The Lord will change his heart," she said. "You just wait and see."

She was more generous in her faith than I was. I didn't see any reason to believe God would answer. If He was going to answer Dear's prayers He was late and His slowness meant a good-hearted woman filled with faith was needlessly living in hell.

There *is* evidence that my father, Archie Lee Cooper, was once a totally different man than the one I knew. He grew up in Verbena, Ala., a town of almost 700 people, straddling Highway 31, midway between Montgomery and Birmingham. It wasn't a place that my brothers or me knew well since the only times we went to his home were on rare fishing trips for cod and carp on the Coosa River. My father's taut dark body resembled a scythe's handle when he worked in the Alabama cotton fields--a dark curve, long and lanky, bending towards the earth. Of course, he didn't see poetry in dragging pounds and pounds of cotton in burlap bags from dawn to darkness in a blistering heat. Nor did he want to become a permanent black curve, always working and bending to the whims of white people, a metaphor for submission. Archie dreamed of traveling from Verbena to enter Tuskegee Institute. He was sure the school driven by

Booker T. Washington's practicality and George Washington Carver's genius would change his life. But my father never found out if that was true. Instead of attending college he moved north to Birmingham, carrying his dream with him.

In Birmingham, he joined a Baptist church and played trombone in the church's band. He also strutted down the aisles as an usher. Daddy once saved a few coins to buy a piece of sheet jazz music entitled "Five to One." One of the church deacons walking pass his house heard him practicing the song on the back porch. The very next Sunday the deacon called Archie before the congregation to have him apologize for using the church's instrument to frolic with the devil.

It seems my father was always popular with the ladies. They liked his smooth brown skin and his silky voice and they loved to watch the 6'3" music maker glide down the aisles. Dear was one of the admirers. Dear told me: "He was so different back then, before the war. He had long black curly hair and a voice so smooth you just wanted to rest in it forever." I tried to picture Daddy as a lady's man. But I couldn't get past the image of the man who stood before me, his mouth full of missing teeth except for a few yellow and gray dangling fragments. Dear said in the ole days he didn't curse none, either. "He was a perfect gentleman, didn't smoke, drink or nothing. And he always talked about going to Tuskegee. I think he joined the Army so he could get the money for that school. But when Archie got out of the Army something was terribly wrong. My man had changed and not for the better. He drank more liquor than the law or the Lord allowed and couldn't open his mouth without cursing.

I'll tell you, the man the Army took from me was not the man they gave back."

An alarm crept into Dear's voice when she got to this part of the story: "He quit coming to church. Him and my Daddy can't stand preachers. If they don't agree on nothing else, they shake hands on that. Your granddaddy said Satan is in the pulpit.' Said, 'The preacher ain't good for nothing but eating up your best pieces of fried chicken, taking your hard-earned money, or laying up with some 'saved' sister."

When I was growing up Daddy rarely if ever talked about his time in the military or about his childhood. It was only in recent years he opened up to me. He said as a teen he was shy and withdrawn. A friend convinced him that if he took a drink or two he would loosen up and feel a bit more relaxed around the girls. It worked. Daddy said he really loved talking to the girls but wasn't able to unless he had a drink or two first. When he joined the military, he said there were times when all they did was sit around and drink and tell lies. Aside from driving a supply truck, one of his duties when he was in Korea was to travel from his camp outside of Seoul and go into the city and trade stolen cigarettes in exchange for young girls. He said officers kept females hidden under the floorboards of their quarters for weeks at a time.

There were occasions when soldiers grew overly possessive of the physically appealing young women. One day a soldier learned that a young girl he was seeing was also keeping company with other servicemen. In a jealous rage, he accidently killed her. Dad's commander ordered him to dispose of the body by taking it to the back of the base and throwing it over the fence.

According to my father, it happened on other occasions too that young Korean girls met their deaths at the hands of U.S. soldiers. Finally, my father refused a direct order to dispose of the bodies, which resulted in him losing the two corporal stripes he had earned.

As a child my brothers and I often talked about running away and we asked each other how Dear could tolerate our father's drunkenness and meanness. Once she was entertaining her club members in the living room. Daddy, drunk as he could be off home brew, stumbled through the back door. My brothers and I heard him coming and turned off the lights and pretended to be asleep. Daddy always said: "When I come home, I want it quiet enough to hear a rat piss on cotton." If it wasn't quiet, he'd yell, "What have you been doing all day? You been sitting around with your thumbs stuck in your asses!"

On the night Dear was entertaining, Daddy clicked the lights back on and in a slurred voice called us sons-of-bitches and headed toward the bedroom gagging and throwing up his guts. We heard vomit splashing on the floor. Then he reeled into the bedroom, opened a dresser drawer and pissed all over Dear's things. When he finally got to the bathroom, he fell asleep in puddles of his own vomit.

Dear didn't know he was home until one of the club ladies went to the bathroom, threw the door open and hurriedly retreated to the living room. Dear politely asked her guests to leave. Then she called us to help her.

"Len, Alfred Lloyd, Archie Lee! Y'all come here and help get your daddy off this floor!"

We jumped out of the bed wearing just our underpants. We struggled to get him up as he flopped across the foot of the bed. As she was getting him undressed, he woke up and started cursing.

"If y'all don't get your black asses back in that bed, I'll stomp corns on your asses as big as a nickel and kill every last one of you bastards!"

We made a beeline for our room. We were all too familiar with the storm that was rising in the next room. My brothers slid beneath the covers and I scampered under the bed and crawled to the farthest corner against the wall. The balls of dust, roach carcasses and rat droppings didn't matter when Daddy was in what he referred to as his "coma." Dear usually got a beating on Dad's "coma" nights.

"Our Father, which art in Heaven," I whispered, faintly. I knew this passage backwards and forwards. But on that night the words escaped me.

"Bitch! I'm the boss in this fuckin' house! I'll put you, your clothes and your no count chulluns out the gotdamn door!" he screamed. I heard him slapping Dear. I heard the thumping sound as she fell against the wall.

"Don't you hit me again!" she yelled back.

I lay on my side with my knees up to my chest and my ears covered, rocking and begging, crying to God to let this last lick be enough. It seemed the more I prayed the worse the beating became. I wondered if it was possible that Daddy had a good reason for hitting Dear. Otherwise, it seemed to me God would have interceded and saved her. The preacher said that God's ways are not our ways and that His works are mysterious. I didn't understand God's point in letting Dear, one of His loyal subjects, get smacked around. I was taught that to question God was a grave sin, but it was a sin I committed frequently.

Daddy eventually drifted off to sleep and I crawled out from under the bed, back onto my pallet. I heard Dear sobbing in the bathroom. I asked Dear once why she didn't just take us and leave. She was convinced that someday Daddy would again be the husband she once knew. But I didn't feel her hope. Toward the end of every week I experienced overwhelming dread in anticipation of the weekend. Meanwhile, I figured I undoubtedly had offended God by asking Him to help Dear. Why else would he allow the fighting to continue?

Anytime there was an upheaval in our fragile lives, my friend Billy and I stole off in the middle of the night to the clearing next to my grandmother's house. We called it "Problem Hill." We lie flat on our backs in the tall grass, looking toward the sky, asking God for a sign. Once Billy thought he received one. His eyes were glowing bright as new marbles. I reminded him that his sign was just a shooting star. We both made a wish. No point in wasting a perfectly good shooting star.

Billy's father was much like mine. Billy was what we called "cock strong," unusually strong and muscular for his age. But he wouldn't harm a fly. He was leery of people outside of his family. The adverse effects of his home life were more evident on him than mine were on me. He was teased horribly about how badly he smelled, or the over-sized safety pin he used to keep the back of his Converse sneakers together. This was not some foolish fashion statement; Billy's mother honestly couldn't afford to buy shoes or sneakers for him at times. People stared and often made belittling comments, but he never let on that it bothered him.

That hillside near my grandmother's house was Billy's and mine for hours as we beseeched God for everything from money to imploring His help to get our mothers to leave our drunken, no count fathers.

I once prayed in earshot of my father for Dear to divorce him. My boyish prayer riled him up the same way my overheard plea had. He beat me with an electrical extension cord this time. The looped welts on my skin turned white after crusting over and the scab fell off. The kids in school laughed and joked, but it was just a matter of time before some of them came to school bearing the same markings of a troubled home.

Sometimes when my father was drunk he whispered in my ear, "You ain't my child." At other times, he just blurted it out for no apparent reason. I heard my friends' parents repeat this in a playful tone. I smiled and pretended the words didn't hurt when Dear's church choir members teased me with this when I was visiting their homes to play with friends.

"Len, who do you favor in that house?" a friend's father once said as the mother looked on. The adult daughter continued the taunt, "I think Len favors the milkman or the postman." Everyone laughed heartily. I smiled, but inside I died a little. Still, as painful as those moments with friends teasing me were, they didn't compare to the pain I felt when my own father told me I was not his blood. Daddy's words were intended to wound and injure me and they always did.

He spat out the words. "Boy, you know you ain't mine."

He was probably right, I thought. After all, I was the darkest one in the family. My hair texture was nappy and hard while Alfred and Daddy had deep, rich, shiny curls. Archie and Dear were light-skinned and I was always teased about how black I was. I asked Muh once if Daddy was my real father. I was still in grade school at the time.

"Where you git that from, boy?" she replied.

I hunched my shoulders up and down, (a child's way of saying, "Don't know"). This response always angered Dear and Muh, who preferred we articulate as opposed to gesturing.

"Sho Archie is yo Daddy," Muh said.

I am not certain she was telling the truth, but I needed to believe her for that moment and that was all that mattered. Muh's negation of Daddy's venomous comments took some-but not all-of the bite out his words. As a child, I kept many painful experiences to myself. The identification of the author of this comment was added to the ever-growing collection of secrets. As I grew older, Daddy uttered these words with less frequency. Eventually, he stopped saying it. But the words echoed inside my head for years.

One evening Daddy came in late from work and in a soft, controlled tone accused me of looking out the door to watch for him and then racing for the kitchen and starting to wash dishes when I saw him coming. Nothing I said convinced him otherwise. He ordered me out of my clothes and told me to lie across the bed.

"If you move one inch, I'll tear your ass up all night," he said, angrily. "I don't give a damn!"

Daddy doubled the long brown electrical extension cord. He beat me across my back, pausing between each lash. The cord tore across my shoulders and then my waist.

I rolled over, looking at him, pleading. "Daddy, please!"

The cord made a whistling and slashing pop as it tore across my flesh.

"I have all night, boy," My father reminded me. "You better keep still. I don't have a damn thing to do and nowhere in the hell to be. I don't give a shit! Now git your ass back over there!" He was furious.

I tried to keep as still as possible, but I couldn't stop moving. Every time I flinched, my father got angrier and angrier.

He beat me harder. I felt fire tear across my back. Across my legs. Across my arms. Buttocks. Neck. I flinched.

He paused--and then started again. And again.

The only part of my body spared was my face and head.

"I'm not lying, Daddy! I'm not lying!" I pleaded.

He ignored me. But he slowed down. He was tiring. I don't know how long he beat me. He stopped when he could barely stand or raise his arm.

"Go get the damn alcohol," he demanded.

My brother remained quiet and soaked the torn rags in the isopropyl and gently touched the broken loops on my back. I could hardly catch my breath through my sobbing.

Although the beatings were the worst acts of meanness, they weren't the only ones. In Daddy and Daddy-Yo's houses the women seldom sat and ate with the men. Dear stood in the doorway until we had our fill, then ate what was left. Some days there was nothing. At those times, Dear cried. It was not as if she was weeping for a feast that passed her by. Many times she prepared fried potatoes for breakfast, boiled potatoes for lunch and the juice from the lunch potatoes with corn bread mashed in it for dinner. No, I knew she was crying for something other than food.

Daddy never made more than $80 or $90 a week driving the delivery truck. He sometimes gave Dear $5 or $10 to run the household and he gambled or drank up the rest. One afternoon my friends and I were playing basketball when all of a sudden the game came to a halt because my nosey, hell-raising neighbor, Mrs. Juette, was making a commotion. She was about four-feet nothing and almost as wide, but she knew how to make a large racket. "Len! Come get your daddy out of my flower bed right now!" she shouted.

Up until then it was an ordinary afternoon. On any given day after school up to 15 kids stood around waiting their turn to get in to the foursquare or basketball game. I felt all eyes on me at once as I limped away, wounded from embarrassment. Juan and Billy, my closest friends, offered to help me, but I knew I had to take this familiar walk alone. At the flowerbed, sure enough, there my father was lying at the base of Mrs. Juette's front porch, all sprawled out in between her roses and begonias.

By now the adult neighbors gathered. My brothers and I struggled to get daddy to his feet. We carried him past the onlookers to our house a block away. Daddy spat out grass and dirt along with expletive after vile expletive. I hated daddy for putting us through this humiliating ritual.

My Granddaddy constantly reminded us of the sorry lot we had drawn for a father and told us that it was never going to change.

I truly believe Daddy-Yo would have killed my father if he had presented him with little cause. Whether Dear loved Daddy or not was irrelevant to him. Daddy-Yo always said that Daddy was not only a poor excuse for a man but for a human being as well.

One night Dad came in as drunk as a skunk, coughing

up all the words we were not permitted to say or think. My older brother ordered us to turn out the light and jump in bed immediately when he heard Dad staggering and cussing towards our room. The room was pitch black and we pretended to be sound asleep. I heard Dad utter, "I got something for you little bastards."

On rare occasions Dad got distracted from wreaking havoc in our lives and just passed out across the bed. This night we would not be so fortunate. I heard Dad fumbling around with something in the kitchen. We were all too afraid to move. Alfred and I alternated looking from the doorknob to Archie, waiting for instructions. I peeked from under the covers with my eyes fixed on the doorway once I heard Daddy coming closer. I looked to Archie once more for something, anything. In a rush, the door flew open with a loud crash.

"I told you little mothafuckers I had something for you!" Dad shouted, pointing the barrel of the shotgun towards Archie.

Before I could scream, there was an explosion and fire shot from the barrel. Within seconds, there was another flash. I froze. Something warm and wet ran down my legs. I felt something tugging at the back of my arm as I stood in the middle of my pallet on the floor. I saw Alfred's silhouette against the Alabama moonlight. Archie seemed fine; he pulled me off the floor and pushed me through the window before climbing out himself. Wearing nothing but our white briefs and in our bare feet, we ran around the house and across the street to our grandparents' house. Of course, Daddy-Yo used the moment to make his point about just how no good and worthless our father was. Muh comforted us and scolded Daddy-Yo in her own way.

"Sam, you know it ain't right to talk bad about Archie in front of these boys," Muh said. "No matter what you say and do and no matter how bad he is, he is still the only daddy they got. It just ain't right."

Daddy -Yo always had a simple retort. "You can't fool them boys, Bea. They know what kinda daddy they got."

Within the hour my drunken father was out in the street in front of Daddy-Yo's house yelling for us to "get our asses home." As it turned out, Daddy had lit two firecrackers and dropped them down the barrel of the gun. Daddy-Yo placed his 38-caliber pistol in the chest pocket of his worn, blue overalls before going outside. I watched from the front bedroom window. He walked toward Daddy, talking along the way. "Archie, if you make one more step, I promise it will be your last," Daddy-Yo ordered.

Daddy stopped in his tracks and continued yelling.

"You boys get your asses over here! Now!"

As I watched, I thought of what Daddy-Yo always said: "Don't draw a gun on a person unless you intend to use it." I actually prayed Daddy would take one more step toward Daddy-Yo. One more step meant freedom for Dear. No more late night beatings. No more having sex with a husband reeking of vomit and waste. One more step would release me and my brothers from our torment. No more extension cords or braided tree branches. Secretly, I begged, "Please Daddy, do this one thing for us, for me."

I would have taken unspeakable pleasure in seeing my father, lying face down in the dirt, gasping for his last breath. But God's justice was again deferred. We remained at my grandparents until Dear came for us the next morning.

Daddy kept company with people whom Dear

despised. Once a week and sometimes more, Daddy made his way to Mrs. Burrell's house to spend the greater portion of his meager $90 weekly wages on his favorite drink: scotch and sweet milk. In our neighborhood you could count on a having a shot house within a short brisk walk of about 15 or 20 minutes. Mrs. Burrell and Ben Fuchs sold more liquor than all the others combined. Louise Winfield lived just a few feet from our back porch and down the path in a green, wooden double-tenant house. After spending months drinking at Mrs. Burrell's, Daddy would suddenly switch gears and start spending his precious drinking time at Ms. Winfield's house. I suspect Daddy got behind on his tab to Mrs. Burrell and decided not to return until he had enough to pay the outstanding bill.

Ms. Winfield had been a fixture in my life since the day I was born. Dear gave strict orders for us to be respectful of her, but nothing more. Everyone whispered and said she was strange, the unusual sort. Daddy came right out and called her a "bull-dagger," whatever that was. Louise was short and stocky and wore men's clothes. Every day I had to pass her house in order to get to my school and every day she was out front saying hello to all who dared to make eye contact.

"Hey Cooper boy!" she yelled in her deep, gravelly voice, while fanning her hand and arm way up over her head in an undulating motion. There she stood; dressed in a man's flannel plaid shirts, corduroy pants and penny loafers. Sometimes she wore men's hats with full brims like the ones men often wore to Sunday services. Louise cannot be adequately described unless I mention her teeth. With each word spoken, her tongue whipped through the opening in her mouth where at least four of her front teeth once resided. The two teeth on each side of her mouth were green, yellow and brown. But I barely noticed Ms. Winfield's teeth because I had grown accustomed to seeing my father's mouth, which was in much worse condition. In my neighborhood adults didn't get their teeth fixed. If a dental problem arose, no matter how small, that tooth was usually extracted without giving much thought to the possibility of saving it.

Ms. Winfield, the bull-dagger and Daddy's friend, took a shine to me--and I hated her. Whenever I passed her, she politely asked me to go to Joe Miller's or Mr. Ben's store to buy a pack of Pall Mall cigarettes. I ran home to ask Dear and each and every time I asked, Dear found something else that was certainly more important than running nickel errands for an aging "dike."

As years passed, I became less afraid of Ms. Winfield. At some point, I had visited every house within several blocks from where we lived in my North Birmingham neighborhood of Enon Ridge and Fountain Highs. I *never* once set foot in Ms. Winfield's house. In the summer it seemed that no matter what time I passed her house, day or night, her mother, a robust, toothless woman, was sitting on the front porch in an old rickety wooden rocker.

"Hey Len," she said, politely while gumming each and every word. She sat, legs gaped wide open, knees pointing east and west. She tucked the excess fabric from her tent-like dress between her legs whenever she saw me coming. I am still thankful for that to this day.

"How's your momma and daddy, your Grandmaw and Mr. Sam and Mr. and Mrs. Cooper doing?" The same question was asked and answered weekly for no less than 16 years. The only time I can remember not having this brief conversation was when the police car was parked in front of Ms. Winfield's house on Sunday mornings. Daddy said they were there to collect hush money in order for the Winfields and others to continue selling liquor without a license.

As I became older and a bit more brazen, I joined in the chorus of taunts my friends unleashed on Ms. Winfield, the bull-dagger. From a distance we screamed, "Montana!" I don't know where that name came from, but every time we yelled it, it sent Ms. Winfield into a tirade and right over the edge. She chased us and we ran like hell! We all thought it was fun.

One day a group of us were hiding in the wooded area next to our house when we saw her coming. As soon as she passed, we jumped out screaming at the top of our lungs.

"Montana! Montana!"

And the chase was on. She turned toward us and ran only a few steps. This time she just stood and watched us as we kept running for our lives, choking on laughter. My buddies kept running all the way to their homes. I decided to circle the neighborhood in order to avoid Ms. Winfield en route to my house. I was approaching the path that led to our house from a side street about a block away. There was still enough daylight to see exactly where I was going. I had walked this path all of my life so there was no need to pay any special attention to the direction I was traveling. In this half-block trail during the summer months you could find strawberries, black berries, apples, peaches and plums growing wildly. Fruit trees and berry vines were in abundance in our neighborhood.

As I sauntered up the path, not paying any attention to the road, I walked right into Ms. Winfield, standing in a way that obstructed my path. It was too late to run. I thought, "Maybe she didn't realize it was me with the others who had been teasing her so unmercifully for the past few years."

But that was a ridiculous thought.

We both stood there in silence for what seemed like eternity. It looked as though she had been crying. I just prayed she would let me pass. Our eyes were focused on one another.

"I have known you and your brothers since the day your momma brought ya'll home, Len."

She paused mid-sentence, as if she had decided whatever advice or scolding she was going to render would go unheeded and it was pointless for her to waste good effort on the likes of me.

"Not you too, Len?" she uttered, rushing pass me.

I often wonder why she never told my Daddy how I was one of the ringleaders that teased her without mercy. Maybe she was more compassionate than I was at the time. Certainly she was aware of what went on in our house and maybe she just wanted to spare me.

At any rate, that evening when I met her in the path I could see up close how painful our teasing was for her. Suddenly, I felt sorry for her, because many times in school I was the target of relentless teasing from classmates and I understood the pain taunts caused. So soon after this incident, when I ceased calling her Montana, the others followed suit and reframed from mocking her as well. Without any big discussion, we all became respectful of her and her mother.

As mean and odious as Daddy was at home, in front of white people he was as mild and obedient as a puppy. Daddy delivered yeast by truck for a large company. When an emergency delivery needed to be made, Mr. Moorman, his boss, did not hesitate to call our neighbors at any time to have them dash over and tell my father to make the run. Daddy never refused. Mr. Moorman needed little cause to fire him. Occasionally, Daddy took me with him. Mr. Moorman and the other white men who worked for Standard Brands could slay the savage beast in Daddy just by their presence. Dad was humble and submissive around white people, not mean-spirited, vindictive and aloof like he was with us.

Dear made constant excuses for Daddy's bad behavior. She sometimes blamed a decades-old incident for his meanness. Dear said that when Daddy was a boy, a wagon ran over his grandfather's foot. The big iron wheel with its wooden spokes almost cut his foot in half. Daddy said growing up he heard the story told over the years by family members. The doctors and nurses at the nearby white hospital saw his grandfather's life ebbing away as blood poured through make-shift bandages around the foot. Still, they refused to treat him. By the time his grandfather could be seen by the black doctor, great granddaddy had bled to death.

For me, daddy's meanness never required a long, complicated or introspective explanation. He simply didn't love or want any of us. He laughed and spoke nicely to all his drinking buddies, but never towards us. What father who loves his children would address them in a vile manner, using names such as "sorry asses," "black bastards," or "piece of shit"? No, it wasn't so complicated. I believed he simply hated everything about his family.

Daddy knew the power and wickedness of white people. In their presence, he only spoke when spoken to, punctuating each sentence with a respectful "Yes, sir" or "No, sir," then capping it off with a mild debasing grin.

Naturally, I wanted Daddy to talk to Mr. Moorman and the other white people like he talked to us: strong, assertive and sure. I didn't think about the trouble his insolence towards white people could cause us. As a child, I needed to know that my father hated others and not just his wife and sons. It was hard for me to understand why he showed respect for those who despised him, while having only contempt for those who loved him. Yet, even as a young boy I felt Daddy's nervousness whenever we were outside of our community as night fell. In the growing darkness, not a word passed his lips.

In silence, I prayed as a 10-year-old. Reverend H. L. Freeman, pastor at New Salem, said from the pulpit: "God answers all your needs, if you just ask him." Well, I asked over and over again to the point of begging for God to change our lives-Dear's, my brother's and mine. I prayed that white people would have kinder hearts and that Dear would leave Daddy. But things got worse.

There were more bombings, policemen turned vicious dogs on children, and firemen knocked down teenagers with torrents of water from their powerful hoses. Daddy used his fists so often on Dear's face that we expected to look at her and see bruises and black eyes. Did God hear me? With millions of people all over the world asking Him for help, maybe it wasn't possible for Him to hear the voice of one nigger-child in North Birmingham.

When I was in God's House I saw people who spoke with Him and said that He touched them. The women's eyes rolled back in their heads, their bodies trembled like leaves caught in a strong wind. I thought that one day one of these ladies might die right next to me. I kept my fears to myself. Although I didn't understand it, I knew the Holy Ghost had touched them. What was I doing wrong not to be visited by God's messenger?

I didn't realize it when I was just a boy, but I was setting up a pattern in my thinking that would last for years, a conclusion that somehow or for some reason I was outside of God's purview. At times in my young mind, I questioned whether or not God existed at all, whether He heard my prayers or knew about my troubles and pain. Or was it that He did not care? I began to ask these questions to myself, silently.

Meanwhile, I witnessed some church members talking to the dead. At funerals, mourners looked up, prayed, cried and talked to the deceased spirit. I looked up with them and saw only rafters, ceiling tiles and light fixtures. God talked to almost everyone in my church except me. He touched people in ways I didn't understand. Then I was struck by a near paralyzing fear. God wouldn't answer the prayers of a sinner. Perhaps I was not saved and was already destined for hell. I was mischievous in church. That's why Dear made me sit in the front near the mourner's bench, where the old folk knelt and prayed in a language I didn't understand. Once, one of the elder deacons gave a loud, emotional prayer. Tears rolled down his face. The congregation, sensing the spirit moving in him, urged the deacon on. Lifted by the crowd, the deacon let loose with a Holy Ghost step in time with the crowd's exhortation and the cadence of his prayer. He spun around in a fashion that would put the Temptations to shame, and thrust his thumbs in his vest pockets.

He threw his head back to bellow out another "JEEE-SUS!" and his upper denture plate flew out his mouth and rolled under the communion table. Everything seemed to move in slow motion. Trying not to draw too much attention, he attempted to retrieve the dentures quickly with style, while keeping the Holy Ghost cadence. But the dentures had rolled too far under the communion table for that. One of the ushers had to get down on his hands and knees to rake the pink and white false teeth out with a broom handle. Dear gave me the "evil eye" from the choir stand and dared me to laugh. I covered my mouth with my hand, excused myself and rushed outdoors, where my friends and I laughed loud and freely.

So now I wondered if maybe I had not been touched because God didn't like people laughing at his deacons. Was I a sinner? Reverend Freeman, one of God's messengers, said that all sinners went to hell. I definitely did not want to burn in hell forever.

I had an experience that assured me I could not tolerate being near fire. My father sometimes amused my friends and me with a lighter fluid trick. He poured the flammable liquid over his fingers, put a match to it, and let it burn for a few seconds before extinguishing it by vigorously shaking his hand. I tried it one day and never felt such intense pain before in my life. If I couldn't stand the pain from burning lighter fluid for a couple of seconds, how could I endure my flesh and insides burning in an inferno without ever being consumed? No, I didn't want to go to hell.

The preacher said, "If you sinners don't straighten up and fly right, I see you belching up sulfur and flaming embers." I believed his message without doubt and promised to be more obedient to the preacher, my parents and God.

My middle brother Alfred had constant nightmares about the devil coming to get him in his sleep. He sometimes woke up sweating, screaming and occasionally, wetting his bed. When he rolled over onto the pallet with me I was glad to have his company. He never knew I was more afraid than he was.

Reverend Freeman said that Jesus was the only person that could save us from Satan and his hell. I lay on my mat, awake sometimes until the sun came up, with the name of Jesus on my trembling lips. In my grandmother's house there was a picture of Him kneeling against a huge stone with his hands clasped, pleading toward heaven. The glowing halo and the ray of sunlight beaming down on His sad face made me love Him more. Sometimes I looked at that picture while begging for the blessings from God that never came. As far back as I can remember every 11 o'clock worship service began with the hymn, "What a Friend We Have in Jesus." Other than an occasional joke about a colored Christ, no one ever seriously talked about Jesus being anything other than a white man. Not only was He white, but so were the angels, saints and the entire heavenly host. We sang in our church: "Wash me whiter than snow." These experiences marked me for life and gave me an even higher wall to climb over. What was I to think of myself, a black boy with nappy hair, when everyone holy and sacred and good was white? Also at New Salem, every adult said, "Children are to be seen, not heard." It was disrespectful for us to question adult actions and decisions. I overheard the Sunday school teachers tell Dear that I was rude and impudent and in need of strict discipline, which meant a good whipping.

I was often punished for embarrassing my parents in church and school.

During Christmas practice, I entered the pastor's study without knocking. One of my girl cousins, who was also my age, was sitting in the reverend's lap and he had his anointed hand all the way under her dress. This man taught me all I knew about God, Christ and being saved from hell's fire. Still, I knew he had no business doing that. My cousin didn't seem bothered. I ran as fast as I could to the church basement, with the reverend following right behind me. He found me near the water fountain in an isolated hallway. He spoke with me about the incident, but I was so nervous, confused and stunned that I can't recall what he said and I told no one what he did until I told my father more than 40 years later.

"That man fathered more than a half dozen children in and around that church," my father said with disdain.

Contradictions swarmed around my life like hornets swarming around a new nest. There was little stability in my home and the church provided even less. My heart craved for a place where it could feel safe and secure. But there were none. My fear of God was much stronger than any love I felt for him. That's how I felt, too, about white people and Daddy. I never thought about going to heaven because I was too occupied worrying about staying out of hell. I also couldn't understand Dr. King's kind of freedom because I was so worried about white people's power. And I didn't think of family love because I was too busy trying to dodge my father.

CHAPTER 5: HOPE AGAINST HOPE

The dream of freedom that Martin Luther King, Jr. desired for *all* Americans was slow to take effect in Birmingham. The Civil Rights Act of 1964 initially changed very little in my hometown and state. Whites fled from Birmingham to the outer suburbs. Across the state, private Christian academies sprung up like lily-white dandelions in places where once there was nothing. On paper, there was equality for all, but in Alabama everyone knew who was still in control.

In May of 1967 I was two months shy of my 14th birthday and in my last days at Carrie A. Tuggle Elementary School. Ms. Brown was my homeroom teacher. One morning she passed out what was called a "freedom of choice" form, which was part of the desegregation federal court order. The forms allowed black children to attend any high school in the county of their choice. Ms. Brown asked each of us to stand and tell the class which high school we would attend in the fall. Most of the kids stood and proudly said, "Parker High School."

Parker was part of a long tradition in educational excellence in North Birmingham's black community. My mother and father attended Parker and I was expected to follow. Enrolling in any other high school was never a consideration for me. When my turn came to tell what school I was going to attend, I decided to score some points with the class and make a big joke out of the process. This was a costly mistake that followed me for years and set my life on a different course.

Ms. Brown called my name. I shot up from my chair and in a loud voice, proudly stated, "Ramsay High School."

Ramsay was the pride of the white community. I would have to take two buses to travel four miles across town. Parker was a good two miles from my house if I took the short cut through the city's landfill. The class was spellbound. No one spoke. Eyes flittered from me to Ms. Brown, then back again. A scowl came over her stern face.

"Leonard Lanier Cooper, you are too *stupid* to attend a school like Ramsay," she said.

My eighth grade classmates erupted in uproarious laughter. My fate was sealed. I was going to attend Ramsay to save face with my friends. I often reflect on that spring morning and wonder how my life would be different had Ms. Brown laughed along with us or said nothing, instead of unleashing her stinging rebuke of my playful choice of high schools. Perhaps I would have returned to my seat and the joke would have ended there. Instead, I was humiliated in front of all my friends to the point of feeling trapped in my decision. I had no other choice but to attend a school I knew little about.

I told my brothers what happened and word got back to Ms. Brown that we called *her* stupid. For the remaining academic year, Ms. Brown rarely spoke to me.

Twenty years later, when I visited my grade school, I saw Ms. Brown and attempted to exchange pleasantries with her.

"You and your brothers said I was stupid," she uttered and scurried away.

In 20 years, it seemed that it still had not occurred to Ms. Brown, the *adult* and *teacher*, that her maligning comments hurt an impressionable 13-year-old and altered his life. She was too wrapped up in the fragility of her own feelings to realize just how much damage her words caused. It was incredulous to me that in two decades someone I once looked up to, someone who wielded great power and influence over children, had not gotten over being called out of her name by a hurt little boy.

By the time of my return visit, I had worked diligently to overcome old thinking, and to be someone whom I had not been allowed to be in the Birmingham of my childhood. I figured most people, surely those black teachers who helped shape me, had done the same.

CHAPTER 6: FROM BLACK TO WHITE

I persuaded a neighborhood friend named McCurtis Kelly to attend Ramsay with me. It was an easy sell. He had heard about the unabated violence that plagued Parker High and feared for his life. McCurtis's concerns were not without merit. I witnessed several shootings and knife fights near the school when I stopped by to watch my brother practicing with the marching band. I once helped a neighbor home after he had been shot several times with a small caliber pistol near the school. When Parker High played any of the surrounding black high schools, you could bet on a shooting or stabbing to follow, regardless of which school was victorious.

McCurtis, better known as "Stu Meat," and I also decided to attend the summer sports program at Ramsay. Daddy-Yo temporarily suspended my farm duties, except for the weekends or times when he decided whatever I was involved in could not possibly be as important as my field responsibilities.

Stu Meat and I took the No. 18 Fountain Heights bus and transferred to the No. 12 Highland Avenue bus to get to the south side. Naively, we were not fearful for our safety. The first person we encountered on our premiere trip was an olive-toned girl, who we later found out was second generation Lebanese. Her name was Mary Isis and she was kind and unusually accommodating. She assuaged any concerns we may have harbored. Many people from our neighborhood predicted we would be skinned alive once we set foot on the hallowed, white school grounds.

"Go to the men's locker room, which is in the athletic department on the opposite side of the school," Mary said, vigorously shaking our hands. She appeared genuinely glad to meet us.

We thanked her as we left and made our way around the side of the building to a flight of green steps that led to the locker room. We entered the heavy wooden doors and walked into the athletic department and then the locker room. To the right were the varsity lockers. To the left were the coaches' offices. Halfway down the cement aisle was a huge washer and dryer surrounded by more wood framed, wire mesh lockers. Stu and I forged onward. I scanned the surroundings in hopes of finding one friendly face. Stu was oblivious. I had it in my mind that each step brought us deeper into the bowels of pure hatred.

We saw a lone student standing at the end of the walk near the entrances to the showers. We continued walking. We were almost midway down the hall when several players jumped out from behind the lockers. They grabbed Stu Meat. They forced soiled jock straps over his head and onto his face. I turned to help him, but this little runt they called "Fikes" stepped out and hit me in the gut. He was short and stocky and felt as hard as stone. I didn't let on just how much the punch hurt. I fought to keep from doubling over. It felt like my rib cage had caved in. Head coach "Mutt" Reynolds, sneering, stood with other assistant coaches, each refusing to stop the fight.

There were too many attackers to allow me and Stu Meat to get in any real punches. I just covered my head and face, as my forearm and elbows deflected the assailants' strikes. They probably could have hurt me badly, if they truly wanted to. I suppose they were making a statement, marking their territory.

Finally, one of the coaches blew a whistle, as if he was calling off dogs. The coaches didn't bother introducing themselves.

"One of you show these boys to their lockers in the back corner," Coach Reynolds said.

Stu Meat and I wore our gym shorts and white t-shirts underneath our regular street clothes. We thought it would be foolish to get undressed in such a hostile environment. It was still fresh on my mind that a little more than two years earlier, a white man had drowned my cousin.

Alabama belonged to whites. Always has and always will.

For much of the morning, we engaged in touch football and basketball and then had lunch. It appeared that Stu Meat and I were the only two blacks at Ramsay. Although I was always suspicious, it seemed to me Stu Meat was too trusting.

We found out on that very first day that the white students and coaches were free to call us "niggers" or whatever vile racist labels they wanted to use. Over the weeks we heard the faculty often refer to us as "nigras," while many of the students still called us "niggers." In fairness, there were a couple of white boys who didn't seem to mind us being there. No matter what anyone called us or how we were addressed, we answered respectfully. Eventually, before the summer was over, they addressed us by our last names. Perhaps addressing us any other way would have been viewed as endearing. To most of them, we were animals, to be treated as such and not to be afforded even a modicum of respect.

When that first day came to an end, I was content to put on my clothes without having a shower. A couple of days later, the whites taunted us. "You nigras smell like animals. My goodness, you guys stink."

I didn't care what they said; I just wanted to leave. Stu Meat insisted we prove them wrong and take a shower. I surrendered my better judgment to his unyielding persistence. We removed our blue gym shorts, white t-shirts and sneakers. We didn't have towels, but Stu Meat didn't mind that. My eyes swept the surroundings. I was guarded, as always-and prepared. I was well acquainted with the hatred and treachery whites were capable of when it came to black folk.

We walked pass the row of open commodes near the entrance. As we entered the showers, I whispered in Stu Meat's ear, "This is a bad idea." Several of the white boys were already soaped from head to toe. One boy yelled while pointing, "That's the nigra side over there."

Everyone seemed to stop. All eyes followed me and Stu. Something was unmistakably wrong. I whispered to Stu Meat, "Let's just leave now!" He laughed and pumped the soap from the dispenser, splashing it all over himself. I noticed the color of the soap in our dispenser was different from the pink soap in theirs.

"No!" I screamed as I grabbed Stu Meat's hand to stop him from covering the rest of his body with what was obviously urine. Stu Meat laughed and continued, even trying to put some on me. I forcefully grabbed Stu Meat and wrestled him out of the shower. He refused to believe that anyone would do such a hateful thing. Stu Meat had always been extremely naive. I had known him from the cradle; his mother and Dear were best friends in high school until his mother moved to California.

The first day of school at Ramsay provided a preview of what was to come: some days were mundane and indistinguishable while others were pure, unadulterated hell. I searched desperately for a reason not to conclude that all whites were awful people and void of compassion-or at the least that all the white people in Alabama were awful. Black parents, teachers and civil rights leaders alike extolled in my soul the virtues of being black and taught me that I was as good as any white person in Alabama and deserved respect. I heard and understood the words, but convincing me of the validity of such preachments was another story.

The morning after Martin Luther King, Jr. was killed, some teachers were giddy with happiness and many of the white students could not contain their glee.

"We got y'all boy last night," one boy said to me in the hallway.

For black people, the day of King's assassination was a day of immeasurable darkness and sadness. For whites at my school, it was a day of joyful celebration.

On another afternoon some friends and I were at the school playing basketball. Three or four white students asked to challenge us to a game. "Black against white," one guy said, and we agreed.

When the game ended, one of the white guys said, "Y'all won the game, but you're going to lose the fight."

"Fighting over a silly basketball game?" I remarked.

My friends hightailed it out of there. I remained; amazed that anyone would consider fighting over a foolish game. The white students surrounded me. The next thing I knew I was hanging on the chained-linked fence by the flesh on my back. The prongs on the fence ripped a two-inch tear below my shoulder blade. Another white student passing by helped me down and assisted me to the coach's office. Coach Reynolds covered the wound with a large stretch adhesive bandage.

"Football players get scratches and scrapes all the time and there's no need to worry your momma and daddy," he said.

I followed his advice. A couple of days later, while dressing, Dear saw the large bandage and ordered me to stand still so she could remove it part way. She ripped it down and almost in the same motion, covered the wound and rushed me off to the doctor's office. The doctor told her the healing had already started and it would be best to allow the injury to heal on its own. He said the scar was going to be rather unattractive. Then he scolded her for not seeking treatment for such a deep tear. Dear tucked away the prescription in her purse and we left without her offering an explanation.

My parents seemed proud that I was playing football for the Ramsay team. There were about 90 black students at the school out of a student body of 1,000. I never got to know any of the white students very well, but the black population was like a second family.

Eventually Stu Meat quit the athletic program. He did not leave because of the racist antics on the coach's staff or the football team, but rather due to the daily rigorous exercise regimen that was mandatory. At night he suffered excruciating leg cramps. After a couple of weeks I was making the trek alone.

On one of the slow days, one of the assistant coaches asked me to watch his seven-year-old son. We sat near the base of the stone wall adjacent to the football field. Walking down the street were several young black men.

"There goes a bunch of niggers," the little boy said.

I grabbed him firmly by the arm and angrily asked, "What do you think I am?" I paused. "What do you think I am?" I asked again.

"You're not a nigger, but those are," he said, innocently.

A thousand questions stormed my thoughts, but none found the path to my lips. I am ashamed to say it now, but on that day I found solace in knowing that this young soul separated me from other blacks.

CHAPTER 7: WHAT ABOUT YOUR FRIENDS

My best friend, Juan Johnson, didn't think much of my going to a predominately white school because he said he didn't see any evidence that whites cared at all about educating black students. Juan, who was the fastest and smartest among us, always viewed his self-worth to be well above the rest of us in the neighborhood. Juan's daddy poured steel for the Tennessee Coal and Iron Company. As grueling as the job was, holding such a position in Birmingham meant providing amenities that most families only dreamed of attaining in a lifetime. Juan's family had several new cars and they were the first to own a color television. He was the first of his peers to have a motorcycle, a bright red Yamaha his sister crashed into a tree the first day he had it. Juan was never considered a nice or thoughtful person, and in truth, it didn't bother him one iota what others thought of him.

Juan's mother, a compassionate and caring woman, was always there to rub salve on my physical and emotional wounds. Although I was in high school, I was still getting the occasional beatings from my father for what I viewed as minor infractions. One week, when I was in the 10th grade, my Father promised me that I had a whupping coming. Sometimes he let a day pass before he got around to whupping me, often for something I did not do, anyway. When the day came that week, he sent me down to the thicket next to our house to fetch a tree branch. At times I made as many as three trips to those woods because my father rejected my branches until I found one he felt wouldn't break so easily under the force of his beatings.

This time I gathered the limb but made a detour to Juan's house. His mother was home alone. She and I sat at her kitchen table trying to determine the best way for me to avert an unnecessary beating by my father. I can't recall the infraction that brought me to her that day, but I do remember her torment. I stood at her door for at least an hour, trying to decide whether to leave or stay with her.

She knew if I stayed it would only prolong the inevitable; if I left, the belt, electrical cord or tree branch waited just up the street and around the corner. Regardless, with either choice the end result was the same.

"Len, what can I do to help you?" she cried.

I gave her a half smile. "There's nothing you can do, Ms. Johnson. There's nothing anyone can do."

"I'm so sorry, Len," she said.

I walked away but kept looking back for some sort of reprieve, I suppose. She stood in that door until I turned the corner. Juan also bore witness to the daily events of me growing up in a "broken" home, but, unlike his mother, my suffering amused him.

In my house, Daddy finally stopped whupping me in my sophomore year of high school. The last time my father beat me, I was recuperating when I looked through the window and saw Juan walking towards our front door.

"God I hate him!" I said to Juan while we sat on the front porch. This time Juan looked genuinely concerned, so I decided to tell him exactly what happened. "Daddy came in drunk and started yelling at me again. He took off his belt and began beating me without saying why." Juan laughed. He stood and then danced around the yard in jerky motions, as if to be reacting to lashes from a belt. I stared in disbelief that he found all this funny.

I stopped talking. I didn't want to give him another moment of pleasure at my expense. I was slowly dying and crumbling to pieces inside and my best friend thought it all humorous.

"Juan, if I live to be a thousand years old, I swear before God almighty a drop of alcohol will never ever touch my lips," I said.

Juan invited me to his house to cool off and relax a bit. While I waited in his living room He went to the kitchen to pour cold drinks for us. He handed me a bottle of 7-Up that was about a quarter full and kept the Mountain Dew for himself. I turned the soda up to take a big swig and realized it was whiskey, not a soft drink. I ran to the kitchen and spit it out in the sink. Juan laughed hysterically.

"So much for that promise of never tasting alcohol," he said between guffaws.

How could my best friend play such a mean trick on me and find so much pleasure in my anguish and grief. I wouldn't dream of doing something as mean-spirited to him.

I was a grade ahead of Juan. Until I met him, I never had friends below my grade level because that was considered uncool. Juan attended Parker High, the predominantly black high school near our neighborhood. He thought I was crazy for going to a predominantly white school because he did not believe that white people cared about educating black people and doubted that they were trying to do their best to educate me.

We spent little time hanging out after school during the school year. As soon as summer rolled around, when I was not working my grandfather's farm or involved in the summer sports program in my high school, Juan and I spent almost every waking hour in his basement playing monopoly, electric football or fooling around on the creek bank.

During the hot summer months, kids came down in droves from the northern states to visit relatives living in the South. I absolutely adored this one girl, Patricia, who came to visit her cousins every summer. Each year, I tried to muster up the nerve to say just one word to her. The summer after my freshman year at Ramsay I decided I was finally going to do it. Juan was my new friend then and he pushed me to try all sorts of things. Talking to girls was always trouble for me, but for Juan it came natural.

"What's the worst she can do?" he asked, as we headed toward Junebug's house, where Patricia was staying for the summer.

Juan didn't get it. The humiliation Patricia might heap on me with her rejection paled in comparison to the laughter and teasing he would unleash. Nevertheless, I jotted down and rehearsed some of the things I wanted to say. Juan and I waited on the front porch, as any good southern boy would do when he "comes-a-calling" on a young lady.

She came out of the house without me hearing her. It just seemed that I turned around and there she stood, more beautiful than she was in all of my dreams. My nerves faded fast. The passing moments were awkward, as the three of us chitchatted. Oddly enough, it was soon apparent that she had no particular interest in what I had to say but she hung onto every word that parted

Juan's lips. She even laughed at his tired-ass jokes.

We both thought Patricia was stunning, but I was hurting too much inside to remain one second more. I came up with a lame reason to head home. Wounded and dejected, I limped across Junebug's front yard. Surprisingly, Juan ran and caught up with me before I reached the end of the driveway.

We ended up at Juan's house, soon followed by one of Patricia's buddies. For a moment I was thrilled, just knowing she was about to deliver the message I had waited two long, sweltering summers to hear.

"Patricia likes you and wants you to come back," she said.

I was ecstatic. But then I realized the comments were meant for Juan, not me.

"Tell her I am not interested in her in that way," Juan said.

I was surprised. Then delighted. From that day forward, Juan never spoke to Patricia again unless in my presence. He didn't have to explain his actions to me; it was crystal clear why he dismissed her. Juan had given our friendship priority over dating the prettiest girl to visit Birmingham every summer. This snapshot of a friend's unwavering loyalty is a story I have shared and carried with me all my life. Even my children have heard it.

My guess is that Juan has no recollection of this incident because the moment was trivial and unmemorable to him. But it meant everything to an awkward 15-year-old making his way through the wreckage of a broken home and shouldering a marginal feeling of self-worth.

Juan's family was devoted to their church, which was a short ride from their house. Occasionally I attended church with him. By this time, going to church was no longer a requirement for my brothers and me. When we reached high school, our mother left it up to us as to what path to choose for our spiritual and religious fulfillment. For a year or so, I rarely graced any church, except when it was a special occasion or friends invited me. To me, Dear's Baptist faith was riddled with contradictions and problems I didn't understand. For instance, young girls who were unfortunate enough to get pregnant out of wedlock were forced to come before the congregation to beg for forgiveness and apologize for their transgressions. Meanwhile, the boys in question were free of such humiliation. At least the Catholics offered counseling and had special programs for young unwed mothers.

One afternoon, Juan and I, along with several of our friends were out walking along a secluded road in our neighborhood. We came upon a red and white 1957 Impala we all recognized. Lo and behold, sprawled out on the back seat was one of the Baptist church Sunday school teachers and a good deacon from the church. He was one of the same deacons who I had heard shout "Amen!" as they paraded a young girl before the congregation for getting pregnant before marriage. As we paused by the car, my friend Navi slapped on the trunk with his hand, which made a loud noise. Then we ran off as fast as our legs could carry us.

CHAPTER 8: A LEAP FROM DEAR'S FAITH

Even as a young teenager, I knew I wanted no part of Dear's church. So it was time for me to look somewhere else for spiritual growth and fellowship. When I was much younger, I had questioned the Bible's version of creation and many other miraculous events in the scriptures. I was also suspicious of the women in my mother's church who shouted and passed out every Sunday on cue. Even as a boy, it seemed to me that their emotional reactions were staged and I was not going to let them pass off their Sunday theatrics as genuine religious experiences. In my youthful opinion, those emotionally charged services simply lacked sincerity and conviction.

The Baptist Church's link to emotions and sensationalism ran me to the Catholic Church, which appealed to me because it did not accept scripture as absolute truth. Also, the Catholics didn't pass the collection plate for the third, fourth and often fifth time as the Baptists did and I loved what I considered the "sophistication" of the Catholic Church.

My brothers, indifferent to my decision to leave Dear's church, stayed with the family religion, which for generations had been Baptist. Dear thought my decision was a poor choice, but she nevertheless left it to me to decide what religion called to my soul. My father said nothing when I told him I was leaving the Baptists. He didn't care whether I went to church or not or what church I attended. The Powell family, which included nine children, was one of the few Catholic families in my neighborhood. Most of the other families were Baptist or Methodist. Mrs. Powell, who was one of Dear's childhood friends, took me to the Catholic Church for the first time when I was 16 years old. I walked around the corner from where I lived to meet the Powell's at their house that first Sunday morning. We all piled into their extra-long station wagon. Our Lady Queen of the Universe Catholic Church was situated in the heart of Dynamite Hill, the site of many bombings during the civil rights movement. On both sides of the entrance stood a tall, whiter than snow angel with broad wings, clasping with both hands a large metallic pole with a grand cylindrical lamp affixed to the top. I was in awe. Mrs. Powell affectionately held my arm, keeping me close to her side. She didn't wait for my questions. At every turn, she offered explanations for actions she thought I did not understand. She explained why parishioners made the sign of the cross on their chest or bowed down on one knee while entering and exiting the church. I believe my mouth was open with amazement and excitement all through the service. My eyes went from one station of the cross to the next. The stations were miniature marble scenes of the major events leading up to the crucifixion. I closed my eyes and let my senses take hold and capture every smell, every sensation. I loved the calm, orderliness of the service. I was thankful that there was no place for spontaneity. No one was passing out. No screaming and shouting. No jumping. I knew almost immediately: I had found a church home!

After the Mass ended, I roamed throughout the sanctuary, admiring and touching the faces and hands of the life-size marble statues of Joseph, Mary and the baby Jesus. I sat alone in the dimly lit church on the back pew and thanked God for my new direction. In the Catholic Church, I loved the ornaments, the smell of incense from the thurible and the occasional Latin chants. For me, it was a pleasant change from being fearful of someone passing out or dying in the midst of having a Holy Ghost seizure or being threatened and reprimanded for asking questions about scriptures and rituals I didn't understand. Everything was new from top to bottom, which allowed me a new beginning. People *expected* me to ask questions. The black girls in the Catholic Church seemed prettier, with their light, even-toned skin and long, flowing hair.

When I arrived Father Paul and Father Fitzpatrick served as priests at Our Lady Queen of the Universe Catholic Church. Father Paul often said from the pulpit, "God loves you black folk, too." And no one in the congregation made an issue of his comment.

For two years, I met with Father Paul weekly receiving convert instructions. Then, finally, I was baptized in the Catholic faith. After two years of instructions at the church and working closely with the congregation, the event was rather anti-climactic. I didn't bother telling or inviting family and friends. The ceremony was an accent mark on the Sunday morning liturgy, with all the new members standing before the parishioners alone with a person designated as their Godparent. Mine was a young man assigned by the priest in haste and that I hardly knew.

Once in the middle of the Christmas High Mass at midnight, Father Paul stood with arms spread wide behind the altar, reading from the sacred book before the congregation. In an instant, his face turned red as he made a mad dash to the adjacent room known as the sacristy. The sacristy was reserved for the priest's vestments, unconsecrated bread and wine or whatever else was needed for the mass. As Father Paul ran from the sanctuary he nearly tripped on his long white priestly robe. Some of the men raced behind him, slamming the door shut once they entered the sacristy. Without explanation, the president of the parish council stumbled and floundered his way through the rest of the service. There was no explanation for Father's hasty exit from the pulpit and the onlookers murmured throughout the rest of the mass.

"Go in peace to love and serve the Lord," the council president said as the mass ended.

"Thanks be to God," the crowd responded.

Before the church emptied word was out that Father Paul was drunk and had vomited in the sacristy sink. The glitter and luster of the Church began to tarnish for me. My own father used to abuse alcohol. As Father Paul ran in front of the congregation, I saw my father running from our kitchen table and throwing up in the bathroom sink. I was embarrassed for Father Paul and sad for myself, as the image I created of the saintly priest crumbled. I saw a problem in the Catholic Church that I had never before witnessed in my mother's church. By leaving my family's place of worship, I left behind some concerns that were now being substituted with different ones. I decided not to return to The Queen.

For weeks I stayed away and refused to go back to Father Paul for convert instructions. I had perfect attendance in my new church until this incident. One of the elder ladies in the church invited me to her home to discuss the "human" side of the priesthood. I arrived at her home late in the afternoon on a Saturday. She lived in a two-story stone house in what was once an affluent black neighborhood not far from the church. Her home had the smell of an old house, but it was not an offensive odor. She invited me to sit in the living room, which was off the small hall leading to other areas of the house.

"Can I get something for you? Something to drink?" she offered.

"No Ma'am I'm fine." I responded.

Mrs. Boyd had taken an interest in me since my first day in the parish. Every Sunday I was greeted with a hug and kiss from her. It appeared she was genuinely excited to see me. For the next minutes we exchanged normal conversation until she broached the topic of Father Paul.

"It was very unfortunate what happened with Father at the midnight mass, but you have to understand things in a bigger context, she said."

"What is there to understand? Father Paul is a drunk that can't hold his liquor. I think that just about sums it up," I replied.

"I wish it was that simple. "Father Paul has no one to share his troubles or concerns with. That's the way it is with most priests and nuns. You can go to your family and friends or girlfriend, but when Father Paul gets home from a difficult time, who does he turn to? God?" she said, lifting her voice. "Well Len, sometimes God is busy and may not have time for you at that moment."

I sat in silence and listened. Maybe I was being too harsh on him. I didn't know what to think. Mrs. Boyd did not know that I was an unwitting spectator and participant in a world turned upside down by alcohol abuse. The moment I learned of Father Paul's drinking problem, he and my father became one in the same. On that afternoon, I was too young in my spiritual development to find forgiveness for my father or Father Paul.

"Go back to your instructions classes," she continued. "If you still feel that strongly about what happened, talk to Father Paul."

Her argument did not alter my views on how priests should conduct themselves and for certain it could not excuse Father Paul's actions. But I needed a reason-any reason-to return to the church that I very much wanted to be a part of.

I went to see Father Paul a few days later. He was clearly embarrassed when I broached the subject of his drunkenness at the midnight Christmas mass.

"Although a priest is representative of the church and the person of Jesus on earth, you must never forget that we are still men and make mistakes," he said.

I understood clearly what he was saying, but his mistake was monumental in my eyes. As he talked, I nervously pulled at the dead callous skin on my palms, focusing on the floor. His high-pitched voice quivered with each word. Then a few moments of silence ticked away.

"Shall we continue with the instructions?" he whispered.-I agreed. I loved my new church, The Queen, too much to be deterred by any old closet alcoholic priest. Father Paul was my anchor in the church, but after that incident I saw him as a drunk who had little to nothing to offer me. I often reflect on this moment and think how for me one incident negated all the good this priest tried to do in my community. I did not understand true forgiveness or the complexities of human beings. I wanted my father, my religious mentors and all other human beings to be perfect, or at least not to have the kinds of flaws I considered major and ungodly. My life would prove to me that forgiveness is a process, that it is certainly more than uttering the word. I didn't know this as a young man, so I judged Father Paul too harshly, crippling any real possibility of ever getting to know him. I believe in the end my unwillingness to forgive was much more damaging than his temporary lapse in judgment. But for the time, I just wanted to get through Father Paul's instructions and baptism. After that, I concluded, would have no further need of him.

Although the Catholic Church held me spellbound, I knew it wasn't free from the racial strife that plagued the city. Sunday morning is the most segregated time in America and Birmingham was definitely America. Like my parents, I was well aware of the deep-rooted polarization of the city and how both simple and intricate choices were often made along color lines. There was not much mingling between the races even among religious denominations, including the Catholics. Mrs. Powell told me a large bomb was found and disarmed in the vestibule of my new church back in the 60's. Before the civil rights law came in to effect, white ministers and white guest speakers might drop by the black church on special occasions, but blacks could not do the same at white churches. Black ministers did not drop by white churches. Blacks were turned away at the door. In the Catholic parishes, special sections were roped off for Negroes if the event called for a racially mixed audience. But by the time I finished my instructions and was baptized, which was during my junior year of high school, there were no noticeable remaining vestiges of racism in my church, the black members and visiting whites sat together and we had both black and white speakers.

CHAPTER 9: THE POOL

My junior year of high school ended pretty much the same way as it started-with little or no fanfare. I was content with being the nondescript, invisible and irrelevant one. As in previous years, I once again enrolled in Ramsay's summer sports program. The highlight of the summer of 1970 was when I was introduced to Rodney, a transfer student from the neighboring all Black high school the previous year. He took pride in being a wannabe player or ladies' man. At any given time, he was embroiled in three or four so-called "serious relationships." He often asked me to run interference for him when he became too entangled in his self-created web of lies and deceit. My services were most needed on weekends and I was always there to oblige.

The role of a sidekick never set well with me, but I *was* a loyal friend. Rodney was a terrible liar and leading a duplicitous life didn't suit him. He really had a good heart and struggled with his self-prescribed deceptive antics. But the lure of pretty faces and curvaceous hips was always too much for his heart and wandering eyes to resist. There were times when the pains of his conscience got the best of him, resulting in a full disclosure of his transgressions. When he was with a girl he truly believed he had a future with the truth rushed forward like a forceful autumn wind, with him hoping his admissions would free him of suspicions and accusations. The girls were not always so understanding and forgiving. He broke hearts, and tears flowed. But he always managed to convince the girls to give him one more opportunity. I was always there to help pick up the pieces.

At the time, neither of us knew the far-reaching implications and future ramifications of decisions made on any given indistinguishable Alabama summer day. Yet Rodney and his family played a pivotal role in many of my life choices. During the summer sports program at my high school, my friendship with Rodney paralleled the relationship I had with Juan. Yet Rodney was not judgmental and vindictive, as Juan had proven himself to be at times.

Every day at noon when the athletic program ended, Rodney ventured down to the Underwood Park pool in Birmingham's South Town project region. His house was on the outskirts of the low-income, brick garden apartments.

I was pleased when he invited me to tag along to the pool. I didn't have money to swim so I sat outside watching Rodney through the wire mesh fence do full and half gainer dives off the one-meter springboard. It looked so easy, so effortless. A couple of times Rodney had a few extra coins and paid my way in to the pool. I was delighted. He spent much of his time in the deep end as I flailed around in the shallow water that ranged from three to five feet deep. I submerged my face under the water, kicking and pulling only to come up and realize I had moved a few inches or not at all. It was even more disappointing when I lifted my head from beneath the water and planted my feet firmly on the bottom and found that not only had I not moved, I had lost ground.

My father shared with me his theory on the mechanics of swimming.

"The deeper the water, the better chance you have of actually swimming, Len," he said. "In deep water the pressure from beneath pushes you up, keeping you afloat, and the force behind you propels you forward."

I believed his baseless nonsense. I had grown weary of the years of picking cotton and taking care of hogs, cows and crops. I was primed and in need of a vocational change. I figured if I could find a "real job," like being a lifeguard or a job that paid real money, my grandfather would free me from the plow and crops during the summer and minding livestock in the middle of the winter.

One day Rodney was preparing to head across town to McAlpine Pool for a two-week lifesaving and water safety course you had to take to become a lifeguard. He invited me to come along. I had watched Rodney swimming in the deep water for weeks and I had memorized his swimming techniques: Freestyle, backstroke, breaststroke and not to mention, treading water. Armed with my vast knowledge of swimming, coupled with what my father told me about how your body must be in a prone position in deep water for the pressure to push you up and keep you afloat, I was ready.

For the first exercise, the trainer instructed all perspective lifeguards to divide into two equal groups on opposite ends of the diving well. The water was glistening as it splashed against the shining metallic gutters. I was with the group labeled "rescuers," while people on the other side represented "victims." The instructor walked us through a few minutes of land drills. I was in top form and looking good for the onlookers that gathered on the other side of the fence.

There were a couple of girls in the crowd that I had met earlier and desperately needed to impress.

"Good technique, Len," the instructor said, reaffirming what I already knew to be true. The trainer even used me as a land example. From his tower, he yelled out instructions and explanations, as I walked through the motions of approaching a drowning swimmer and correctly placing the victim in what was called "the cross chest carry."

"Very good, Mr. Cooper!" he shouted while looking down at his clipboard. Then the moment came to separate the men from the neophytes. I knew without a doubt that when the day was over, I would be selected among the few to move on to the actual lifeguard course.

"Victims! Rescuers!" the trainer yelled from atop his lofty perch.

The guard tower was a throne that wielded immeasurable power in the pool and surrounding neighborhood. I watched the first victim jump in and pretend to be drowning. The rescuer jumped in on queue. After the pair struggled to the side of the pool, it was finally my turn to shine. After instructions, the trainer ordered the victim in to the pool.

"Rescuer!" the trainer screamed.

I jumped in the water with a splash. To my surprise, there was no bottom like in the shallow end of the pool I was accustomed to. The more I tried to get leveled off, the more I sank and the more water I splashed. I remembered what my daddy told me and called to mind what I had observed during all those weeks of watching Rodney. I had recorded his every move, every muscle twitch in my memory. But nothing worked.

Now there were two victims in the pool, but one of us was not pretending.

The trainer dove into the water from the tower, swam under me and came up from behind. He had his arm across my chest, as he side stroked, carrying me on his hip. He finally made it to the pool's edge after a brief tow.

"Mr. Cooper, before you think about becoming a lifeguard, maybe you should consider learning how to swim first!" he barked.

Everyone laughed, even the two girls outside of the fence. I didn't see one thing funny, as I tried to conceal my shame and embarrassment. After the training session had ended, Rodney offered to help me learn to swim. He did not laugh or look disappointed at me. I was grateful.

I was determined to learn to swim. My friend Juan wanted to learn also. We began making daily trips to our neighborhood pool. We stayed clear of the deep end but got close enough to watch swimmers who seemed to know what they were doing. We gave it our best effort, but nothing seemed to work. Then one day a big, burly lifeguard called me over to the guard stand.

"You are trying too hard," he said. "Watch. This is what you are doing." He flailed his arms like octopus tentacles. "You are fighting the water."

I was sufficiently embarrassed, but thankful for the help.

"Swim slower, splashing as little water as possible," he said, demonstrating a correct stroke slowly and methodically. I stood near the guard tower, mimicking his every move.

On the first try I managed to move a few feet. Juan was enjoying the same progress. By the end of the week, both of us could swim the full length of the pool. The pool was

L shaped and we stayed well clear of the multicolor rope, separating the deep end. So one day the same burly guard called us over. "Why don't you go over to the deep end?" he asked.

"You've got to be kidding!" I replied.

"If you don't jump off that diving board you will have to leave the pool and not come back until you are ready to at least try!" he yelled.

I slowly climbed the metal ladder leading to the diving board, which extended over the eight-foot deep diving well. All eyes were on me. I cautiously approached the front edge of the board, placing my weight on my back leg so as not to accidently fall in. I shook with fear as I walked on the plank and my feet slid across the sandpaper-like surface covering the light green and white fiberglass. The board bounced slightly, and I considered calling the whole thing off. Terrified, I cased the bottom and the distance to the ladder, conveniently located next to the lifeguard. I looked at Juan and Juan looked at me. I stood there on the edge of that board, partially frozen with fear and my eyes fixed on the lifeguard. The guard stood in his tower and gave us a land demonstration on how to swim up and level off before attempting to swim out. I was ready-and scared. I crept slowly even closer to the end of the one-meter springboard. Now, the tips of my toes were hanging over the edge. Finally, with my eyes closed, I just walked off. Suddenly, as I entered the water, the loud laughter and splashing from kids frolicking about the pool came to a sudden halt. All I could hear is the bubbling sounds in my ears and mostly silence. I was suspended somewhere between the surface and the bottom.

I know the jump happened quickly but so many thoughts ran through my head. It was as if time slowed down. I felt liberated as I entered the water. It was still, quiet and peaceful. Then I remembered where I was and what I had just done. I swim hard and fast as if my life depended on it. I imagine water was flying everywhere. I swam for my life.

Juan would not be out done. He jumped next.
My fear of the water was gone! I looked at the lifeguard and he was just grinning. I didn't thank him verbally, but I spent the rest of that day diving.

Mr. Herman Whitehead, the director of Birmingham Park and Recreation Pools, also taught me 11th grade chemistry. I was not able to acquire one of the coveted lifeguard jobs, but Mr. Whitehead allowed me to work in the basket area of the neighborhood pool. My job was to provide bathers with the green mesh baskets to store their belongings. All day I was surrounded by loads of sweaty clothes and smelly, crusty socks. The only time I had access to the pool was on my off days. This was not adequate time to practice and I was determined to rid myself of the humiliation I endured at the lifeguard recruiting class. So I concocted a plan.

One day during lunch I took the pool keys to the nearby hardware store and had a copy made. The keys had stamped right on the side 'do not copy' but the man in the hardware store didn't see the marking or didn't care. During off hours and at night, I locked the gate and practiced in the shallow end. I had a modicum of comfort in the pool, so I didn't dare to venture too close to the deep end, especially since I was there alone.

I took the lifeguard training and failed the test once more, but I never stopped practicing. The next time I took the test I received the highest score in my group.

The following summer I passed the Water Safety Instructors course under Herb Schroeder, said to be the toughest trainer in the state. This accomplishment allowed *me* to certify and train lifeguards.

I was assigned to work at the pool in my neighborhood, which was considered one of the most dangerous areas in the city. I took an immediate interest in teaching poor kids not only how to swim, but to swim well. It wasn't long before word spread that the East Thomas swimming pool had a swimming program second to none. I personally went out into the neighborhood soliciting anyone interested in learning to swim to try our classes.

For several years, my neighborhood pool was staffed with lifeguards who had a genuine interest in teaching people to swim. During the sessions, scores of onlookers hung on the fence watching the lessons. Often those same onlookers signed up for the next available session. The children's classes in the morning filled up as well as the adult classes in the evening.

Mr. Whitehead, the director, asked me to be in charge of organizing the swim team to represent East Thomas. I was eager. I knew all the kids that frequented our pool. It was not so important that they knew how to swim *well*, it was my mission to simply teach them *to swim*.

For the next few weeks I recruited unenthusiastic kids ranging in age from 5 to 18. Most of the parents weren't so eager either to have their children participate in an activity uncommon to the black community. I was determined to change their perceptions.

It was a very hard sell. I offered the children free admittance to the pool for each day they attended practice drills. On the first day of practice about 20 kids showed up. The sight brought tears to my eyes. They huddled poolside, lips dry, shivering from the evening breeze, the little ones with teeth chattering. Some were dressed in pretty floral or striped nylon swimwear, but most were dressed in old tattered shorts and cut-off jeans. A couple of them had huge safety pins securing the waistbands to keep the shorts from falling down. Most of the children were kids whose parents couldn't afford to pay the quarter for admittance during recreational swim hours. I often assigned chores to the children, such as picking up paper or emptying the trash, to cover the charge of admission. The director stopped by unannounced on a couple of occasions to find the pool full of kids and very little money in the cash register. The director commented only once about how the number of patrons in the pool did not square with the daily receipts. I believe, from our conversations, that he understood many of the neighborhood kids could not afford the luxury of spending hot summer days poolside.
It was mandatory that all swim team members also attend swim lessons in the morning and practices in the evening. Much of the time I spent with the team was on my own time. I didn't mind at all.

The East Thomas Swim Team was made up of kids from across the economic spectrum. Some were kids of drug dealers and addicts; some were children of teachers and doctors. There was even a son of a federal judge.

The first year of competition with the 13 other pools throughout the city was a disaster. We finished second to last. The team competed hard and lost graciously, time after time. They learned early on how to be a proud loser. But I knew they needed desperately to see and feel the sweet harvest of their hard work.

The following summer there seemed to be a feeling in the air that something remarkable was about to happen. Many of the team members returned from the previous year, but parents also brought their younger children and insisted they be involved in the classes and particularly on the swim team, even if they couldn't swim. There were an equal number of boys and girls. At our first swim meet, we had to face a team that had demolished us the previous year. Ted Adams was by far my best and fastest swimmer. Ted was from a well-to-do family that could afford to have a pool in their backyard. His father was a prominent attorney in Alabama who was later appointed to the federal bench under President Reagan. None of this mattered to Teddy. He was proud to be on the team and never missed a practice or a meet. As he poised himself on the deck for the beginning of the race, the throngs of onlookers grew silent, waiting for the starter pistol to fire. Ted purposely false started by diving in too soon, gracefully, effortless, slicing through the water the length of the pool. I noticed the expression on the faces of his competitors. They were confused, perplexed. Teddy was the fastest swimmer I had ever seen. The crowd gasped at his sheer speed while the other swimmers appeared to have lost heart as they looked back and forth at each other. Ted and I exchanged winks. We both knew the race was over. The opposing swimmers wouldn't stand a chance in such a flustered, already defeated state of mind. We won that day and that event set the pace for the rest of the season and tailored the outcome of every swim meet.

These rich and poor black children from Birmingham's north side celebrated by kissing and hugging one another. A prominent dentist who had three children on the team shared a sustained embrace with a scrawny single poor mother, whose hair was wiry, unkempt and filled with lint. That day, any economic and social gap that existed between the swim team members and their families vanished. That summer the East Thomas Swim Team was invincible. In our second season, East Thomas finished first in the city!

In addition to teaching classes and coaching the swim team, I was always the first to arrive in the mornings. The pool was situated well off the main road and far back in the corner of the park. It was my duty to inspect the facility before the gate opened to the public. Some mornings I found large green metal trash barrels and old car tires submerged in the deep end of the pool. The resident druggies and drunkards looked down upon me from their gathering point on a small hill next to the railroad tracks. During pool hours, they insisted on entering the pool without paying the fee. Sometimes they climbed up on the roof and sneaked in without the guard seeing them or the guard pretended not to see them in order to avoid a violent confrontation.

One day these undesirables (less tolerant of us, who were supposed to be there) lobbed wine bottles from the hilltop on to the pool deck. The glass scattered into what seemed like a million pieces. The pool was immediately evacuated as the children carefully tiptoed to safety outside of the pool area. Every inch of the deck was hosed down and the bottom of the pool vacuumed.

The violence around the pool was unabated at times. A young man sought refuge in the pool after being stabbed between the eyes with a broken Coke bottle. When he ran towards the pool entrance, I recognized him as one of my former swim team members. I quickly opened the gate and ordered it be locked behind him. He fell into my arms. His blood drenched me as well as a portion of the pool deck. I covered his wound with a white towel. Each time the cloth was removed, blood squirted out from between his eyes like a miniature fountain. The police and ambulance arrived within minutes. These violent scenes played over and over, like bad movies. In time, many of the serious troublemakers that hung around the park ended up dying in some act of violence. Others ended up in prison. A few changed their lives for the better.

CHAPTER 10: THE SINS OF MY FATHERS

During career week for seniors, the guidance counselor discouraged many black students from applying to major universities, steering them toward black colleges and the Armed Services. When my senior year rolled around, there were more black students attending the school, which presented me with mixed feelings. I suppose in some way the increased numbers of blacks kept the whites in check, at least the ones I had trouble with in previous years. The influx of new students changed everything. Suddenly the school was predominantly black and the new students outnumbered the returning students both black and white combined. They took over pretty much everything from student government offices to sports. The nearly 100 blacks from previous years were absorbed into this new wave of black faces. Many in the new majority hated being there while some of these same black students strutted around like conquerors. I managed to make friends with a few of the new arrivals, but many kept to themselves.

When time came for me to consider a college, my choices were rather limited. I was not a superior student in high school, except for one marking period in my senior year. For some inexplicable reason Ms. Galloway was of the mind that I could compete academically if given the opportunity. She fought for me to enroll in her advanced biology class, although the boys' advisor vehemently opposed. That was one of the few times I made an A in a high school course.

Attending college was not a part of my life's plan, at least not until Juan made it clear that he had set his sights on becoming a doctor. If we were to remain friends, I knew that meant I had to attend college as well.

After graduation, I spent the next two years at the local junior college taking remedial courses and beefing up my sagging transcript. I managed to save a little money to buy a car in order to drive the twenty miles to school. The car was often unreliable and I depended on my middle brother and friends who knew how to fix cars to do repairs at no charge.

I decided on a pre-dental curriculum with a biology concentration. During this time, my parish priest gave me additional responsibilities in the church, especially on weekends and when youth events were scheduled. The thought of entering the seminary and becoming a Roman Catholic priest had been with me for some time, but I kept the desire to myself. My academic performance continued in lackluster fashion. My father made it crystal clear that he was not going to contribute one cent towards my college education. Dear helped the best she could by paying a portion of my tuition from the money she made sewing draperies for a local company. After two years at the junior college, I transferred to the University of Alabama in Birmingham. The tuition was considerably higher. At one point I was working all night on a full-time job and taking a full course load. I managed to sleep a bit every *other* day. This continued for months. In the middle of preparing papers or assignments, my father often intentionally started a fight, insisting that I was wasting my time.

While at the university, I was fortunate to land a position sorting checks at the Federal Reserve Bank. I was assigned the night shift, which started at 9 o'clock in the evening until 5 o'clock in the morning. My classes at school started promptly at 8 o'clock in the morning. After my shift, I raced home, often in a futile effort to complete an assignment and occasionally grab an hour or two of sleep. My father had different plans.

"Len! Git up from there and come take me to work," he demanded while pacing from the kitchen to his and Dear's bedroom. "Daddy, I've been up since yesterday morning and I need to finish this paper before class at 8 and after school I have to go right back to work." I explained.

"I don't give a damn about any of that!" he shouted. "Just git up off your ass and come take me to work!"

This scene was repeated over and over again while I was studying at the university, often with a threat of being thrown out into the streets. "You should be paying rent, anyhow, with your grown ass. Now git up off your behind and do as I tell you!"

I sometimes found my finished and unfinished papers torn up and thrown in the trash. "I don't understand," I said standing before my father with the torn pages in my hands. My father's eyes never looked in my direction. "Daddy, Why? I don't understand, I don't understand any of this." There was silence. I resorted to leaving my job at the bank in the mornings and headed straight for class. I took No-Doz pills to keep me awake for days at a time.

My instructor arrived early and saw the pills on my desk. I arrived in the class an hour early and was exhausted from being awake for nearly two days. The instructor entered the room shortly after I took my place and walked past me. "These things will kill you," she said, removing the pills from my desk and placing the box in her purse.

"I need those!" I pleaded, as she left the room. I fell asleep just before my 8 o'clock class and didn't wake up until noon. I had no recollection of the class ever being in session. I had slept for hours.

On days when my car would not start, my grandfather and father refused to provide me with transportation. I never understood their aversion to higher education. Daddy-Yo attended college for a while and Daddy dreamed of going to college himself, so why did they view education beyond reading, writing and simple math as a waste of time? They never said the words, but in later years when asked about it, my inquiries were met with silence or indignation. One day I decided to come right out and ask Daddy-Yo why he refused to help with my tuition or contribute anything towards my education. He looked calmly through me and said in his deep resonant voice, "Git on way from here boy! What you're saying is nothing about nothing!"

To him, my inquiry amounted to nothing, and he wasn't going to waste a second giving it the least consideration.

There were occasions when I had to walk several miles to the campus, resulting in tardiness and missed assignments. Rarely would an instructor allow me to make up the missed exam. The failing grade was factored into my overall grade point average. On many occasions, Daddy or Daddy-Yo could have helped me, but both always refused. I reached deep inside of myself, trying to find the good or lesson to be learned from Daddy and Daddy-Yo's behavior. They were supposed to love me and I tried desperately to see and understand the logic behind their actions. There was nothing to understand, no lesson to be learned. My father and grandfather had no interest in my success or failure. Neither of them ever put a dime in my hand just for me to spend as I pleased. Never. I was convinced they did not care whether I lived or died, succeeded or failed. I was of no value outside of what I could do for them. And their disdain for me made me hate my own life.

CHAPTER 11: SAY GOOD-BYE TO LOVE

Nothing was going right except my relationship with Laura, a nursing student from Aliceville, Ala. We had been dating for about a year. As a matter of fact, my friend Rodney from the pool introduced us. For my 21st birthday, she invited me up to her second-floor dorm room for what she referred to as my "very special gift." In my mind, I was set on doing some heavy petting as we had done so many times before. We discussed the possibility of going all the way, but I was content with the kissing and caressing. So on this special day, I was not convinced that we would actually have sex.

It was against the rules for men to visit the nurses' dorms except at designated times on the weekend, so this was special indeed. I made my way up the stairs with her, tipping past unsuspecting hall monitors. As we headed to her room, outside of the allowed time, she took me by the hand, and we carefully eased past other nursing students. My heart felt as if it would burst. I didn't care about the risk of getting expelled because all that good kissing and hugging waiting for me was worth all the risks, even the risk of getting expelled from the university. Yep, we were very much in love.

In the room, we kissed and hugged as we had done many times before. But this time was different. She was encouraging, willing and taking charge. It wasn't like I had not had sex before. After all, I had my first encounter when I was six. But that episode was followed by a 15-year lull.

That first experience scared me away from sex. My friend André caught me on top of Mildred Douglas on the ground under her house. We both were fully dressed through the entire experience. But instead of André stopping me, he went to my mother. I remember Dear calling my name at the top of her lungs from our tiny cement back porch. "Len! Git yourself in here right this second!"

I jumped off Mildred, leaving her all sprawled out behind the brick supports, and ran as fast as I could. I saw

92

André running across our back yard pass the fig tree and hedge bush to his house.

"Git your narrow ass in here!' she yelled while holding the screen door open. "What were you doing under that house with Mildred!" my mother yelled.

I couldn't answer. Everything I wanted to say was shackled to my fear and embarrassment.

Mother persisted. "Don't make me ask you again!"

My father was standing in the doorway to the kitchen, waiting for my answer. He didn't appear to be as angry as Dear.

I answered her interrogation with a whisper. "I was doing the pencil."

My Daddy excused himself, trying to muffle his laughter.

"What did you say?!" she angrily whispered.

"The pencil," Dear and Daddy both knew what I meant.

The next thing I knew my father had called several of his drinking partners and invited them over. They gathered in our tiny living room and he called me from the back, where I had been banished. I was not going to get a whoopin; I provided Dad and his buddies with too much entertainment.

"What did you say you were doing with that girl under the house?" my father asked.

Five pairs of blood-shot eyes fixed on me and paced my every move.

Again, I whispered through my humiliation, "I was doing the pencil."

They erupted into deafening laughter, with my Daddy leading the pack. Dear was furious with me, but mostly angry with Dad for not straightening me out.

Such conflicting and contradictory views from opposing authorities in a child's life can be confusing. Dear did her best to raise upright boys that respected women, even the ones that didn't sometime respect themselves. In grade school, if Dear knew I liked more than one girl she scolded me while bent over at the waist, with one hand on her hip and the tip of her finger pointed close to my nose. "Len! One at a time! Do you hear me! One girlfriend at a time!" she said. Her idea of the birds and the bees talk consisted of leaving a box of dried unwrapped condoms on the chest of drawers in our room. The box didn't come with any explanation from our parents. I didn't know what they were, but they sure did make decent water balloons.

So at age 21, when time came for me to make love with my girlfriend Laura, I drew on that last experience as a six-year-old and was more than ready. I was in love.

She acted like a woman who was possessed. Those few moments seemed like hours, as we teased and explored each other's bodies for the first time. There were moments when the anticipation was so intense; I thought I might pass out. No matter how much my heart raced, it was a welcomed sensation I would never forget and later tried to repeat as often as I could. Yep, she knew precisely what she was doing. The intimate hour spent in her room was everything I imagined from a strictly physical perspective. All the while we were entangled, I asked myself why she was so at ease and comfortable if this was her first time. I tried to push those thoughts to the rear of my mind, but they insisted on being heard. Afterwards we lay in each other's arms and in time, drifted off for a brief sleep. The present Laura gave me on my 21st birthday was special indeed and will never be forgotten.

I didn't ask my beloved any questions about her past experiences because I was too afraid to hear her answers. She once told me she had never been with anyone before, but following that hour of passion on my 21st birthday, I didn't believe her. In the same month, she returned from a trip home to Aliceville. She recounted how she had been with her ex-boyfriend named George in order to determine the depth of her love for me. Did she really think I was that naïve to believe such foolishness? I figured she wanted to be with him and needed a reason. So it was painfully clear that the first intimate moment we shared, one of us was a virgin, but it certainly was not her. With each detail about her time spent with her old boyfriend, I died a thousand deaths. I was destroyed. I was too upset to even ask her if she received her answer or clarification regarding us on that trip.

Her trip home and that intimate time spent with George was always in the back of my mind. I never fully recovered from it.

Young foolish hearts are quick to forgive, but not to forget. We continued trying to remain a couple until the question of the priesthood entered into the picture.

After two years of my less than impressive performance at the university, it was time for Juan to apply to medical school and for me to apply to dental school. Based on my grades alone, I did not stand a chance of being accepted. Juan was a superior student but decided if he did not enter medical school at the University of Alabama-Birmingham the first time he applied, he would apply again the following year. He also applied to other universities. If a perspective medical school granted him an interview, he visited the campus although he had no real interest in attending any other university outside of Alabama. I accompanied him to his interview at Vanderbilt University. While he was at the medical school, I spent time with a close family friend at Meharry Dental School. To my surprise, I was receiving serious consideration at Meharry with a possible probationary acceptance to the school. I wasn't the least bit excited with the prospect of actually going to dental school. My college performance was abysmal and in truth, I did not want to spend my life filling cavities and pulling teeth. A dose of honesty was long over due. The reason I wanted to become a dentist was because Juan wanted to be a doctor. It was as simple and as foolish as that. During Juan's interview at Vanderbilt and my time spent with a friend at Meharry, I decided to pursue my priesthood aspirations. I needed to go back to Birmingham and end my relationship with Laura.

Juan and I returned to Birmingham that same afternoon. I never mentioned a word to him about my decision to enter the Catholic seminary. I knew his objections would drown out any voice of reason. The first order of business was to tell my girlfriend.

Laura was home in Aliceville spending time with her family. I made the two-hour drive to southwest Alabama all the while gathering my thoughts and imagined her crying uncontrollably once I broke the news of my decision to become a priest. I finally arrived at her house, which sat on a small hill at the end of a winding dirt road with sparse wooded areas on both sides. She greeted me with a hug and kiss after I emerged from the car. I went inside her home and exchanged niceties with her mother and father, before she and I returned to the car. We parked in a wooded area normally reserved for our kissing and what ever followed. On this day, there would be none of that. Laura slid closer with eyes closed and melted in my arms. Our lips touched and nothing more. Laura knew something was different. In the past, I couldn't keep my hands off her. This time I was standoffish, distant, aloof. Laura pulled away from me and stiffened her back.

"Len, what's going on?" she suspiciously asked.

"Laura, I don't know where to begin."

She slid across the car seat away from me. I stared at her through my silence.

"Len?" she uttered once more.

"I have decided to become a priest."

"What!" She replied in shock and surprise.

"A priest," I continued.

"What about dental school? What about us?"

"I'm sorry," was all I could say.

"If you wanted to end this, just say so!" Laura said as her voice elevated in anger.

"Take me home! Take me home now!" she angrily replied.

The drive back to her house lasted for an eternity (or maybe 10 minutes or so). She opened the door before the car came to a complete stop.

"I've done things with you I am only supposed to do with the man I marry!" She said before walking away. I had a sick feeling in my gut. It was like I had robbed her of something precious. Perhaps I did. That was the last time we spoke.

All the while I wrestled with completing my undergraduate studies at the University of Alabama in Birmingham, I imagined entering the priesthood. It was a dream I kept to myself for years. Juan was furious about my decision to become a priest. As a Baptist, he believed Catholic theology and tradition was contrary to Scripture.   He and I spent many late nights debating the pros and cons of the other's faith. His arguments had merit but not enough to dissuade me. I made my decision to become a priest. I was going to enter the seminary. I believed I had a true vocational calling.

My role in my home parish, Our Lady Queen of the Universe, encompassed spending weekends trimming the hedges, mowing the lawn, polishing the dark green slate floors of the sanctuary and making sure all was in order for the Sunday mass. Of all my responsibilities in the parish, I resented most getting down on my hands and knees shining the floors. It reminded me of the work done by my mother and many other black women in my neighborhood. For the time my mother took the No. 11 bus, traveling across town to her job in the elegant homes of white folk, she spent much of the day on all fours washing and scrubbing. She prayed her children would not have to toil as she did.   At night she complained about how her knuckles and knees throbbed and ached.

Now it was my turn to bow down before a different master. Nonetheless, I was as submissive as my mother.

I was also in charge of the church's youth program, which often met several times a week. I did not seek to be applauded for my efforts by the congregation. This was my outward expression of love, devotion and loyalty to a God and church I placed above everything. To serve God for the measure of my days was my only desire, my focus, and my all.

There were times when I stole away from the troubles at home, school and Birmingham and went to my church, the only place where I found a moment of solitude. Some nights I'd find the church open, with the only light being the flickering flame of the tall white sacred Pascal candle in the corner next to the altar. I found a place, sitting in my new church, surrounded by the solemnity and remained alone for hours. This was the only place where I could talk to God and not be interrupted. I never heard His voice, but I held on to the hope that He would hear mine. The still. The quiet. The darkness. These gave me the moment of peace I needed, as Jesus on the cross and all the marble statues looked on.

Once I decided to concentrate all my efforts towards the Roman Catholic priesthood, the bond with my parish grew stronger as I spent time at the church. The blacks that went to the Queen of the Universe Catholic Church were richer, better educated and better connected socially than those at New Salem Baptist Church. The white priest's social circle consisted of white businessmen, bankers and educators from other parts of the city. Those closest to him in the congregation were included in that circle. Monsignor Foster invited select members of the parish to accompany him to the homes of some of Birmingham's wealthiest and most influential citizens. Everyone seemed to show respect and reverence for the priests. The elite social circles and respect were just benefits of wearing the collar.

There were days when I should have been studying for a chemistry or genetics exam, but instead I was taking communion to the sick or manicuring the church lawn. After Sunday mass in June of 1976, I asked Monsignor Foster if I could have a word with him. He instructed me to come to the rectory after service. He was still wearing his priest outfit when he invited me to sit on the recliner in his TV room. He offered me a glass of wine. I respectfully declined. I had no problem with him enjoying a glass or two. I was comfortable talking with Monsignor Foster so I got right to the point.

"Father, I've been thinking about this for quite some time and I believe I have a ministry to join the priesthood." Father Foster continued sipping from the crystal glass as if he didn't hear a word I said. "Father Foster, I said I would like to study to become a priest," I repeated.

"Leonard, I heard you the first time," he replied.

"Are you in the least bit enthusiastic about the possibility of me attending seminary?" I asked.

"Not really," he said, donning a brilliant smile. "Why did it take you so long?"

His acceptance meant everything to me.

It wasn't long before Monsignor Foster was on the phone with Bishop Joseph Vath. Father had made it clear in earlier conversations with me that he held the bishop and the chancery in little regard.

Later that week, after the Chancery Office received word that a young black man was interested in the priesthood, one of the bishop's emissaries met with Monsignor Foster at the church rectory to validate my sincerity. I remained in earshot of their conversation. I couldn't understand everything that was said, but it was obvious the representative was agitated.

"We've never had a black priest in Alabama and I'll be damned if we're going to get one now," he said. My muscles tightened. I felt stiff, cold. I waited for my parish priest to excoriate his distinguished visitor. I expected him to deliver a personal reprimand on my behalf.

He sponsored me for the seminary, was my shepherd and spiritual advisor. I waited with my hands gripping the back of a straight chair so tightly my palms ached. I listened. Waited. Listened. Waited. There was only silence.

Life in Birmingham, Alabama before and after the civil rights struggle had taught me that racists, regardless of which side of the pulpit they stood on, often masked their evil doings with feigned acts of kindness. I hoped and prayed that Monsignor Foster's benevolence emanated from a good heart and not just because he was assigned to work an all-black parish and had to make the best of an otherwise undesirable situation.

These men of God were planning my life and weren't giving me the courtesy of representing myself. I had made many sacrifices to enter the priesthood, both economic and personal. I was Baptist born and raised in the Bible Belt South and had eschewed both family and community tradition by not only desiring to becoming a papist, a pejorative term in that area, but by wanting to become one of his spokespersons as well, a Catholic priest. I was asking to join people who I knew did not understand me. I had once heard my bishop, the one who sent the emissaries; describe as "radical" the attempts by black priests to bring black-oriented music to the Church. He didn't understand that he was being insensitive to the heritage of the 25,000 black Catholics in the North Alabama Diocese.

Although a door separated me from the two men holding my fate, I overheard the stinging renunciation. The bishop's emissary had always been gracious and respectful towards me, so this angry outcry was more disappointing than surprising. Monsignor Foster offered nothing in my defense.

I slipped out of the back door of the rectory and waited in the dimly lit sanctuary of the church. I never mentioned to Monsignor Foster that I overheard their conversation. I had come to love Monsignor over the past seven years. Every Sunday I assisted him at the altar wearing an off-white cassock he had custom made especially for me. I made rounds with him daily when he visited the sick and destitute. When he was unavailable, I took communion to those who could not attend mass.

Monsignor Foster was the only white person I had ever trusted. For fear of offending him, I was too afraid to confront him about the comment made by the bishop's representative and about his own silence. But I was even more fearful of the response Monsignor might give me.

He was an excessively formal, almost rigid man. His recessed brown eyes, dimpled chin; thick waved hair and well-manicured hands clearly gave one the impression that others did his bidding. Outside of our parish, Monsignor Foster's inner circle was white. His family had been in the banking business in New England. If he was forced to choose between defending me or going along with the church's position, I was sure he would side with the church. I was satisfied in not knowing Monsignor Foster's true feelings.

The Monsignor did tell me that since the decision was made that I would be accepted into the priesthood vocational program, the chancery and other priests often referred to me not as just a priesthood candidate, but specifically "their black priesthood candidate."

"Since your decision to become a priest you've been viewed as a novelty by some clergymen and loathed by others," he said.

I believed that whites *outside* the Church wouldn't readily accept a black man, even a black priest. But with religious and church folk of all denominations the presence of a Catholic priest commanded respect. So I optimistically hoped that seeing the Roman collar would dilute any venomous response people had to my black skin.

Shortly after Monsignor Foster met with the bishop's representative, I met with Father Frank Mucello, the dioceses' vocational director at Thompson Restaurant on 20th Street in downtown Birmingham. This was in June of 1976. The vocational director's job involved all things having to do with seminarians.

"I wish we could ordain you today to show some of these people the Church isn't full of racists," Mucello said, peering gleefully across the table.

I said nothing. Even I knew that the Church could not exempt itself from racism through the ordination of one black man. I was not prepared to become a symbol of racial equality in a church that had only 300 black priests out of nearly 70,000 nationwide.

In situations where I was the only black, I wore my color self-consciously and uncomfortably, like a bad haircut. For nearly two months I attended many such occasions, meetings with curious priests and parishioners. There were seven other young men studying for the Diocese.

Mucello and the bishop made it painfully clear that the Diocese had big plans for me, plans that ran counter to the plans I envisioned for myself. Upon ordination, Mucello said, he wanted my first assignment to be at Our Lady of Sorrows, which was a very affluent white parish located "over the mountain."

There was a time in the past when blacks were hassled by police and angry residents for simply driving through that section of the city. It is still predominantly white, though blacks can safely drive through. I suppose my presence would make a statement, be sort of a marker pronouncing how much had changed over the years. But I was not swayed.

My family and friends worried that my soul was lost because I was adopting a faith that needed a man to mediate between God and me. One night Juan's uncle, a minister visiting from Washington, D.C., conducted an impromptu prayer service in Juan's living room.

"You're a marked man and God is calling you," he said sternly, pointing at me during the rousing service.

I was quiet and tearful during the emotionally charged evening. My heart was beating faster and faster. The minister's words only gave additional confirmation to what I was already feeling. I reached for him and there was a long embrace between us.

"God called you, but not into the Catholic priesthood," he later told me. I smiled and offered no response.

To these people of faith, the whole point of the crucifixion was to establish a direct line to God. They figured they could pray for themselves and didn't need a priest to handle the transaction. I did not insult their intelligence by offering a weak explanation such as the one provided by the Church defining the role of the priest. To Catholics, the Pope is Jesus on earth and the priests are his sole representatives in the person of St. Peter.

Those close to me who were not Catholic did not hesitate to voice their dismay with my decision. Little did they know, I had a few concerns of my own. I asked myself if a black man could find solace in a white church without losing his soul and distancing himself from his heritage. A large number of black Catholics in my parish despised Negro spirituals and gospel music, integral parts of their heritage. It was painful to watch them genuflect and leave the sanctuary when the gospel choir began to sing. Questioned about it, they responded with indignation, "If I wanted to hear that loud music and clapping, I would have stayed in the Baptist Church."

I was aware of remarks made by priests and parishioners from other congregations. The tepid reception I received from white priests was expected but not from some in my own parish and other black congregations. Since announcing my intentions to study for the priesthood, I grew accustomed to the bad behavior of some godly people. I was hurt and disappointed when some blacks questioned my sincerity because I was a convert and some said I would introduce black Protestantism into the liturgy. Monsignor said, "Some priests openly questioned how you will fit in or be accepted by a predominantly white Diocese, Len."

Meanwhile, even black congregants vehemently opposed spontaneous responses and fiery sermons, two elements I planned to incorporated in my church masses by having visiting choirs and guest black priests who spoke with the cadence of Baptist preachers. Members of my own church reminded me, "Once you are ordained Len, the sermons and Protestant music will have to stop."

I was single-minded about the priesthood. Nothing could assuage my yearning for ordination. I imagined I would live in southern Indiana for years to become a priest and then come back home to Birmingham and live the rest of my life christening babies, hearing confessions and burying the dead. The Roman Catholic priesthood not only promised to fulfill my spiritual hopes, but it also meant freedom: I'd receive an upgrade, socially, and the bonds that accompanied being black would be loosened.

In black parishes, the Stations of the Cross had white characters and no black ones. Jesus on the cross was always white.   It seemed to me that we were worshipping the images of our oppressors.

It was time for me to put aside all my inhibitions and enjoy all the love and attention heaped on me by my parish. Before my departure for seminary, I dined with different families from my parish. The ladies in the congregation, proud of my decision, called my mother to find out my favorite dishes and then sometimes spent hours slaving over scorching burners. They prepared hams, roast chicken, succulent vegetables, and sumptuous desserts of homemade cakes and pies. By the time I left for school, I had gained an additional 10 pounds.

The bishop and Father Mucello agreed to attend my going away banquet at my church. Father Mucello had once attended a gathering in my honor, but the bishop always canceled. My concerns and suspicions grew, but they were overcome by a deep-rooted overriding desire to be a priest.

Monsignor Foster told me the bishop and Father Mucello sponsored a dinner for the other seminarians. Neither my family nor I were invited to the affair. Monsignor Foster made his dissatisfaction with the chancery office known at every opportunity, especially from the pulpit. His hostility existed long before I decided to enter the seminary; the treatment my family and I received from the bishop's office only made it worse, it seemed.

Neighboring black parishes collected special offerings on my behalf. I was the black Catholic community's favorite son, the toast of the town, the first and only black from the Diocese to ever enter the seminary.

Deacon Willie Moore was the closest any black person had ever come to being a black priest in Alabama. He served the Diocese as the only black lay deacon and was under the tutelage of Monsignor Foster, our parish priest. He wasn't taken seriously by the Diocese and was viewed as nothing more than a glorified altar boy. He turned the pages of the Sacramentary as Monsignor Foster read and the good deacon held the paten (a round brass plate) under the parishioners' mouths as they received the host wafer during communion. Now and then he delivered the message from the Gospel and read from the Leaflet Missal. When it came to matters concerning the Diocese and the Church, his views were never solicited. Deacon Moore was supportive of my becoming a seminarian and offered words of encouragement. He had complete faith and confidence in the leadership of the Church and asked me to do the same. Blacks seemed quite content with one lone white priest being the leader of a congregation of hundreds of black families.

I was not bothered too much by the disproportionate representation, but I hoped and prayed: "God, let my presence someday be the catalyst to change the disparity."

The week before departing for seminary, I received a barely readable form from Father Mucello, listing all the personal items I should bring with me. It listed toiletries, linen and other personal items. My family never met the bishop or any of his emissaries. Monsignor Foster believed this was an outrage. My parents had no idea where I was going or what the next eight years of my life would entail. For the first time, I felt truly alone.

Monsignor made it known in many of our conversations just how little he cared for Father Mucello. Monsignor's discontent escalated as he witnessed the director's treatment of me. He referred to Mucello as "that whining little weasel." Mucello often referred to me, even in my presence, as "the candidate with special needs." I never understood what he meant by that. Once, I even asked him to explain.

"Don't worry Leonard," he said. "Everything is being taken care of."

But Monsignor believed the man was racially insensitive. I was the first black in the state to be sponsored by the Diocese for the Holy Orders, which might be seen as a sign of progress by some. Yet, this was Birmingham, and I was forced to ponder if some things about the "Old South" would never change. Mother had taught me "my place" in segregated Alabama. Now I had to learn "my place" in the Catholic Church.

Father Mucello never showed me a catalog or put me in touch with the one seminarian from the Diocese that was returning to St. Meinrad for his second year. These were traditions normally offered to white students. I had no say in anything dealing with my vocation.

It was 5:30 a.m. on August 22nd 1976, a bracing morning when the fog and dew lingered in the air as my long-standing friends Juan and Michael waited with me. The three of us huddled together on my $11, black footlocker. We kept close to stave off the early morning chill. We waited alongside I-65 for more than a half hour for the ride that would take me to Saint Meinrad Seminary and Arch abbey in Indiana to study for the Roman Catholic priesthood.

The small town of St. Meinrad consisted of a few hundred people and was located about 70 miles west of Louisville, Kentucky. After my work was completed there, I hoped to return to Birmingham and to my parish of 300 families and serve as their pastor.

"This is wild, man," said Juan with indignation. "Was it asking too much for them to drive four extra blocks to pick you up at your house?"

I had known Juan and Michael for the greater portion of my life. Juan was vehemently opposed to my going to seminary and didn't miss an opportunity to voice his disapproval. Juan regularly took me to task by asking indefensible questions such as, "Why it is that true Catholics cherish and almost revere relics, and precisely, what does it have to do with Jesus and salvation?" I floundered and groped for an answer, knowing nothing I said would dissuade his assault.

"Don't tell me you don't find something just a bit strange about that and maybe even a little satanic," he once said.

Michael was a cradle Catholic and belonged to my church. He fully supported me and never challenged the church's position. Michael saw me as his spiritual mentor and knew the value of having a black priest in a predominantly white culture.

Father Mucello had conferred with the driver and agreed that my neighborhood was too dangerous for a lone white person to brave at this odd hour. It didn't matter that whites never had any trouble in Birmingham's black neighborhoods.

The wind from an occasional passing car swished against my neck and I raised the collar on my Windbreaker and thrust my hands deep into my cotton-lined pockets. My companions reflected on the uneventful passing of my 23rd birthday two weeks prior and wondered how it felt to reach a ripe old age.

"Dang Len, you're getting up there," said Michael. "Won't be long before you'll be pushing 30 years old."

Juan, Michael and I waited anxiously, very aware of each second that ticked by. Juan's subtle anger about my decision subsided for the moment, but was replaced with a menacing silence. He occasionally glanced towards me, then down the dark highway. He loved me and did not want to make this time more difficult than it already was. Michael said, "I love you, man, I love you, man," over and over again, his words sounding like a mantra. A car approached out of the darkness -and we knew it was time.

The car came to a halt and the driver emerged to make room for my things in the trunk.

"I guess this is it," I said.

"I love you, man." Michael said as we held each other close.

Juan was biting his bottom lip as he often did when he was at a loss of words. We stared at each other then locked as one in an embrace. There was nothing more to say. We quickly separated and without looking back, I opened the car door and slammed it shut behind me. In an instant, the long winding road north ushered me into the darkness and into the unknown.

It was about an hour-and-a-half drive to Huntsville, Ala., which is 85 miles north of Birmingham, near the Tennessee state line. Huntsville is known for the Red Stone Arsenal Space Center. The driver was a young man about twenty years of age. He was cordial and respectful as he drove silently, giving me time and space to navigate through my sadness. My heart and thoughts were still with Juan and Michael, as the reality took hold that it would be months before I saw the familiar faces of home. I gazed into the darkness knowing that the passing of every crossroad, every mountain, every hill and dale, took me farther and farther away from everything that ever meant anything to me. I fought back the tears as the sun began peeking over the horizon. This was my first time being away from home for more than a couple of days at a time.

After a few minutes, the driver, who I only remember as Jim, broke the silence with a brief introduction.

"So Len, what do you think about being a seminarian and going to St. Meinrad's?" he asked.

"To tell you the truth, Jim, I know nothing about the school, the students. Zero!" I responded.

"We have a long ride ahead and I can answer most of your questions," he said.

Jim was a second year student at St. Meinrad's College and Seminary and based on his enthusiasm, seminary life suited him.

"I am surprised Father Mucello didn't put you in touch with me sooner," he continued. "As a matter of fact, there are several other new students from Birmingham."

This revelation was not news to me. What I gathered from Jim and what Monsignor Foster told me, there was an ongoing relationship among the seminarians from Birmingham. But I had been left out. For the next hour or so I gathered bits and pieces of information about the school from Jim.

Before going to Indiana, Jim and I were scheduled to meet a group of new candidates at the Fanning family house, which was home to one of the students near the space center. When we arrived, breakfast was finished and they were standing around in the yard waiting for us.

"My name is Len Cooper," I said.

"Yes, we all know. Father Frank told us all about you," one of them said, extending a hand.

"I'm sorry, but I don't know the first thing about any of you," I said.

The six young men looked back and forth at each other as if not knowing how to respond to my comment. There was an obvious familiarity among them that I did not share. We all stood together just outside the house as they repeated the same small talk questions again and again. I couldn't tell if they were uncomfortable with my blackness or if they were just being overly nice.

Either way, they couldn't hide their surprise at seeing me. I think the shock was not because of my blackness; they weren't expecting me to be six feet five inches tall. The small-framed Vietnamese student looked at me from toe to head as if to be scanning a giant sequoia tree. But I didn't mind.

The group returned to the indoors. I was offered breakfast but politely refused as any southerner with proper upbringing would have done. In some circles in the South we were taught to accept a meal on the third insisting. You politely declined the first and second offer. I am not sure where I learned such a strange rule, but somewhere in my upbringing I was told this and I adhered to it despite the fact that I was starving. I waited for the host family to once again offer me some of the cold leftover grits and eggs on the table, but no one did. I suppose they never heard of this three-meal-offering rule. I excused myself to the bathroom while the son said goodbye to his two younger sisters and parents.

The ride to the seminary was rather sedate, as the driver lagged behind the two cars leading the way. The silence lasted for what seemed like hours. If I didn't initiate a topic of conversation, the void was once again filled with silence. Jim enthusiastically answered my inquiries about the school and surrounding communities.

"So this is your second year in the priestly program, Jim. I suppose you have already decided on the priesthood as a vocation?" I asked. He sidestepped the question. "The first thing you see from a mile away are the two steeples towering over the tree tops," he said with excitement, through a brilliant grin. He was very proud of the seminary. He told me about the soccer team, the beauty of the countryside and described some of his favorite teachers and students. He didn't ask a single question about my background. I wondered if the vocational director back in Birmingham had prepped all of them on how to treat me or instructed them to stay clear of probing questions. Either way, it all seemed very odd.

For hours we rode through Tennessee and Kentucky, then into hilly southern Indiana. At last we were on the winding roads approaching Saint Meinrad College Seminary, which revealed gothic structures looming above the mountain surrounded by patches of farmland. Arriving in the guesthouse parking lot, we followed the signs directing us to our new home.

All of us stood in awe of the towering steeples of the 19th Century Abbey Church. The grounds were impeccably manicured and the rolling hillsides resembled a large checkerboard of various shades of green and yellow squares. Swarms of bats circled the church's loft. Scores of Benedictine monks dressed in long black cassocks, thick black leather belts, and hoods walked in procession from the Byzantine church, singing Gregorian chants. The scene conjured up every horror movie I had ever seen.

Some of the guys in my group savored the atmosphere, closed their eyes and swayed to the rhythms, intoxicated in adoration. I was ready to get the hell out of there and go back to Birmingham, but my pastor's advice pounded inside my head: "Give your vocation a chance, one day at a time." I thought: It will be a major accomplishment if I can make it to dinner.

Two novice monks filed out of the line, approached us and offered their assistance in finding our quarters. Both had the traditional corona cuts, bald except for a one-inch wide swath that goes around the head, just above the temples.

Novice Roger, one of the monks who came to help us, led me to the building and through two huge wooden and steel doors. As soon as the doors shut, I smelled an overwhelmingly stale odor in the halls, like the smell of an unventilated house. The walls were lined with hundreds of black and white antiquated photographs of former monks and seminarians. I noted that they were all white, but had no serious concern about that. My room was on the third floor next to the theologians, who lived in the older part of the building. Those in higher grade levels and theology were assigned smaller, isolated rooms with no frills. Perhaps because they were closer to ordination, they were being prepared for a life of austerity. Near my room were several doors marked, "Cloisters." They led to the restricted area where the monks lived. I would find out that these monks were quiet, enigmatic, and kept their distance from us. Some monks lived there for a short while; some came to St. Meinrad right out of the minor seminary, also known as a high school seminary, and lived there for most of their lives. A few were aged and confined to wheelchairs or beds. I felt a profound loneliness come over me. My eyes panned the grounds. Women were visibly absent. I naively thought I might address certain female ministerial needs in my pastoral training. But I soon discovered that in the seminary and in priesthood in general, women are of no real significance and virtually non-existent. That was unnerving because even at a young age I understood the importance and contribution of women to providing a well-rounded environment. I imagined seminary college would be like the Catholic University of America in Washington, D.C. or Notre Dame in South Bend, Indiana, where new seminarians took courses with regular students in a co-ed environment. Now, I accepted the fact that my involvement with women was going to be restricted while in seminary. I was going to be confined to an isolated, all-male school stuck in the mountains.

I had an unsettled feeling in my gut. Everything was diametrically different from what I expected, but one thing was certain, I was beginning to realize I did not want to be there.

As we walked down the long corridor, I heard what sounded like loud party music. Impossible, I thought. I was, after all, in a seminary. Yet as the doors leading to the underclassmen section swung open, stifling cigarette smoke, ear- shattering hard rock drums and screaming guitars greeted me. I did not expect to hear Eric Clapton's "Layla" and Jimmy Hendrix's "Are You Experienced?" I was taught in my mother's church that cigarettes and rock music were tools of the devil.

I saw a poster of a scantily clad Farrah Fawcett pinned up on the back of the door next to the Blessed Virgin. Young men ran around chasing each other down the hall and through the study lounge, while some sat on the floor, crowded in front of a small color T.V.

I saw a little sign with the face of the Virgin Mary and the words "Inaccurate Deception," what I imagined was supposed to be a witty reference to the "Immaculate Conception." The announcement of a "Rector's Convocation" said instead: "rectum's convocation." There was also a handwritten sign that said, "God promised not to destroy the world with fire, so he built St. Meinrad instead." The monks escorting me didn't seem at all bothered by the displays. I was thoroughly confused.

My two guides directed me to my small room and vanished. I closed the door behind me in hopes of gathering my thoughts and trying to make some sense of this place.

I learned that more than 500 men lived there. I looked through the window of my dingy room to see what appeared to be men walking around beneath the evergreens and gardens. The waning daylight was mocked by the dry-weather lightning that flashed in the distance. My emotions were stretched and pulled to the extreme. My chiseled smile masked the tears just below the surface. I greeted the other students cordially, but I was dying inside. I had been on campus for less than an hour and already I was looking for a reason to turn around and leave. I could still hear my mother lamenting and see her tears over my decision to come to seminary. This is not the life she envisioned for me, and now I questioned myself.

Eventually, I could learn to appreciate the towering trees and emerald green mountaintops. But what was going on inside the seminary was contrary to my beliefs. I thought seminary was going to be calm, peaceful, and tranquil. I envisioned a prayer-like environment with soft chants playing in the background, men having spirited religious, theological and philosophical debates. Instead, here I was trying to understand why there was so much profanity, loud acid rock music and half naked guys chasing each other up and down the hall. Before my first meal, I was in the midst of a vocational crisis. Nevertheless, when I was outside of the building, among the shrubbery and gardens, I experienced a penetrating peace and tranquility that filled me up and seemed to put me in the presence of God Almighty. But inside, the building I only smelled the musty stench of sweat and soiled linen at times masked by the heavy smell of disinfectant.

Nothing was familiar to me. Not the music. Not the things these men talked about. I desperately needed something I could relate to. There was no contemporary gospel music, no Motown sounds or any music I was accustomed to hearing. No colloquial lingo going back and forth, like good friends hanging out in front of the barbershop. Nothing.

I knew from experience that with this many white people in one place, it was just a matter of time before someone made a racist remark. When it happened, I wouldn't have a clue as to how to deal with it. At home, if confronted with racism I had my supportive family and friends. But now the closest black person was 50 miles away. Within a few hours of being at the seminary, I searched frantically for ginger ale to sooth my knotted stomach. I had seen and heard enough to know that I was not going to last in the priesthood program at St. Meinrad.

The bishop and Mucello often spoke of how important it was for the Church and the Diocese to have me ordained. They desperately needed a black priest in the Birmingham Diocese to promote race relations. I was prepared to be disobedient if the bishop asked me to be that spokesperson. Disobedience was a major offense, often punishable by dismissal from the priesthood. I wanted to serve in the *black* community!

Before I arrived, my roommates, who were out, claimed three of the four beds in the room. The only one remaining was a top bunk in full view of anyone standing in the hall looking in while the door was open.

Apparently, they had been there for a few days before I arrived. There were two bunk beds and in each corner of the room was a stacked chest of drawers with a small counter and mirror on top. The beds were unkempt and the vanities in disarray.

The sun had almost set as I sat on the windowsill alone. I am not certain what I was expecting to find in the seminary, but certainly I wasn't ready to move into a big frat house. I was actually hoping for a level of spiritual maturity that's often absent in the secular society.

Out the window, I watched men walking toward the campus lake with towels on their shoulders. Just a few days before I had quit my lifeguard job in Birmingham at the neighborhood pool where I had worked for the past five summers. I felt the tug of familiarity; of something I could do well, a place I could fit in and maybe find comfort. I rummaged through my trunk to find my Speedo swimsuit, goggles and towel. I ran barefoot down three flights of stairs; pass the moss- covered cemetery wall and tombstones to the lake. Twelve young men were playing a game they call "greased-watermelon" football. I stood on the sidelines with mud squishing between my toes, watching two teams try to score goals with the Vaseline smothered melon. Finally, someone hollered at me.

"Hey, you wanna play?"

I shook my head yes. I was delighted. My troubles and acute homesickness vanished momentarily as we tussled for control. Then the melon squirted out in my direction. At last, I had a chance to score one for the team and pick up a few points with the guys.

Dashing for the goal, the opposition converged on me, but so did my own team. They dunked me in the water up and down, laughing. I felt hands firmly on my buttocks, squeezing my penis and scrotum. Surely this is accidental, maybe some sort of hazing ritual, I thought. I struggled to break their hold.

I pushed the red and green pieces of broken melon away. But they ignored the watermelon; they were after me! They held me under the murky water. I felt the grit of the stagnant lake closing off the back of my throat. I forced my way to the top, throwing vicious punches and missing with all of them. Grabbing my towel and goggles, I ran off into the woods.

I heard laughter as I ran deep into the thicket of trees, far enough until I felt I was certain not to be followed. I bent over and heaved but nothing came out of me except a deep, sickening burp. For the first time in my life I questioned my own manhood, wondering if I inadvertently gave a wrong signal with my body language, an inviting glance or a consenting tone of voice.

Was there something about me that the seminarians at the lake found attractive, willing and enticing?

I was discarding one by one every belief I had about seminary. I viewed it as a place that extracted the best men society had to offer. I believed the men there gladly sacrificed everything dear to most people and assumed a life of service and total submission. At seminary, I thought every waking hour would be spent in prayer, meditation and preparation for the day when we received our pastoral assignments. But I found human frailties were magnified in seminary and if I was to survive, something had to change. The Catholic Church and seminary weren't about to undergo a major transformation for one black boy from the foothills of Appalachia.

The taboos of homosexuality were engrained, cultivated and nurtured in me since I could remember. When it comes to sexual orientation, I am a product of the ultra-conservative black community, which said simply: Homosexuality is an abomination and if you subscribe to this perverted lifestyle, you are deserving of whatever wrath that comes upon you. In church, I listened attentively to all the words of condemnation and the scriptural references on how God created man specifically to be with woman-without exception.

On that first day at seminary, after being jumped on, dunked and fondled, I ran from the lake to find security in the darkness of the woods. I sat on the ground, resting on the moistened pine needles, shivering and hungry. I reflected back on the conversation I had with my oldest brother in the alley behind the Hyatt Hotel the day before I left Birmingham. He asked, "What is the possibility of a black man becoming Pope of the Church?"

"Probably less than none," I replied.

I offered him logical reasons for my desire to fulfill the Holy Orders and he returned with convincing arguments for why priesthood is a waste of time for any serious minded black man.

Now in the woods, I was rethinking my decision and second-guessing my defense of it. I remained in the woods until well after dark. I entered the building through a side door and made my way upstairs to the third floor. I noticed a light in the office of a monk who was a teacher. Before I could get pass him, he frantically waved his hand, beckoning me to come into his office.

"Do come in and join me for a chat please," he said, motioning his hand as if to hurry me into the room. "I am Father Blaise. And you are?" He pointed towards the chair for me to sit.

I was still in my swimsuit with a towel draped around me. "Leonard Cooper," I said, as we shook hands. "I arrived just this afternoon."

We continued with the usual introductory comments until he asked the question I knew was coming. "So Leonard, what's your impression of the school so far?" This seemed to be a typical question asked of newcomers by both staff and students.

Rather than give him the specifics about what happened to me at the lake, I said, "I have nothing against how people choose to live their lives, but I am surprised by the number of effeminate males here and how aggressive they can be."

"I don't understand," he replied, no longer smiling.

"I arrived just prior to sundown and already several students have made unwanted sexual advances towards me," I said.

"Mr. Cooper, you must be mistaken," Father Blaise replied.

I could see by his expression he was growing annoyed with my accusation.

"We have never had problems of that nature here at St. Meinrad. Maybe it is your interpretation or maybe something you may have said or done led to this."

I sat quietly and listened until he offered his conclusion.

"Maybe you needed to be touched and accepted by other men," he said.

I knew his comments were absurd. I needed to understand why I was attacked at the lake; why the school allowed such an environment. But it would be pointless to ask such questions. So in less than a minute, I had heard enough.

"Excuse me, sir," I said, standing to leave.

I spent a very uncomfortable night, feeling as if I could be attacked in my sleep. I lay atop my blanket, pondering whether I had made a terrible mistake in my innocent search to find meaning and a place where a young black man could be respected and even gain some power. The next morning I awoke to find that the rector of the school had appointed Father Blaise as my spiritual counselor.

"Isn't that just great," I thought while reading the posting on my room door.

I settled into my new life, determined to succeed. For the duration of the summer and early autumn, I learned to adapt to living as a seminarian. My classes consisted of philosophy, Latin, psychology and church history. My roommates and I tolerated each other. We did not interact with one another at all. We didn't eat together. We did not sit together during Mass. I was never invited to join them for off-campus functions, nor did I ever socialize with them at the on-campus pub. They hung out together, never inviting me to come along. It was uncomfortable and awkward but I resolved myself to accepting that this is the way it was going to be as long as I lived in that room.

I later learned there were three other black students and a black monk, who was a professor. Over the next few months, I grew closer and closer to them. We visited each other's living quarters, ate together, exchanged music and debated theological ideas.

The black monk, Father Cyprian, unofficially counseled me. I spent more time in his office than with my assigned spiritual advisor. In truth, Father Cyprian was accommodating and a good listener, but I had to remind myself he was first and foremost Catholic and a product of the monastic community. He provided a listening ear, but nothing more. Still, we hit it off well.

It was rare to see any females on campus other than the women workers in the cafeteria and laundry rooms. One of the few females I initially encountered was a nun dressed in laymen's clothes who conducted my psychological interview. During the sessions she lit up an occasional cigarette and in the evenings she enjoyed a beer or two at the campus pub known as "The Unstable." I thought her behavior was a bit odd for a member of a religious order, but nonetheless I didn't give it much thought. Nearly two months had passed since I arrived at the seminary and I had not seen any black females.

Around mid-October each year, two weekend days were reserved for parents' weekend. This was a time when the campus was flooded with proud parents and siblings from all parts of the country. Dear, my grandmother, Ma Bee, who is the mother of my parish, and her daughter Gina, made the 381-mile journey to see me. I advised the women not to attempt to make the trip alone, so they hired a longstanding family friend named Tommy to do the driving. All morning, I waited eagerly for their arrival. Around noon I got a call from my guests, who had already checked into their quarters at the campus hotel. I couldn't wait to see them.

As I raced across the campus, I saw the four of them walking in my direction. In one motion Dear and I embraced and the tears flowed. I was expecting her to shower me with words of love and affection. She whispered in my ear; "Len, you have to leave this place *today!*"

I didn't know if her tears were because she was happy to see me or if they were out of concern for me. I pretended not to hear her plea. Instead, I lost myself in her love and the adoration of Muh, Ma Bee, and Gina.

Gina, who was 16 years old, blurted out, "Tommy won't leave the room."

This meant Tommy was held up back at the campus guesthouse where they were all staying. I looked to Dear for a response, but she glanced at Muh and Ma Bee who waited for her to provide an explanation.

"Dear?" I directed. Her eyes trailed a group of extremely effeminate men parading past us. The culture I grew up in had no use for men with feminine tendencies and if a man exhibited such behavior, he was avoided at all cost.

"We will talk later," Dear uttered.

For the entire weekend Dear took food to the guesthouse for Tommy. She said he told her if he ventured out, "queers" would overpower him. There was nothing anyone could say or do to convince him otherwise.

After dinner, students performed in the auditorium for all of the guests. The program had a Broadway theme. Tommy was a trombonist in a local band in Birmingham, so I thought the lure of music might get him out of the room. I called him to extend the invitation, but he rejected it immediately.

"Look Len, I'm not setting foot out of this room until Dear is ready to leave," he said. "And why are you here? Are you a queer? Everywhere you turn, there is a queer and that doesn't bother you?"

I tried explaining the situation, but he refused to listen. "Tommy, I am here to become a priest. If I leave, that will be the end of it. Can't you understand?"

"No! What I understand is for you to be here and stay here you must be one of them," he said.

I realized then that he viewed me as just another gay man he needed to avoid. He stayed in that room the whole visit and refused to see me. I later found out he never removed his pants and never showered. Dear tried all weekend to coerce him out of the room, but he refused every attempt.

When Tommy and I we were children he spent many days sitting with me and my brothers on our front porch. We all practiced the trombone for hours. Neighbors stopped and sat on the lawn, just to hear Tommy and my brother play. Tommy was one of the best. But now from the tone of our telephone conversation, I knew things between us had changed forever. Was it coincidental that Tommy severed ties with my family once returning to Birmingham? After that trip, I never saw or heard from him again.

I could not escape the advances of my fellow seminarians, no matter what I did. Father Blaise, my spiritual advisor and the monk who advised me following the incident at the lake, counseled me weekly and sometimes daily. He returned again and again to the idea that all the sexual attention I was receiving was somehow due to my behavior.

It was well-known throughout the seminary that I was angry about the intensity of the homosexual atmosphere. I made it clear I would do whatever it took to put an end to any unwanted advances and if it continued it would be at that student's own risk.

Every couple of weeks, instead of the usual steam tables and serving lines for dinner, sit-down meals were served with white linen napkins and tablecloths. One evening during sit-down dinner I left my plate of food unattended. When I returned a seminarian whispered, "That guy over there cleared his nostril in your dish."

I looked at the guy and recognized that he was someone I had a run-in with a few weeks earlier. It never occurred to me that he would go to such lengths to get back at me. I left the dining hall. I was so angry I could have seriously injured the guy. This would have made matters worse, so I kept my anger to myself.

Most times seminarians displayed their disapproval of me by offering a few terse words – "He's just a convert, he wouldn't understand," or "Why do you dress that way? You will never fit in looking like that." One student went as far as reporting me for reading the autobiography of Angela Davis. I was full of repressed and seething anger. Instead of sleeping in my top bunk, I spent most of the night napping in the brown cloth recliners in the lounge. I couldn't stand my roommates and they had absolutely no use for me.

Much of my time was spent alone in my shared study cubicle or walking in those parts of the forest that seminarians and faculty rarely used. Behind the main building, I found solitude in a rock garden with multicolored sandstones and an array of flowers. I sat for hours on a wrought iron bench there, sorting through the turmoil raging within me.

My moments of peace lasted as long as I remained on that bench. As soon as I entered the main building it seemed trouble met me in the hallway.

If my roommates saw me in the study cubicle, they found other places to study. I recalled for some reason being so frustrated one afternoon that I slammed the cubicle door, went to my room and changed into my running shorts and shirt and ran outdoors into a freezing rain. I stood in the middle of the downpour, not caring about getting soaked or being cold. I needed to get off "The Holy Hill." I ran down the street and off the campus alongside the highway. I ran for miles, drenched from head to toe in what felt like ice. I wasn't bothered a bit. I continued running and with every breath, the freezing winter rain caused my throat and nose to throb. I continued running harder, faster, until the steeples of the Abbey faded in the distance. I turned off the main road to a grassy pasture where I fell on my face in a prostrate position. I just lay there for a while. I felt the droplets pounding on my legs, back, and then my face. At that moment, I felt that God had abandoned me. Maybe Juan's uncle was correct. Maybe I was being called to a ministry, but not the priesthood.

I had long believed that God was truly with me, although I never had an experience of being in His presence. I surrendered my life to God and the church based on nothing tangible but rather based on pure faith. But on this day I spoke to God and He did not hear, I reached for God and He was not there. Maybe God doesn't dwell in St. Meinrad or in me anymore, I concluded. So I gathered my wits about me and made my way back to the school.

"We saw you running out there in the rain. Looked pretty stupid to me," a student said as I passed a study lounge. I continue to my room, changing out of my wet clothes and headed for a steamy shower.

Later that night I met two of the black seminarians for pizza and soft drinks at the "Unstable." I was a couple of years their senior so they often came to me with their concerns. I didn't want to involve them in my day-to-day troubles with the staff and student body, so I seldom talked about my problems. But it was impossible to keep my situation a secret, so when they broached the subject, I skillfully steered the conversation in a different direction. In time, I would confide in them, but for now I only told Monsignor Foster, my parish priest, of my plight.

The Monsignor recommended that I come home for a much needed break.

I caught a ride with a fellow seminarian from the Birmingham Diocese. He drove me all the way to my front door. I ran into Dear's open arms, feeling that what was waiting for me was more love than any son could wish for or deserve. But immediately I saw that something was terribly wrong. I could see she had been crying and one of her eyes was slightly swollen.

I ran through the house searching for my father.

"Enough!" I yelled at Dear. "This is enough!" I had grown tired of collecting my mother's tears.

But my father wasn't in the house. I ran outside, walking up one side of the street and down the other, still in my priestly garb, which consisted of a black shirt and Roman collar. It was just before dark.

"Len! Alfred is down on 5th Street fighting. Jump in the car and go bring him home." My grandmother hollered from her front porch, directly across the street from my parent's home. I followed her instructions and headed to fetch my middle brother. I was not accustomed to being the aggressor in physical confrontations, but this day was different. After seeing Dear, I was in the mood for a good fight regardless of the outcome. I drove a little more than two blocks. When I got there Alfred was sitting on the edge of a wooden porch with his head hanging down towards his knees. He had dirt and dried grass in his hair. Five or six other men were standing around taunting him.

"What the fuck are you doing here!" he shouted.

I ignored him. I looked at the faces of the men standing around him. "One against six should be just about even," I continued. "Which of you wants to get his ass kicked first?" I calmly took the collar off and threw it on the front seat of my blue 1971 Caprice Chevy. "You see, I don't give a shit! I'll take on all of you, or each of you one at a time! Doesn't matter. Just make up your fuckin' minds!"

The men all walked away, mumbling under the breath words I didn't understand. Soon they all disappeared between the rows of dilapidated houses. Alfred continued his tirade of cursing and walked away, refusing to get in the car.

"I didn't ask for your goddamn help," he yelled. "Take your ass home 'cause I ain't going no damn where with you." I drove home and sat on the front porch, hoping and praying that my father arrived while I still had the courage and outrage to confront him.

Finally, my father drove up in his old broken down pukey green and white station wagon. He was as drunk as ever. He got out and staggered past me, mumbling, "Summa-bitch."

I was used to it. This was a scene that had played out for years. The only difference on this day was that I was no longer a child who was a son-of-a-bitch, wallowing in fear with roach carcasses and rat droppings under my bed. I was now a six foot, six-inch-tall "summa-bitch" that weighed over 200 pounds.

My father stormed through the screen door and started in on Dear.

"Marie! Marie! Goddammit!" he yelled.

I wasn't far behind. All afternoon I was consumed with the idea of bringing to a tragic conclusion Dear's miserable existence with my drunken father. The idea of killing my father had crossed my mind many times. Besides, Birmingham wasn't known for sending blacks to jail for ridding the city of one more "no count" nigga. The beatings *had* to stop. Dear's tears had to be dried. Dear had no champion. There was only me and if I didn't stop Daddy, who would?

Barely inside, he pinned Dear over the cedar chest and against the wall in the bedroom. I walked right pass them, straight to the kitchen drawers that held the butcher knives. I heard yelling, crying, screaming. I grabbed a knife. I was numb. I returned to the bedroom. I grabbed my father's arm, as he was about to strike Dear. He had his other hand firmly around her throat.

"Summa bitch! What the fuck do you think you are doing," he yelled, spitting food particles and whatever else was trapped between his raggedy-ass teeth right into my face. I had decided long ago that no matter what my father did directly to me, I would not raise my hand towards him. But on this night I needed added restraint to keep that promise to myself.

"Now you listen to me!" I said, holding a death grip on his forearm. With my other hand, I pushed the sharp edge of the 12-inch blade against his stomach. "When I let go, I want you to hit her one more time!" I yelled. "Do you understand? And when you do it, I promise you; the police will come for me, and the coroner for your sorry ass! Do you understand that I don't give a shit about going to prison if it means Dear will have one day of peace without you?"

Dad drew his fist back farther. "Summa bitch!" He spat out the words several more times, as if they weren't intended for anyone in particular.

"Len, what are you doing!" Dear hollered.

"Momma, this ends tonight, right now," I calmly replied. "Don't worry; it's going to be alright."

My attention and anger turned toward Dad again. "Now please hit her, you worthless piece of shit. Please! Do it!"

I pressed the blade even harder against his mid-section. He tried to move my arm, but I was much bigger and stronger. He kept motioning, as if he was going to strike her. I didn't flinch or bat an eye.

"Put that knife down, Len!" Dear begged.

I heard her, but I didn't. I was unable to respond to her. Dad kept threatening. I remained resolute. Finally, he took two steps back and fell on the bed in a sitting position and started bawling. Dear removed the knife from my clutched fist and ran to the kitchen. I calmly went out and sat on the front steps. I heard my father sobbing, uncontrollably. I felt nothing for him.

My oldest brother told me he had a plan to kill our father but he chickened out at the last minute. I had no such inhibitions. After that night, I thought it best I move in with my grandparents. Several days went by and not a word passed between my father and me. Apparently, he only recalled the events of that night after his drunken stupor wore off. Prior to my returning to the seminary, it seemed his inebriated state was fully over, he came to me as I loaded my belongings into my car parked in front of my grandmother's house. I noticed Daddy standing in the gravel road next to the car, eyes focused downward toward the ground. "What did I do that was so bad that you would kill me so easily?"

I just looked at him without saying a word. He never looked at me. I couldn't tell from his demeanor if he was too ashamed or embarrassed to lift his eyes. For the first time in my life I wasn't afraid of the shell of a man standing before me. His words meant nothing and did nothing to sooth the tempest still churning inside of me. His words rang empty and hollow. I didn't care.

"I promise I am going to do better by your mother," he said.

"Dad, if you hit her again, I swear before living God, I will come home and put an end to this once and for all. I swear!"

"I believe you Len, I believe you would," he said in a weakened tone and resigned, raising both hands in front of him as if to surrender the moment. We left it like that. Neither of us ever mentioned that day or the violent days before it again. Dear looked on from behind the screen door as I gave her a half smile and nodded. It was time for me to go.

I returned to school, driving my own car. During my early days in seminary I rang up huge long distance telephone bills. I was barely able to pay the charges with the little change I earned on campus working in the biology lab or the little money I saved from working at the pool. I spent hours on the phone commiserating with friends back home and Dear, checking on her well-being. Although it was not the official position of the seminary, you were discouraged from maintaining ties with the life you left behind. During several late night meetings, my spiritual advisor reiterated this position, as if I didn't get it the first time. I saw my situation as unique. I needed to hear my mother's voice free of fear, free of pain, free of tears. I needed to know that Dear was safe and well. I could not imagine that another seminarian had any reason to raise a twelve-inch blade to his father.

I called Dear twice as often as she called me. There were times when I called her following morning prayers and again, just before bed. She was always delighted to hear from me.

"Dear, I swear the beatings from Daddy are going to end, even if it means I have to make the eight-hour drive home every week," I added during one call.

"Don't worry," Dear said, "I'm fine. I'm doing just fine."

But after that evening of confrontation, I noticed Dear's voice was filled with contentment each time I called.

Dear kept me apprised of Dad's attempts at making amends for all those years of beating, cussing and anguish. I was not impressed, at least not until she told me he had made an appointment to get his teeth fixed. That was significant. All of my life I had only known my father to have those fragments of dangling yellow and gray enamel, barely hanging on to his darkened, diseased gums.

"Your daddy is driving me to Sumter County to visit my cousins," she said during one call.

I was encouraged to hear all the improvements Daddy had made in his life and Dear's. For the first time, Dear seemed happy for longer than a few days. And the days stretched into weeks. And the weeks became months and years.

"Your Daddy joined the church's deacon board," Dear told me.

I got news that he bought her a new car and took out a loan to build a new house back on the farm.

I met her excitement with skepticism until I asked, "What about the drinking?"

She replied, "Not a drop in weeks. He even stopped smoking."

I never heard Dear so happy. I was happy for her. I knew it was impossible for me to have a sound, healthy relationship with my father because I was the one who stripped him of the little misguided dignity he thought he had. Still, I was happy Dear's long night of terror was finally over.

Months passed without incident. Dear was never bitter about spending years with a cold, callous abusive husband. And now she basked in the warmth of Daddy's love and devotion. One thing she liked most about her own newfound love for Daddy was lazy Saturday mornings. She rose before the 5:30 sun and fixed breakfast for the two of them, fried eggs over easy, toast made with white bread, fried bacon or ham, grits with a pool of butter on top and black coffee. Dear said when they arrived at the lake shortly after breakfast. Daddy unhitched the small aluminum boat from the trailer, allowing it to splash into the shallow clear water. They remained there until the oppressive heat became unbearable. Dear said sometimes they left early after Daddy reached the quota of allowed catch for the day.

When I was at home, Dear grinned like a high school girl recounting their special dates and how she sat calmly in the back of that boat with the daily newspaper folded in half, reading aloud story after story, from politics to sports as Daddy cast his rods. I imagined Dear perched atop the wooden cross board, probably adorned in one of her many colorful one-piece shift dresses with her arms exposed. Dear said Daddy offered a commentary every few minutes as the small metal boat drifted from side to side between the shore and tall green and brown reeds spotting the banks. She enjoyed giving me every detail.

"For lunch we usually share bologna on white bread or canned sardines or sausages," she said.

She fixed lunch right there on the boat, slapping the bologna on a piece of bread, topped off with a couple of slices of individually wrapped pre-fab cheese before handing it over to Daddy. The meal was not complete without cheese and crackers. Dear didn't have to tell me just how much she enjoyed this time with Daddy; I heard it ringing in her voice. She was alive again!

Daddy also insisted that Dear handle all their financial matters. Daddy was still working as a truck driver. When he received his wages he gave the check to Dear, who in turn gave him an allowance. They purchased a new home and two cars. The deed for the land was in Dear's name.

Dear got a part time job as a cleaning lady for the local post office. Daddy accompanied her on Saturdays and did the mopping, sweeping and dusting while she sat nearby with knitting needles in hand. Years passed and Daddy never again raised his voice or his hand at Dear.

Having my own car in seminary was a Godsend. Not only was I able to travel throughout the region, I was able to drive home whenever I needed. One time the choir director from my home parish called to ask if I could return to Birmingham to sing in our church's choir concert. The drive was eight hours each way and I gladly did it. I went home for whatever flimsy reason I was presented.

As I was leaving home on one of my visits from seminary, Dear stood near the doorway clutching to her chest her massive 18th Century Bible. The book was rarely removed from its place in the oak and glass bookcase that we rescued from the curbside after a neighbor discarded it. Before that, Dear stored her oversized Bible in the closet behind bags of quilt scraps. It was always wrapped in an old white towel, protected from household accidents and me. She bought it used, after admiring it for some time at a store called Birmingham Book and Magazine.

As a small child, I admired it from afar. It had a rustic black leather cover and tarnished brass lock hinges. I was nearly 10 the first time Dear allowed me to handle the Bible.

As long as I could remember, this book was a part of her life and mine.

"Len, I wish I had something nice for you, but this is all I can think to give you," she said, as she released the book from her breast and handed it to me. Tears gathered in the wells of our eyes.   "Dear, I can't take your Bible!" I said as she placed the book in my hands.

"I know you will use it and take good care of it. It's your Bible now," she said. I carefully placed the book on the back seat of my car along with a few other items, waved goodbye and drove off, headed back to seminary.

I resumed the regiment of day-to-day life as a seminarian. There were actually several students with whom I got along well. For a while it appeared things were changing for the better and I was making new friends.   As it turned out, some of the guys who befriended me had other interests. They were on the seminary's basketball team and since I was tall, they wanted me to play. Even the coach, when he saw me in the cafeteria, said, "My name is Coach Alstat. I'm hoping you will try out for the basketball team."

"You sure are tall," said one of the two players flanking him.

Shortly after our chat, I showed up at practice. I was the tallest and blackest person on "The Hill," the nickname for my seminary. What they did not know was that I never truly enjoyed organized basketball. Their invitations were based on a stereotype, but I didn't care. I desperately wanted to fit in, somewhere, anywhere.

Most weekends the coach invited me along with other players to his house for dinner and to watch TV or to some other team outing. I truly enjoyed my time with him and the other players and they treated me like family, like any other member of the team. But during one of the first practices, I frustrated the returning superstar of the team by blocking most of his shots near the basket. In a fit of anger and frustration, he pushed me as I went up for a rebound, causing me to severely sprain my ankle.

For the next few weeks I hobbled around the seminary campus on crutches, missing practice and playing time. When the doctor finally okayed me to return to the court, I twisted the other ankle by stepping in a gopher hole as I ran across an open field on my way to basketball practice. I was out for several more weeks.

Against the doctor's recommendation, the coach placed me in the game before I was completely healed. I didn't offer a single word of protest. I so desperately wanted to fit in, be a part of the team. I told the coach what the doctor said about the extent of my injuries, but it didn't matter to him and I dared not object to his decision. As soon as I grabbed my first rebound and land on one foot, I felt the soreness return to the initial ankle that I injured. I slowed down as I ran up and down the court. I was giving it my best, but apparently it wasn't enough. The coach screamed at me from the sidelines.

"Get over there Cooper and pick your man up!" he yelled. "Come on Cooper, get your behind in position!" I hobbled up and down the court.

Before the end of the first period, both ankles were swollen and the pain was unbearable. After the ball was inbounded again, I was unable to move from my position near center court. I stood frozen, signaling for a time out. I could hardly stand as two trainers carried me to the bench. As I passed the coach, he glanced at me briefly in disappointment. There were no words of comfort or praise for a good effort, just disappointment from the coach and the team. My short-lived basketball career was over and I was back on the crutches.

The coach never invited me to his home again. None of the players asked me to join them on trips to the movies or to just hang out.

My new seminary friendships ended as fast as they began. There were no noticeable changes in the attitudes of the student body once they learned I was no longer part of the squad.

During services in the college chapel, the coach sat with his team for a special mass.

"Good morning Coach Alstat," I said.

"Cooper," he sharply returned, never looking in my direction. I stood before the team waiting for the conversation to continue. There was an uncomfortable pause as if they were waiting for me to leave.

"I guess you won't be spending Saturdays with the Alstat's," said a friend walking with me.

"I do have a 14-year-old daughter at home you know," the coach added. The team laughed hardily at these words. My friend and I looked at each other as we found places on the other side of the chapel.

"You see Len, Alabama crackers are everywhere. When you were on the team, you practically lived at his house and he had no issue with you being around his children. Now all of a sudden he has to protect his little girl from a hormonally driven oversexed black man," my friend concluded.

I felt like a fool.

"I'm glad you're off that damn team," said one black seminarian. "They saw a tall black man and basketball was the first thing that came to their minds. As long as you could run up and down that court and bounce that ball, that's all that mattered. They didn't give a damn about you."

My enjoyment of the camaraderie far exceeded my enjoyment of the games or practices. When it was gone, I truly missed it. I needed something to fill the void left by having to quit the team.

I had many disappointments during my brief time in St. Meinrad's, but I also have relationships and pleasant memories that will remain with me for the balance of my days. I enjoyed the spontaneous fellowship with some of my lounge mates and other seminarians on campus. When we were not in class, much of our time was spent debating theological doctrines, history or world events. At other times, I had fun listening to their music, which was strange to me, or sharing a good laugh. I suppose in some respects I grew more tolerant of things I didn't understand. But few of my fellow seminarians gave me the same courtesy. I treasured my small circle of friends and learned to depend on them for everything, especially day-to-day human social interaction. We went to the campus pub, watched television and created tall tales. But these light moments of unobtrusive pleasure and fun were few and far between. I was frequently depressed, isolated, and sad. Following one of our late night outings and talks, I retired to my study area to catch up on some assigned readings. Deep into the assignment, I forgot about time. It was 2 a.m. when I asked the others to excuse me so I could go to the bathroom. The bathroom was located in a section that separated the college quarters from the theologians' quarters. As I closed the metal door behind me, I heard soft yet passionate moans and groans coming from a nearby theologian's room. My curiosity got the best of me. I hid behind the curtains leading to the bathroom. I was positioned there much longer than I planned as my bladder swelled. It was taking forever before the two men emerged.

I had never witnessed two men having sex and even now, I only heard while they remained inside the room. So far in seminary I had seen two men openly give each other nipple and chest massages, butt rubs and kisses on the lips in greetings. But this was a first and honestly, I was shocked by their lack of discretion as the door to the room opened. They were all over each other, hugging and fondling, their tongues locked. As I watched, I got sick at the thought of two men having sex. I couldn't bear to look at them another second. I bent over slightly and kept my eyes fixed on the floor. A few minutes later I suppose they had tired themselves out, because they started giggling and talking about plans for their next encounter. One man was a theologian I knew fairly well. I didn't know the second fellow, personally, but I knew he was a first-year seminarian from the East Coast. After they left, I finally ran to the bathroom.

Before returning to my lounge to think through what I had witnessed, I needed to talk to somebody. I noticed the lights were still on in the study of one of our lounge mates. Without knocking, I barged in. There he was in all his glory, lying on the floor, penis pointing heavenly, beating off. I slammed the door shut and ran like hell. He started chasing me for only God knows why. I ran around corners, up and downstairs, doing whatever necessary to keep him from identifying me. Finally, I hid behind the altar in the college chapel. I simply did not want to put my lounge mate in an embarrassing situation where he felt he had to explain anything to me.

God may have been present in the seminary, but I couldn't see or hear the God I believed in through the drinking, blatant homosexuality and petty bickering. I still held true to my commitment to the church and priesthood, but each passing day brought more uncertainty that my dream would survive. I looked around and there were few if any, reflections of the God or Savior that was supposed to dwell within. If that light of hope and goodness burned in me, it grew less brilliant each day.

Before seminary, my faith in God and church came from within. I needed nothing tangible or external to prop up all that I held to be true. The question of a priest being gay was not an issue with me. I took issue with all of the predatory behavior and all the unwanted pursuits especially when I said "No" in so many different ways.

My parish priest was gay and I loved him dearly. Before seminary, I was even-tempered, never used foul language, and was always considerate of others. I allowed the priesthood program to change all that. Maybe the rage was lying dormant, hidden deep inside the little boy who was on his way to a Birmingham Sunday school when a neighboring church was blown up along with four little girls he never knew; maybe it settled into his heart after years of watching his grandfather, a brilliant businessman, demeaned repeatedly by whites. Or did the rage rise then cower when that same brilliant grandfather whipped him with a hose as he clung to that old oak tree near the cotton field? Perhaps he recalled lying on his pallet at night and hearing his mother crying in the darkened bathroom. All I know is that my experience in seminary stoked the rage that had been seething in me just below the surface with the potential to erupt at any time.

I loved the church and everything about it. I believed the church was as close as anyone could get to being in the presence of God Almighty, and that is where I wanted to be.   All the drinking, the advances and pettiness were extremely disappointing, but not enough to make me give up. I so desperately wanted to please God.

Monsignor Foster somehow learned that my problems in seminary continued, insisted again that I come home immediately. I left the seminary carrying my rosary, the one with which I said my "Hail Marys" and "Our Fathers" and left on the nightstand with my Bible every night until Christmas. But driving along Interstate 65, I tossed the rosary out the window in a moment of frustration.

I never knew who kept Monsignor apprised of my situation in seminary. I made the eight-hour drive to Birmingham, even though my car's transmission was failing and I could not drive the car in reverse. I confirmed the situations he already knew about and didn't dare mention any others.

"Leonard, I've met with the bishop and had many conversations about your situation at St. Meinrad's," Monsignor said while reclining on the sofa in his TV room. "Everyone agrees that this seminary is not for you, but still they have no intention of transferring you."

"Why, Father?" I asked.

"Leonard, I've asked the same question and both the bishop and the vocational director insist that you remain where you are indefinitely."

"But Monsignor, that doesn't make sense," I exclaimed.

"Leonard, the bishop and Mucello are two of a kind," he said.

"When you go back I want you to prepare your meals in your room and by all means, keep a low profile until the end of the semester," the Monsignor instructed. "After the semester I'll talk to Bishop Vath once more about how you are being treated."

A friend in Birmingham loaned me a miniature refrigerator. There was already a hot plate and tons of canned goods in my study area. I never ate another meal in the seminary's cafeteria unless a friend from the local community was on duty that day. Meanwhile, I was not given pastoral or ministerial duties or outreach ministries, all of which were offered to other seminarians to help them prepare for their future assignments.

Few people sympathized with me. Many seminarians and staffers knew I was not a "cradle Catholic" and to them this was the source of all my problems. Some of my instructors saw me as an agitator, troublemaker and an enigma. When I made the lowest score on my philosophy exam, the professor stood in front of the class and announced it after passing out all the test papers,

"And yes, Mr. Cooper," he said, as he folded my paper, half hiding the failing grade. With a smirk, he slid it on my desk. The students who managed to see my score of 56 eagerly shared the news with the persons sitting next to them. I was humiliated and made a personal promise to myself not to repeat the same mistake twice. A week prior to the next exam, I spent all my spare time reviewing class notes, reading the textbook, seeking outside references and cross references. The next time around, my score was the highest in the class. But the professor didn't mention my score nor did he fold it and slide it across my desk as before. My paper was the first one he handed out and I made certain everyone saw it lying face up on my desk.

"Cheater," someone whispered from the back of the class.

"There is no way he could go from failing to making an A on the exam," another student openly complained.

"I'll take a different test covering the same material," I said aloud to the professor.

"No, that won't be necessary. I know there's no way you could have cheated, based on all the additional information you included in your essays."

My critics were silenced.

My three roommates continued to ignore me. They appeared annoyed by the music I listened to, the books and articles I read, anything of interest to me. The first day I met my roommate Gary he told me, "My father still uses 'nigger' when he talks about your people."

Once I was lounging around outside of a designated sleeping area listening to Roberta Flack and Donny Hathaway. Suddenly, from behind someone yanked the headsets off my head. It was Gary. I turned to find his face a fraction away from mine.

"I'm tired of you and your nigger shit!" he yelled. His eyes were bulging, red and watery. I felt the moisture and warm breath from his mouth, yet I returned the headset to my head, trying my best to ignore him and remain calm.

I could see his anger building as his tirade continued. "You sit out here and listen to that black shit! Reading your black books! I am sick of your nigger shit!"

His words didn't bother me. I could have easily wiped the floor with him, but I decided as I had many times before, that it was best to calm my anger and let it pass. I wasn't afraid.

My fears of whites began to subside upon realization that the seminarians appeared genuinely afraid of me. Gay or straight, many of them stayed clear of me. But each confrontation brought me closer and closer to the boiling point.

Days later, Gary returned to being the gracious cracker from Michigan who remained polite and polished when dealing with 'niggers,' like me. I believed if I had responded to his aggressive behavior with my fists, he would have repeated the scene over and over. I didn't need my roommates to be my enemies.

"I am sorry for what I said the other day," he uttered from behind me while I watched television. "You see this is the way my father talked in our home and I am sorry." All the while his eyes panned the room, careful not to look directly at me.

"Look, I understand," I replied. "Don't worry about it; we are fine."

In truth, we were far from fine. Still, I had to live with this guy who harbored both subtle and overt racist ideas. Rather than involving the administrators or continuing the discussion, I dropped the matter, hoping to make him easier to live with for however long I remained in that room. I never understood his outbreak, anyway. Everyone used the stereo in the common area to listen to music. While I didn't attack Gary or even curse him out or express my anger, I was responding to whites in ways that I would not have dreamed of just a few months prior.

On a quick trip home Monsignor Foster, my parish priest, patted me on the back as if to say "good job" after I finished cleaning the sanctuary floor. Without thinking, I spun around and shouted, "A pat on the back is just a euphemism for 'nigger, you know your place!'"

Then just as quickly, I grabbed his hand and said, "Forgive me Father, I am so sorry."

"Leonard, what's come over you?" he asked.

He decided to approach the chancery one last time, urging that I be transferred out of Saint Meinrad's. I was not surprised when his request was ignored.

Over the Christmas holidays it was rumored that Monsignor Foster would be taking a much-needed leave of absence from the priesthood and church. I dismissed this as just idle gossip. He would neither confirm nor deny the report. Monsignor was clear in his opinion that my experiences in school had an adverse effect on me as a Christian and as a human being.

"When you left for the seminary, you were warm and thoughtful of others, but the seminary has made you cynical and impatient at times," he told me.

I did know that before seminary I took pride in my duties and responsibilities to my parish, but now my duties had become dreaded chores.

Monsignor Foster suggested my return to the seminary be delayed by a semester and he thought it was best that I work with him in his daily duties managing the parish. I was elated. I loved working with Monsignor when he visited the sick or counseled couples preparing for the marital sacrament. Taking a couple months out of seminary was well worth it. I had the chance to do with Monsignor things I thought I would do on a daily basis in seminary, but was never allowed to do.

I enrolled at the University of Alabama so I would not miss time in school. The chancery made it clear to both of us that I was responsible to Monsignor and no one else. It didn't matter where I was or what I was doing, if Monsignor needed me--no matter the tasks, great or small--I had to drop whatever I was doing and attend to his requests. But Monsignor Foster respected me and never abused his authority over me.

During those months at home, I was at my parish each and every day of the week. I spent all day Friday and Saturday preparing the interior and exterior for the Sunday liturgy. That meant cutting the grass, trimming and collecting debris from the expansive lawn, planting new shrubbery, polishing all the ornaments, mopping and much more.

One Saturday I was tending to the grounds when Monsignor came to me dressed in his long black cassock that was draped all the way to the floor. He wore a wide red pleated cloth belt around his waist with a red sash hanging down the side.

"Leonard, I need you to come in and assist at the altar," he commanded.

I was hardly appropriately dressed to be seen in public, much less to stand in the sanctuary before members of our parish and guests. My hair was in braids, plus I was sweaty and smelly.

"Please Monsignor, excuse me this one time," I begged as I looked down at the clumps of earth stuck to my knees.

He did not reply. I refused to move. He walked away. Cars began filling the parking places along the side of the church as well as out front. I returned to my work more vigorously, and then felt another tap on my shoulder. It was the bride, Angela. She was a good friend of mine.

She was simply stunning in her long white embroidered dress and veil.

"I am not going to get married unless you come inside," she exclaimed.

I slowly rose to my feet, careful not to accidently touch her. I was drenched in sweat and humiliation.

"Look at me," I said.

She stared at my dirty toes poking through my worn sneakers; the soil caked on my arms and legs, the too short cut-off jeans and the sweat. I smelled bad. Yet she embraced me tightly in her dress that was whiter than a blanket of fresh snow. This act of kindness and affection melted my heart. I dropped my tools and ran through the side door to the sacristy to get dressed. In a moment, I was in the procession alongside Monsignor.

At the altar, Monsignor addressed the congregation.

"My dear people of God, Leonard is home on leave from the seminary for a brief time. A few minutes ago, he was out back on his hands and knees working in the flower garden. I told the bride Leonard was home and she insisted he be here. I know how much he loves this parish and I know how all of you feel about him. I could have ordered Leonard to assist me, but I knew if Angela asked him, he would come running gladly, because this is how much he cares about her, about all of you."

The congregation erupted in applause.

As it turned out, the rumor of Monsignor's impending departure wasn't just a rumor. But his last day as pastor of Our Lady Queen of the Universe had not been determined. Monsignor Foster asked me repeatedly to reserve an afternoon so that he and I could meet to discuss my vocational concerns.

I finally made the appointment. I knew he despised tardiness and so I showed up early. As I entered the rectory, I was amazed to see the church's director of music sitting on the edge of the sofa with his ankles crossed the way women sit at times. The two of them had already finished off three bottles of wine. I was confused since I thought the meeting with Father was about my vocation and to address any questions regarding Father's departure from our parish.

"Leonard, John and I were discussing a conversation that took place between the two of you recently. I know that he has expressed a personal interest in you and I am hoping you didn't take offense," said Monsignor Foster.

"No offense taken at all," I said. "I explained my position and as far as I am concerned, that's the end of it."

John released a deep sigh and Monsignor cut his eyes toward him. Monsignor tried to convince me to not be so hasty in my objections to John's advances.

"Leonard, if there is the slightest possibility that you would consider getting to know John, then maybe we should discuss this further," said Monsignor. "Maybe you need some time to think about this?"

He was going to say more, but I interrupted him. "There is nothing to think about. I've known John for many years and love him dearly. But as a romantic interest, that's not going to happen."

John's eyes nervously scanned me up and down from head to toe.

Monsignor Foster finally asked, "Leonard, what act of love is wrong?"

I was shocked and disturbed by Father's attempt to convince me to reconsider John's proposition. I never gave either of them an indication that I was interested in men. Although it was rumored throughout the parish that Monsignor was gay, I had never known it was true until this moment.

"After all I have to deal with in the diocese and in the seminary, you two should understand better than anyone," I said, angrily. "Never speak to me again about this. Please!"

My loyalty to Father Foster and the church was unwavering in spite of the revelation regarding his sexuality. The remainder of the academic year and summer was spent assisting Monsignor with weddings, christenings, baptisms and funerals. I once overheard Monsignor tell the Bishop, "Leonard is already more of a priest than I will ever be."

I was proud to hear the Monsignor speak so highly of me.

The Bishop of my diocese despised the idea that Monsignor relied on me for many of the duties that were assigned to him. The fact that "The Queen" was one of only a few vibrant black Catholic churches in the city meant little to the Bishop and the chancery. He made known his intention to shut down our parish and disperse the membership throughout the diocese.

Often members of my parish and black Catholics I never met requested me by name to administer the Holy Eucharist and prayers for them or their loved ones who could not make it to mass for whatever reason. All of my dealings were with black Catholics from my parish or from black congregations who were aware of me as a seminarian.

The young families and children often asked if I could hear their confessions, but this was too much even for Father Foster to go along with. Only ordained priests can hear confession and give absolution. Finally, I was placed in charge of all youth functions in the parish, which consisted of fundraisers, special liturgies, social functions and more. Father said that during my time at The Queen of the Universe, the average age of membership dropped from 56 to 24. Monsignor attributed this drop to my personal outreach and high visibility in the community. I extended invitations everywhere I went. I invited strangers and insisted that when they come, to be sure to bring a friend. Whether they were Catholic or not did not matter to me. When I was not out doing my own ministering, I was with Monsignor Foster.

Monsignor spent part of his off time with his aunt and mother who resided in an exclusive part of Birmingham. When he paid them a visit he often took me with him. The white-haired ladies were a ways up in age, but well cared for. They had a fulltime housekeeper who looked after their every need around the clock. Like Monsignor Foster, they were accustomed to the finer things in life and proceeded to surround themselves with beautiful crystal and antiques. You could say Monsignor Foster was on a branch hanging from Boston's "old money" tree.

Once, he took me swimming at the home of one of his real estate tycoon friends. A portion of the swimming pool was outside the house and the rest continued into the recreation room. The man's young teen daughter was in the pool with friends and I was invited to join them, but politely declined. I had learned at an early age that whites in Alabama often demonstrate welcoming benevolence, which can turn morally vicious on a whim.

I had never seen, much less set foot in such a magnificent house. I was out of my element and certainly out of place. The real estate developer's home had a huge tree growing right inside the living room. The hall leading to the "kids' quarters" looked more like an exclusive hotel hallway, with decorative wall lamps and thick floral carpets.

Monsignor saw just how uncomfortable I was, so we expressed our gratitude and departed. He later said my posture, jitteriness and constant focusing on the floor made it abundantly clear that I did not want to be there.

"Leonard, you've got to stop this foolishness of feeling undeserving or inferior around whites," he snapped. "Every white person isn't working for Jim Crow or out to get you." He did not understand that one trip to one compassionate white man's home would not sort out a lifetime of exclusion.

The money the Monsignor shelled out for the plush carpet he bought for the rectory could have paid the rent on my parents' apartment for years. Like his friend, the Monsignor was privileged and a man of means. How could he understand my life? When priests in the diocese spoke unfavorably about me in his presence, he defended me.

The priests from the Birmingham chancery didn't miss a turn touting the "difficulties of my past" before other seminarians and religious personnel. Whether it was my vocational director, the Bishop, his assistant, or the finance officer, I heard this phrase more often than I cared to hear it. Their comments almost always placed emphasis on my lackluster educational performance, my limited exposure to cultural adventures and, of course, there was always the issue of me not having money.

Monsignor made an announcement from the pulpit asking anyone who knew of a possible job opening or any prospects of employment to contact me directly. Mrs. White, one of the ladies in the church had a business delivering clothes from the local dry cleaners and she hired me to ride with her to make deliveries and collect money. The position lasted just until she found out that I was Sam Walker's grand boy.

One day at the close of work, I asked her to drop me at my home. She pulled the van in front of the house and asked. "Do you know who lives there?"

"Of course I do: Daddy-Yo, my grandfather," I replied.

"Sam Walker is your granddaddy?" she growled, her once radiant smile suddenly replaced with an angry fretful scowl.

"I'm sorry Len, but you can't work for me if Sam Walker is your grandfather."

"Does that mean I'm fired?"

"I'm sorry Len," she replied without further explanation as she drove off down the street and turned the corner.

I spent the next few spring months searching for employment. I wasn't overly concerned because I knew in a reasonably short period of time I could find a position cleaning city pools in preparation for the summer. I was at the university taking philosophy classes, so I wasn't too interested in finding a real job. In June of 1977, I returned to lifeguarding and teaching swimming lessons for the Birmingham Park and Recreation Board.

It was highly unusual for my grandfather to visit me at the park where I worked. One morning before leaving the house, he insisted that I meet him before the pool opened to the public. All morning my thoughts were rattled, trying to figure why it was so important that I be available to see him. He had taken personal interest in a young girl and wanted me to give her private swimming lessons. But this was way out of the norm for him. Still, out of respect, I could not refuse my grandfather's request, no matter how absurd.

I was in the shallow end of the pool removing debris from the gutters when Daddy-Yo entered the gate holding the hand of a young girl with a light complexion and long, coarse, brown hair. The girl possessed an uncanny resemblance to my mother. "You look like my momma," I exclaimed, looking down at her as I climbed up the ladder and out of the pool.

The muscles alongside Daddy-Yo's neck tensed as he did an abrupt about-face without saying a word. He almost yanked that poor child's shoulder right out the socket as he crashed through the rusty wire gate. When I realized they were leaving the park, I ran after them. Daddy-Yo never looked back.

I learned my lesson early on when questioning Daddy-Yo about his personal affairs.

"Daddy-Yo, why don't you take Muh to nice places sometimes instead of her being cooped up in that back room sewing all day," my brother once asked.

"Boy, that is none of your business and I will remind you to keep it that way," my grandfather angrily replied.

In addition to amassing land and real estate wealth, Daddy-Yo's bank account grew exponentially over the years. Daddy-Yo owned nearly 360 bountiful acres of farmland in Blount County, just north of Birmingham. The farm generated very little income for Daddy-Yo.

Most of his earnings came from his construction business in town. In the late 70's and early 80's, he took his mistresses on exotic trips and cruises to the Caribbean, Las Vegas and Hawaii. None of us were aware of Daddy-Yo's multiple affairs, until word got back to Muh from friends who saw my grandfather shopping and at the grocery store with women other than my grandmother. In the 80's, Daddy-Yo's youthful days were far behind him, and maintaining his duplicitous lifestyle took its toll financially.

"Your grandfather told Muh that his friend was in the hospital dying and the man kept asking for Daddy-Yo, my father once told me. When Daddy-Yo arrived in his room, the man told him that he never trusted banks, so he kept all of his money hidden in the old washing machines he stored in his back yard that were used for spare parts in his washer repair business. He told Sam where to find the money and to make sure his children received it. Your grandfather went to the man's house and got all that money and kept it for himself and never told a soul other than your grandmother. The man died thinking he left a little piece of money for his children," my father said.

"Just before your granddaddy passed, he had somebody drive him up here every other day. He took that old lawn chair and sat out there by the roadside looking over at that house across the street from us and crying for hours," my father told me. Across from my parent's house lived one of the women with whom Daddy-Yo had a relationship. My father said, "He sat out there and cried out loud, 'I gave them everything they got over there and they can't come by and see me for a minute.'"

"After all the money ran out, I took him down home to Cuba (Alabama) and he went from house to house to all his brothers and sisters and relatives, asking for money. When we got ready to leave, he stood by the car and counted the little money he collected. It was about twenty dollars," Daddy said.

"All these years I helped ya'll and between all the families down here, all ya'll can come up with between ya'll is twenty dollars," Daddy-Yo cried.

"Your granddaddy cried a lot in his last years. He needed money so badly, he took a part-time job cleaning the grass around the city dumpsters," Daddy told me.

Shortly before his death, he liquidated everything without breathing a word of his intentions to any of us family members. But more importantly, he didn't say anything about his plans to Muh. My grandmother was under the impression he was away on business or visiting relatives. All the while, he was out lustfully cavorting in places Muh had only seen on television or experienced in her dreams. In the early 1980's, Daddy-Yo sold the 360 acres for $70,000, which comes to a little less than $194.00 an acre, a fraction of its worth. I have no idea what the market value of that land was, but for certain it was worth more than $200 an acre. Daddy-Yo just casually mentioned to my grandmother that he had sold the land. There was no further discussion.

I hated everything about the farm. Land that had been promised to us, land that my brothers and I had toiled most of our lives was gone, except for a few scant acres. My brothers and I envisioned someday converting the farm into a community of single-family homes lining the streets with beautifully tailored lawns and evergreens. Now, with the stroke of a pen, that dream vanished as if it never existed. My grandfather gave me so many dreams, made so many promises, all resulting in so many disappointments.

Even in death, Daddy-Yo was loving and charitable to most everyone except us. He gave 20 acres, the farmhouse, 20 to 30 head of cattle and an equal number of pigs to his mistress. Directly in front of her spread set the two measly overgrown acres he sold to my mother, his only child.

When asked the source of Daddy-Yo's success in several different business ventures, Daddy-Yo's reply was always the same. "I put my Maker in everything I do," he replied, while pointing at the ground where he had planted seeds. "I put my Maker in building that house," he continued, while beaming with pride.

I often wonder if he put his Maker in his decision not to help us when our lights or gas were turned off. Was his Maker in his decision to buy homes for other women or take mistresses on exotic trips while his wife earned her money from sewing clothes for others? And where was this Maker of his when Daddy was beating Dear? Was his Maker in his decision not to intercede on Dear's behalf and spare her from Daddy's slaps and strikes? No, I was not impressed by Daddy Yo's abiding faith in this Maker.

Daddy-Yo was old and feeble when I visited Alabama in 1989. While standing in the doorway looking out across the way, urine ran freely down his legs onto the floor. He was unaware of the accident as I got down on hands and knees to clean the area. A year later, Daddy-Yo was sitting on the sofa in the small den watching television. Without warning, he slumped over and slid off the cushions onto the floor. He was dead.

Meanwhile, at the university, I devoted mornings to trying to stay afloat in my philosophy classes. I had absolutely no interest in the curriculum, so my academic performance was mediocre. I tried to find the writings of Hume, Lock and Descartes remotely interesting, but it was virtually impossible to keep my eyes open at times. Often the professors conducted classes on the lawn in hopes of staving off some of the boredom most of us students felt. But it didn't work. When June rolled around, I reduced my course load. Working at my neighborhood pool was my saving grace.

The pool was my place where I took a break from the burdens of life. Teaching swimming was not as impressive as studying to be a dentist or a priest, or studying philosophy, but it was the one thing I had mastered and loved. The waning days of summer were approaching, as I prepared for my return to seminary.

My diocese recruited another black seminarian. I was elated, but couldn't understand why Mucello, the vocational director, was so eager to have us meet. Before returning to Saint Meinrad Seminary, he arranged a weekend retreat at St. Bernard's College in Cullman, Ala. Father Mucello had little or no need for me by now. I had been labeled a troublemaker. On the other hand, the new black guy, Calvin Pleasant, was mild-mannered, shy, a non-boat rocker. He was as dark as the night and the whites of his eyes were consistently a dull red, as if severely blood-shot.

At the end of the retreat, Mucello had each of us stand individually and share tales of our vocational experiences with the other Alabama seminarians as well as reflect upon the possibility of ordination. When Calvin rose to give his presentation, his delivery was disjointed.

He stammered and stuttered as if his tongue had grabbed hold to every word and refused to let go. Every phrase clamored for expression in the back of his throat. His moment to speak was reduced to grunts and inaudible, broken syllables. After a few minutes, it became painfully obvious that all of his good effort was futile; he wasn't going to get out a word. His chest and stomach jerked with every attempt. I thought he was having a mild seizure. I felt sorry for him as Mucello rose and embraced him in a rather pitiful manner. I despised Mucello as much as Monsignor Foster hated him, if not more. Mucello finally had his token Negro that he could mold and shape into the ideal black priest to represent the Birmingham diocese of North. A sickening reality came over me. I knew my days were numbered as a seminarian and it was just a matter of time before I would be out of the program. Calvin was shipped off to Mount Saint Mary's in Emmetsburg, Maryland, as I headed back to St. Meinrad's. Our paths never crossed again. It was summer's end, so I returned to Birmingham to gather my things before returning to the seminary.

The oppressive August heat beat down on Alabama the day I left to return to school. This time, my departure was not accompanied with fanfare. I loaded all of my belongings into the back of my 1972 Chevrolet Caprice and hit the road. Alone, I made the uneventful eight-hour drive through the Smokey Mountains of Tennessee and the Bluegrass State of Kentucky. This time things were going to be different. Come what may, I was not going to protest or be combative towards my fellow seminarians and the administration. I was going to be a model student. It was as if my slate was cleaned and there was a chance to start all over.

I was determined not to squander it.

I was assigned a different room with different roommates. I had my own car and a new outlook. Life as I knew it was about to change forever and hopefully for the better.

I slipped back onto "The Holy Hill" with little notice from the other seminarians and the monastic community. My new roommates were a couple of years younger than me and we shared little to no common interests. I was 24 years old and considered an elder among the student population. For some inexplicable reason, many students showed me respect after hearing my discussions on growing up under Jim Crow laws in Alabama. I thought this was truly misguided and misdirected admiration.

Others loathed and detested me, rarely missing an opportunity to express how they found my views of the church and me objectionable. At this point in my priesthood studies and preparation, it didn't matter to me whether fellow seminarians admired or detested me. I was committed and focused only on my studies and vocation.

On my return, I was first greeted by one of the other three black students. Damio's mother was white, his father black, and he claimed his black identity whenever it proved to be advantageous. He was sitting in the lounge chair just outside of his sleeping quarters with another student who was seated on the floor in front of him. Damio caressed and massage the young man's chest as if they were lovers. I reminded myself of my newly acquired attitude, which meant whatever they were doing was of no concern to me. Besides, I still considered Damio a close friend, no matter what.

Father Blaise was no longer my spiritual advisor. I was assigned to Father Cyprian Davis, the only black monk in the monastery. Father Cyprian grew up in Washington, D.C., and I was honored to sit in counsel with him. In our first meeting he was well aware of my deteriorating situation in the seminary.

"Keep a low profile at all times," he advised me.

I followed his advice for all of one week.

The editor of the campus newspaper approached me with the idea of writing several articles. He often heard me discussing issues related to growing up in the South and my personal views and problems with Catholicism. I was delighted for the opportunity to write. Father Cyprian thought it was a terrible idea.

I was assigned to write the first article, which primarily dealt with growing up in Birmingham, during the Jim Crow era. The second article would highlight my experiences as a black Catholic in Alabama. The final piece was an examination of my personal views of the Catholic Church.

All three of the articles were published around two months into my new attitude and new semester. Some of my classmates further shunned me. My views on the seminary and church were not a secret, but once those views were in print, even more seminarians avoided me. The first two articles came off the school's presses with little notice, as I saw it. I got the usual congratulatory remarks and I was invited by students to come to their lounge area to share further my personal experiences in Alabama. I gladly accepted. When the final article was printed, I thought all hell had broken loose. Even my new roommates, who were always courteous, stopped speaking to me.

"If you don't want to be a priest or Catholic, then why are you here," one of them shouted at me.

"Change rarely takes place from without," I replied.

"Suppose we like the church just as it is and don't want it to change?" he sneered.

"If you think the situation in the church is good and this seminary is a healthy environment for aspiring priests, then you are not as bright as I thought," I hollered, as he stormed out of the lounge area.

On the way to mass in the college chapel, another seminarian blurted out, "Heretic," as I walked pass. He was pointing and laughing at me as others looked on. At the conclusion of the service, a robed monk came to me and whispered, "The rector would like to have a word with you." I hastened to his office and found him at his desk reading and marking sections of my article.

"Sit down, Leonard," he commanded. "I'll get right to the point. You need to write another article, clarifying some of your comments and simply recanting others."

"I'll be happy to, Father."

"Good," he replied.

I stopped him from saying anything else. "I will take back every word I wrote, if you can show me where I lied or misrepresented the church's position," I said. "Besides, these are my experiences."

Father stared. Anger consumed his face.

"The editor of *The Daily Planet* asked me to write about my personal observations and experiences and that's exactly what I did," I continued. "These are my opinions and my experiences, so how do I apologize for that?"

"Leonard, some of what you said in that article is extremely inflammatory," the rector added. "I think it would be in your best interest to tone it down a bit and take back some of your harshest criticisms of the church and seminary."

"I am sorry Father, and unless you can show me where I erred or lied, my position remains," I said.

"I am sure your diocese will not be pleased with your choice and I, for one, am sick of you and your bitching, bitching, bitching, now please get out!"

For the rest of that day and subsequent days, I avoided Father Cyprian, too. He had warned me not to write the articles and now he said the subject matter brought me unnecessary attention and that was the last thing I needed. Of course, he was right. I lay atop my bunk regretting the articles, which drove an even deeper wedge between the seminary and me.

Years later, I returned to the seminary to retrieve copies of the articles. The new library meticulously kept all publications from the *Daily Planet* in large binders. But my articles had been ripped out.

One afternoon following class an administrator sent for me, asking that I stop by his office at my convenience. I was prepared for more questions regarding those articles. To my surprise, the administrator asked me to travel throughout the state to promote priesthood vocations and in particular, to talk up the seminary. I found it rather odd and out of character that they chose me to be a recruiter. It was a known fact that I was in the midst of what they termed a "vocational crisis."

To many school administrators, I was viewed as being doubtful about my priesthood calling. But that assumption was far from the truth.

I was certain of my vocation; I questioned the vehicle used to achieve my ecclesiastical objective.

It was no secret that I had little regards for the monastic community as well as Rome. Still, when asked about assuming the role of a recruiter, I gave the offer little deliberation and agreed quickly.

Surprisingly, I enjoyed the work and became good at selling the vocational party line. We recruiters traveled to parishes and schools throughout the state of Indiana. We received an invitation to address the boys of a minor seminary called Notre Dame in Indianapolis. As before, I was given a prepared script and instructed to adhere to it to the letter. In previous meetings, I did as ordered without reservations, without deviation.

I rose to the podium as my eyes panned the crowd of boys ranging from 8 to 17 years of age. The room was silent. I was comfortable addressing the crowd as every eye fixated on me and all ears waited for my words. I was well into my pitch when without warning my words froze on my lips. My eyes dropped, as I closed the text. These boys were young and impressionable, innocent. They needed to hear the truth about seminary life, its glory as well as its ugliness.

"There is so much work to be done and a service to be rendered," I said lifting my head as my eyes scanned the audience. "The seminary is nothing more than a microcosm of the wider society in which we live. Imagine, problems such as alcohol abuse, drugs, statutory rape, racism, lying, stealing, cheating all being part and parcel of the world in which we live. Those same problems exist in seminary, only they are exacerbated by isolation, separation from family, and the fact that many of us who chose this lifestyle are probably wrestling with underlying psychological problems and issues of self-esteem, sexuality and more. Also, we have a large gay population in the seminary."

I looked to my left as a fellow seminarian walked briskly across the stage towards me. He covered the microphone with his hand and whispered, "What are you doing? This is hardly the time or the place for this."

"Tell me, when is the right time and the right place," I angrily snapped. "Tell me!"

I continued speaking. Eventually he meandered off the stage and disappeared behind the curtain.

"Last year, my mother, grandmother and some close friends came to visit me in seminary. Late in the evening, we walked pass the campus pub. The door swung open and out came two monks carrying a fellow monk dressed in his Benedictine robe, belt and rope around his waist. A monk on each side held him by an arm. He was so drunk, he could not stand, much less walk. His oily black hair flopped around his face as they literally dragged him and his disgrace back to the monastery," I said.

At the conclusion of my speech, the boys offered sustained applause. The question and answer session that usually followed was omitted. Our host gave me an envelope containing a check, which was to be delivered to the seminary.

When asked by another seminarian if I had received the check, I told him I had "respectfully declined the donation."

As soon as I returned to the campus and my lounge area, a seminarian was waiting to tell me my presence was required in the office. I did not bother removing my coat as I made my way down the darkened musty halls. I entered the small conference room where I found several students and priests sitting around a table.

The sponsor of the recruitment program paced nervously, back and forth on the other side of the room.

"Mr. Cooper, do you care to explain what happened at that school," he said. "I hear you went off on your own and didn't bother using the prepared text." Now he was yelling. "What do you have to say?"

"Father, I don't know what came over me. First I was reading the prepared speech I normally use, then suddenly I found myself telling those boys about the many challenges of studying to become a priest."

"Who do you think you are? All the others follow their script. What makes you so special that you can just go off and do as you please?"

"Father. These boys need to hear the truth," I replied.

"Leonard, that is not your call and the arrogance of YOU deciding not to accept the donation. Rest assured, you will be disciplined for your actions."

During the middle of his chastisement, I pulled the donation check from my pocket and dropped it on his desk. I was just kidding around with one of the other seminarians when I told him I declined the check. Little did I know, he had reported back to the school before I hardly had a chance to leave the stage. Apparently, the seminarian thought it was important to tell the school administrators that I had deviated from the prepared text and had declined the donation. As time passed, it seemed I spent more and more time clarifying comments I made, allegedly overheard by pious seminarians. I was often called in to the administrative offices to answer charges and questions on issues of which I had no knowledge. I was determined to stay out of trouble as much as each situation allowed. I was offered a part-time position teaching and overseeing the anatomy lab.

I immersed myself in my work, spending inordinate amounts of time in class. I also became involved in additional activities on and off campus. This was the perfect way to keep my idle mind out of the devil's workshop, I figured.

I always wanted to play the piano or organ and thought studying and practicing now would be a great way to fill the void in my evenings and nights and also keep me out of trouble. I was assigned to a novice by the name of Brother Bryan. Our first meeting was in the evening in one of the small music rooms above the theater. The room had a door and was large enough for the piano and a few inches on each side for you to walk around and sit on the bench. Brother Bryan seemed as eager as I was to begin. He was dressed in his traditional sandals and long, black cassock tied with a rough, wide, black leather belt. I slid in from one side and he slid in from the other, right next to me. We began with the minor scales and by the end of the class, we had moved on to playing simple tunes. With one hand he turned the music pages and with the other, he kept time by tapping his fingertips on the piano's frame. For the full hour, he stayed by my side with our arms and legs always touching. With each milestone and accomplishment, he laughed hardily, throwing back his head and firmly slapping my thigh, then gripping it tightly. I didn't think much of it at the time. His grip was firm and closer to my knee. Initially, I view the thigh slaps as being similar to a hard pat on the back for a job well done. After I hammered out a flawless version of the score presented, he moaned softly, making a sound that resembled that of a woman in the midst of sexual pleasure.

"Uuuhhh aaahhh, Uuuhhh aaahhh," he moaned in a feminine tone.

This time the leg slaps turned to upper thigh caresses. I was already in deep trouble with the administration. I needed a way out that wouldn't offend Brother Bryan.

"Thank you, brother," I said while standing and gathering my books and borrowed sheet music. "I have early exams in the morning and I need to get to the library."

That was my first and last piano lesson. Whenever Father Noel, the music director, inquired about my absence from the classes, I provided a believable yet appropriate lie. Perhaps God would overlook this one little lie, I told myself.

There was no refuge for me in the seminary among religious men who only mimed goodness, righteousness and mercy. It had begun with my first spiritual advisor accusing me of possibly unknowingly enticing fellow seminarians. The president rector believed me to be an outright liar. Others in religious authority refused to discuss the matter with me. There was nowhere and no one I could turn to. Seminary was a vastly white environment, nothing more than an extension or continuation of the life most of the students lived before they entered the school. For me, there were also cultural problems that had to do with being black in a predominantly white seminary environment, problems the white students couldn't understand. It frustrated me to no end trying to explain to them what was obvious to me. Racial issues and differences were crystal clear when white seminarians talked about welfare, education and crime and spoke unabashedly about how blacks were a drain on American society. I learned to avoid these discussions.

I became close friends with Wayne, a black seminarian from Ocala, Florida. Some other seminarians said he was a closet gay, but his sexual proclivity couldn't be further from my concerns. Wayne was rude, obstinate and abusive to the staff and other seminarians at times, but never towards me. When one of the monks passed away it was mandatory for all seminarians to attend the burial services. When the announcement was made, in full view of the administrators and students, Wayne climbed on a table and in a loud voice declared of the dead monk: "He can roll over in his coffin and kiss my black ass!"

Wayne was not expelled or reprimanded for his blatant disrespect for the dead monk. There was never a word mentioned.

Wayne continually tested the patience of both his fellow seminarians and the monastic community. He frequented the nearby convent, as did many of the seminarians. The convent housed a couple of hundred potential nuns or females studying for other disciplines. A few priests were barred from setting foot on the grounds of the schools in the neighboring towns. It was rumored that several priests had been accused of having sex with some of the under aged girls. Wayne had been involved with a particular young woman for several months. He occasionally borrowed my car for his dalliances. One day he was moping in the rock gardens when he informed me that the young woman he had been spending time with could be pregnant.

"Man, I don't know what I'm going to do. I really fucked up this time," Wayne lamented. "I have no intentions of ever getting married and if she's pregnant, I'll just leave the school."

"Wayne, before you do anything rash, just wait for the test results," I calmly replied. "And if she is pregnant, you still have several options open to you."

"I know, I know, but until I find out for sure, what am I supposed to do? I can't stop myself from worrying and for damn sure, I'm not saying a word about this to the rector."

In a couple of weeks, the test came back. Wayne was not going to be a father and his trek towards the priesthood continued.

I refused to judge Wayne because of his brief indiscretions. After all, Wayne was always supportive in my times of great distress. One Friday I missed all my classes because I was sick, lying underneath the covers in my upper bunk bed for more than 24 hours without waking. My roommates didn't care about my well-being. Wayne finally managed to awaken me. I begged him to go get the doctor. A half hour later he returned with a small bottle of codeine.

"The doctor was too busy to come, but he sent this medicine," he said

There were no instructions with the medicine and the doctor didn't say he would come to check on me later.

I had been in bed for nearly three days when I crawled out that Sunday to a chair in the communal lounge.

"Man, you look like shit," Wayne said in his gentle demeanor. "And you smell like that between-the-legs funk!" Wayne administered the medicine the best he knew how for several days and also helped me to the showers to get cleaned up. I felt much better a day after taking the medicine, though it made me high. I never found out what was wrong with me. In a few days I was back to my usual self.

With the passing of each day, I was more and more convinced that it was a matter of time before I would be asked to leave the seminary. I ventured off The Hill occasionally to visit a family in the village at the foot of the seminary. In time, the seminary administrators forbade this simple pleasure. The family had young daughters and thought my visits gave an "appearance of impropriety," according to the vice rector. Any objection from me would have been pointless. It seemed as though I spent more time in administrative offices than in my room. Late one evening, I was summoned to the acting academic dean's office. I was accustomed to answering the administrator's questions regarding something I said or something someone thought they overheard me saying.

Upon my arrival and to my surprise, I was told that I had not fulfilled a requirement I needed to move on to theology and the Latin course I needed would not be offered for at least two years. Following this disclosure, I met with the assistant rector of the seminary, who informed me that he was in agreement with the academic dean's decision. He also spoke with my Birmingham diocese vocational director and all parties agreed that I should return to the University of Alabama in Birmingham, where I could fulfill the course requirement immediately. It was my understanding that I would return to the seminary at the end of the summer to start my theological training during the fall session. During my time in seminary, I trusted the monks academic guidance. It wasn't until I returned to Birmingham soon after my meeting with the academic dean and the vice-rector that I realized an elaborate plan was in place to get me out of the priesthood program.

I returned home to Birmingham during the Christmas break of 1977. I hastened to enroll in my Philosophy classes at The University of Alabama in Birmingham. I delayed signing up for the Latin classes until the spring and summer sessions. Once my enrollment was completed, I raced to the chancery and delivered the bill for my tuition.

"Mr. Cooper, please have a seat. Someone will be with you shortly," said the receptionist.

I was stunned when Father Mucello entered the room and directed me to a small adjacent office.

"I understand that you are under the impression that for some reason the diocese is going to pick up the bill for your classes," said Mucello with a stern gaze. "I'm not certain why you are here, but the diocese has no intention of paying for these classes or any future classes you may decide to enroll."

"I don't understand," I replied. "The rector and the vice rector said I could continue my studies here until I complete the prerequisite for theology."

"As far as the diocese is concerned, you accused your administrators of being racists and you were obviously in a vocational crisis."

"But we had an agreement," I shouted.

"And by the way, all aspects of your life are no longer the church's concern. Good day Mr. Cooper," Mucello uttered, as he left the room and closed the door behind him. My heart fell. I stood in the middle of the room, staring down at my list of classes. I could not accept the fact that I was no longer a seminarian from the Birmingham diocese. This was temporary and would be resolved in due time, I thought. I wasn't going to let anyone in the Bishop's office see just how badly I ached and was torn inside.

I certainly wasn't going to give Father Mucello the pleasure. I was convinced it was all a big misunderstanding and Monsignor held the power to straighten it all out.

Later that same afternoon, Monsignor Foster called me at my grandparents and asked that I come to the church rectory.

"Please have a seat," said Monsignor, as I entered his study. "Leonard, I received this notice from the bishop's office. It says the diocese has no further need of your services and that you will not be returning to St. Meinrad in the immediate future."

"The immediate future! If it says in the 'immediate future,' that means there is a possibility of me continuing at some point? Right?"

Monsignor continued reading. "According to the diocese, you left the school in a rage due to a vocational crisis," said Monsignor, handing me the typed document. He sat waiting as my eyes dissected each page. The document described me leaving the school in anger after accusing an administrator of racism and it said no one had knowledge of my abrupt departure. It was all lies.

"Leonard, let me see what I can do after this cools down a bit," Monsignor said. "I will do everything I can to straighten this out, I promise." In subsequent days, Monsignor arranged several meeting at the chancery with the Bishop and Father Mucello. In a few days the chancery eased their position, by saying they would give Monsignor's request consideration, though I was not reinstated. I never knew why the Bishop changed his earlier stance. I was happy there was still a glimmer of hope of me continuing my trek to the priesthood.

Monsignor Foster was initially charged with the responsibility of determining whether I was worthy of returning to the seminary during the summer or fall sessions. But in a matter of months, the diocese reneged on this agreement as well. Monsignor and Father Mucello were never on the same page when it came to my priesthood vocation. Monsignor once told Mucello, "You can never expect to get ahead of someone, if you are always behind kicking him or her in the rear."

Monsignor showed little if any respect for the hierarchy in the chancery office. I mirrored his disdain and contempt for the Bishop and his functionaries. Monsignor found me a job, hoping it would distract me from my priestly woes. He managed to secure a position for me with the Garner Stone Company in Roebuck, Alabama, which is about 30 minutes northeast of Birmingham. It was in the middle of winter and I was to remain home in Birmingham until the fall session. Monsignor drove me to work on the first day of my new job. We arrived early and the Monsignor and the proprietor greeted each other casually and laughed easily in a way that told me they were already acquainted. Monsignor left and I was escorted to a small wooden and tin shed in the rear of the one-story office, where I met with two younger men and several older gentlemen. For the next eight months I spent my days and early evenings cutting limestone slabs, loading trucks with marble slate, polishing slabs and doing all types of stone work in various locations around the city.

"These long, grueling hours are considered as part of your penance, Len, and might work in your favor when time comes for the chancery to reconsider your re-admittance to the seminary," Monsignor said.

I wanted so badly to share Monsignor's optimism, but in my heart I knew that Mucello and the bishop would not squander this opportunity now I was officially out of the program. Still, I took the job and the penance begrudgingly.

The winter winds whipped through that little shack as we worked. The cold was penetrating. Ice formed on the floor near the entrance and around the huge flatbed table, where we laid large pieces of marble stone for polishing. The days that were not spent cutting and polishing huge, flat stones, were spent building on site at churches around Birmingham, building altars, laying marble floors or building stone walls.

One day we were called to reseal cracked or damaged burial vaults in area cemeteries. That was morbidly fun. I brought along my handy pocket flashlight in hopes of viewing the remains inside vaults that were 50 to 100 years old. This appealed to the boy in my twenty-four-year-old body. To my surprise and dismay, they were all empty and some were impeccably clean.

I was assigned to break stones every morning. Winter at the stone company was numbing and punishing. The summer was oppressive and accompanied by drenching humidity. I suppose it felt like penance should. In mid-June, I was assigned to break large sandstones with a huge sledgehammer. The stones were used to adorn homes and businesses.

Every day was a carbon copy of the day that preceded it.

One day I noticed a priest hanging around the gate peering in at me. I was in full swing with the sledge hammer and pick axe when the shop foreman pointed and said, "Len, you have a visitor over at the fence."

I looked over and saw a gray and brown haired priest of about 60 years of age, dressed in full black garb. His deeply wrinkled face broke into a smile. I glanced at him for a moment and returned to my work. Several days that week, the same scene was repeated. When the priest showed up the following week, I instructed the foreman to deliver a harsh message to him. "Tell that holy man I am busy and don't have time for any of his nonsense. Tell him that for me." The foreman said that I should at least give him a minute of my time. I threw the hammer to the ground and walked purposely to the fence.

"What do you people want from me now?" I yelled, without giving him a second to respond. "My life is shit because of you. You have taken everything! Everything! I have nothing left!" I was going to continue my assault but gave up. "What's the use," I muttered, walking away in disgust.

The priest returned for several subsequent days. I saw Mr. Garner and the priest near the road, laughing and talking as if they were old friends. I was called to the office, where Mr. Garner strongly encouraged me to speak with the priest and to hear him out.

"He has come to you out of considerable risk to his own personal standing with the church," Mr. Garner said.

I reluctantly went outside and approached the chicken wire fence.

"You have five minutes," I grunted.

"Mr. Cooper, I understand your frustration and anger," the priest said. "I am well aware of your situation and believe me, I do sympathize with you. My name is Father Borden, from St. Barnabas just down the street there." He pointed. "I oversee the financial matters of the diocese and I just wanted to let you know that you are not alone in this. I know that you didn't misuse church funds as some are accusing you. I'm..."

"Hold it right there, Father," I interrupted. "You mean you knew this and said nothing?"

"I'm sorry, but there's more," he said. "Some are saying you were involved in improper sex acts in the seminary."

"That's ridiculous," I shouted.

"It may be ridiculous, but there are those who will swear to it."

We were both silent for a few moments.

"Mr. Cooper, what am I supposed to do? You are a young man and have the rest of your life before you. I am approaching retirement and cannot afford to have any confrontations with the bishop."

"You people make me sick" I replied. "Always looking out for each other rather than doing what is right. You've had your five minutes, now please leave me the hell alone."

I hesitated for a second as the priest returned to his car and drove away. Then I returned to slamming those boulders with more force than before.

A week or so passed. I didn't see or hear from my visitor. But then he returned to the same spot, hanging outside that damn fence, observing my every move.

"What is it going to take to get you off of my back?" I asked.

"Have dinner with me, so we can talk further," he said.

"What kind of fool do you think I am?" I snapped.

The priest peered at me through the rusty wire fence, not uttering another word.

"Fine," I forcefully replied.

For the next month Father Borden and I ate at nice restaurants or just sat in the park or in his car talking about the problems throughout the diocese. Just like Monsignor Foster, Father Borden thought very little of the bishop. Eventually, Father Borden gained my trust and I decided to invite him inside my inner circle of family and friends. He was always very gracious and polite to my mother and grandparents.

One afternoon we were invited to Ma Bee's for dinner. She came to visit me in seminary and was a prominent figure in my church. Ma Bee was considered the mother of our parish. As usual, she and her family found Father Borden delightful. After dinner, Ma Bee served what she called "highballs." I respectfully declined.

The evening closed as Ma Bee stood on the red brick porch, waving frantically. Father and I sat in the car outside her house as he recounted the succulent Louisiana meal he had just experienced.

"The evening doesn't have to stop here," he said. "You can come back to the rectory with me and spend the night," Father Borden said, reaching over to rub and caress my shoulder. At first, before this evening, I thought his shoulder and neck rubs were just loving affection from one man to another, like that of a father and son, but not this. His firm rubbing motions on my shoulder and neck turned to finger tip caresses, barely touching the bare skin on my shoulder and neck. When Father leaned back, closed his eyes and made soft sighs and groans. I felt my temperature rising with anger. I opened the door without making a sound. I stood outside the vehicle momentarily. My eyes teared up as I returned to Ma Bee's.

I never said a word or even looked back at Father Borden. I suppose for him, all those weeks of dinners and long talks were all for this one moment. I imagine after a few drinks with Ma Bee, his tongue was loosened and the words and intentions flowed freely. All he wanted was sex.

Like many Catholics, Ma Bee was aware of the extraordinary number of effeminate priests in the clergy, but never voiced her concerns. She drew a clear and distinct line between the antics of questionable priests and the Church. But to me there was no separation; they were one in the same. She once insisted that I swear that no matter how many corrupt priests I encountered in the clergy, I would remain committed to the Catholic Church. I had no such blind loyalties. Ma Bee, like many others, had not witnessed the fake piety shown by priests as they contemplated their next move to lure some young altar boy into their twisted sexual fantasies. I saw the storm churning on the horizon and attempted to sound the horn. Time and time again I was silenced, even by those who loved me, and knew the words I spoke were true.

And no one seemed to care about the pain of a black boy from Birmingham who was searching for a safe and heavenly haven, for a God and godly men who could create for him a spiritual reality that would replace his horrible memories of racism and hatred and an unsafe home.

In the spring of 1978, Monsignor Foster, my old mentor, my beloved friend, my parish priest who had always stood up for he, had had his fill of the priesthood. I was walking through a local shopping mall in Birmingham when suddenly standing in front of me was

Monsignor Foster, now known as Mr. Foster. Beside him was a man nearly half his age, wearing a leather cowboy hat and vest with no shirt. There was no need for an introduction, as Monsignor's grin stretched from ear to ear while he glanced over toward his companion. Monsignor was playful and giddy. I had never seen him like that before. To me, it was obvious that the guy in the cowboy hat was his love interest.

Mr. Foster and I embraced, exchanged niceties for a few awkward moments and went our separate ways. I never saw him again. I knew firsthand that he had had difficulties with the chaste part of his priesthood vows. He was a man of conscience and I was happy for him that he had left the church to pursue his personal sexual interest and to live the life he so desired. I admired Monsignor for refusing to live a duplicitous life like many of the priests and students back in the seminary did. I despised the men on "The Hill" who lied in public but in the shadows acted out all their homosexual desires. A few pretended to have girlfriends when suspicions swirled around their sexual proclivity.

Monsignor was a gay and a great man who loved his parish. I saw no contradictions in his life.

Father Pascal Reiss took over the duties of my parish and I was assigned to him after Monsignor was granted his indefinite leave of absence. Father Pascal fought a gallant fight to get me reinstated into the seminary with numerous phone calls and letters and a few visits to the bishops offices. But he failed. The bishop wanted nothing more to do with me.

I decided to take my case directly to the parishes. I met with small groups from various black Catholic congregations in Birmingham, hoping to garner enough support to partition the bishop to reconsider. Members from my congregations and the parish council had several audiences with the bishop and Mucello. But the decision was final. The bishop was adamant about not allowing me to return to seminary and refused to discuss the issue further.

That didn't discourage me. I called a former priest named Dennis Putman, who fell out of favor with the bishop soon after his ordination in the early '70s. He spent years in "priest jail" for his obstinacy. He wasn't actually confined to a cell; the bishop stripped him of his priestly duties and limited his mobility between designated churches. Putman encouraged me to continue the fight to return to seminary and to expose all the sexual antics there.

"But in the end, the bishop always wins," he said.

Nearing the end of the summer of 1978, I arrived at the church early to assist Father in his preparation for the Sunday Mass. I was slipping into my cassock as Father Pascal entered the sacristy.

"Leonard, what are you doing in here?" he asked.

"I am getting dressed for the procession," I replied.

"Leonard, I am sorry, but you will not be assisting today. I've been instructed to keep you away from the altar. Your time as a seminarian is over. I am sorry, but you will have to sit in the pews with the rest of the parishioners."

I was devastated. I slid the cassock back over my head, handing it to Father Pascal.

"I am so sorry, Leonard," he said.

"Me too, Father." I slipped out the side door so I would not be seen or heard. I was not prepared to face my parish as a "regular member." This was my first realization that my priesthood dream was over.

I continued meeting with parishioners in my church and other congregations trying to find a strategy that would get me reinstated. But my optimism was on the decline and so was the number of faces willing to fight for me. One night I had just returned home to my grandparent's house when the telephone rang. It was just after sunset. It was Father George, a priest I had spoken with several times in the past. But this time his voice was laced with a sense of urgency.

"Len, it is time for you to leave town and find someplace else to live and I mean *now*," he said. "This has gone further than accusing you of misusing church funds and sexual misconduct."

"Father, none of this is true," I screamed.

"Whether it is true or not isn't important. There are people willing to support these accusations."

"But *none* of it's true." I repeated.

"Leave town, Leonard, please, as soon as possible. Please!" Father George begged.

A few nights before his call, my mother had received a disturbing message from an unidentified caller who whispered, "Tell Len, his safety cannot be guaranteed any longer."

"Len please leave those folks alone and keep your mouth shut." Dear pleaded. "Just stay at home and don't go back over to that church again. Please!"

My grasp on the situation was beginning to slip, but I wasn't ready to let go. I never expressed any concern regarding my safety or wellbeing, but there were others, religious and laity, who were worried that I would be hurt. To me they were over reacting.

The following morning I got up bright and early, headed downtown to the Delta Airlines ticket agency.

At Delta, I told the lady behind the counter, "I would like to have a one-way ticket please."

"It would be nice to know to where," she said in a deep Alabama drawl.

"It doesn't matter; you decide."

I realized I didn't have any idea where I wanted to go. The day before, I was paid my weekly wages of $86.60, which was all the money I had remaining. I gave Dear the money I earned at the pool. I looked at the picturesque posters on the walls, travel advertisements for cities like New Orleans, Los Angeles, Chicago and Washington, D.C.

"I hear Washington, D.C. is nice," she said.

"That will do just fine," I replied.

The price of the ticket left me with $35.00 to launch a new life in a city where I didn't know a single soul.

Everything that was dear to me was in Alabama. Even as a boy who was afraid the KKK would swoop me away for stepping outside of my black cage or for something I did not do, or when white children yelled "nigger" just because, I never wanted to leave my home; I wanted Birmingham to treat me like it was my home, to embrace me and nurture me the way it did other native sons who did not have dark skin. I thought as a priest I would have it all, the place on earth where I was born, a spiritual home and the respect of all men, regardless of color. But now I had to flee and leave the only person who had tried to make Birmingham a home for me.

The thought of leaving my mother and not knowing when I would see her again was too much to bear. In my gut I knew that once I boarded a plane, years would pass before I would see her face or feel her embrace.

Early the next morning, Saturday, September 1, 1978, Dear and my grandmother had appointments that took them away from the house for much of the day. Dear's pleadings and tears were etched inside my head and reverberated through my heart. After they left the house, I lit an altar candle on the desk, said a prayer and shed some tears. I gathered my few belongings; I headed for the airport hours before my flight was scheduled to depart. I hated the thought of having to lie to my mother. She had no idea I would be gone for good when she and Muh returned.

If I stayed any longer, she would return and ask questions about the reason for my leaving and I probably would lie. I also didn't want to risk giving her the chance to change my mind. No, I needed to leave while they were away.

I had a window seat on the plane, which meant I could press my face against the glass to hide my tears. I didn't want to leave home, but as I saw it, I didn't have much of a choice.

CHAPTER 12: THIS IS NOT MY HOME

The plane touched down in the late afternoon at Washington National Airport. The dreary onset of nightfall matched my deepening depression. I cried silently as I walked through the terminal. I stopped for a moment in the airport lounge, sinking into a black leather seat that faced flickering televisions. I needed to ponder my next move.

My friend Juan's Uncle Chet lived in Upper Marlboro, Maryland, which is just outside of D.C. He was the pastor of a large Baptist congregation, so I figured surely he would be able to find me a place to live, at least temporarily. I called him and sure enough, within an hour or so he had arranged for one of his church's deacons and his wife to pick me up from the airport. I stood outside the glass door of the terminal as a large blue automobile drove up. The deacon was very warm and cordial but the wife was cold and aloof.

Neither emerged from the car as I reached inside to shake their hands. The deacon appeared to be slightly overweight but wore a big booming smile and a loud friendly voice. The madam, on the other hand, was skinny and wiry. I was surprised when I reached to greet her; she turned away, facing the front.

In the car, the man said, "Hi, I'm Deacon Eubanks and this is my wife…"

"I'm Mrs. Eubanks and you can call me Mrs. Eubanks," she interrupted, never making eye contact with me.

They lived in an area called Hillcrest Heights, Maryland, just across the southern border of D.C. The ride was a short one. The car came to rest in front of a well-kept rambler made of white siding and brick.

Once inside the house, Mrs. Eubanks' expression made it painfully clear that she was not happy with my presence in her home. Before I could take my bags down the staircase that led to the unknown, the lady of the house was barking out a list of do's and don'ts for me to follow as long as I remained, as she said, "under my roof."

"You are forbidden to have any contact whatsoever with the Catholic Church," she said. "Whenever we go to church, you have to go."

I soon found out this was almost nightly.

"You are not to come upstairs unless invited and never come up when we are not at home. You are not to use the lights in the house or any other utilities." She rattled off her list at rapid pace. "You can only wash yourself using the sink downstairs. You are not to eat any food in the house for any reason. You are responsible for any cleaning jobs assigned to you."

Finally, she stopped to breathe, and I walked down the stairs to the basement.

I would never know their first names. All the while I was there, it was "Yes sir" and "No sir, Deacon Eubanks" and as instructed, I always referred to her as "Mrs. Eubanks." The deacon seemed to be a man of honor and integrity. One of his sons was active and committed to the church and community while the other son prided himself in mastering the art of being streetwise. This son was determined to avoid getting a real job, but instead he aspired to become a smalltime street hustler. Nevertheless, he was always broke and asking me for spare change, which I didn't have.

As night fell on my first day at the Eubanks', I held on to the hope that maybe they would change their minds and permit me to use the lamp downstairs, even for a short while. Mrs. Eubanks was clear in her position and reminded me with every opportunity to never turn those downstairs lights on, no matter what. Night after night, I sat alone in the dark for hours. There were times when we were away from the house or at the church and she pointed her finger in my face to remind me of her idiotic rule to not use her precious lights. In addition, I was not invited upstairs to visit, watch TV or eat supper with the family. It got so dark in that basement that it didn't matter whether I had my eyes open or closed.

The first night I remained dressed and slept sitting upright. Early the next morning, Mrs. Eubanks, with her long gangly body, meandered about. I heard her hard rubber bottomed house shoes sliding across the floor above me. Suddenly she ran down the stairs as if to make sure I hadn't messed with her precious belongings during the night. She stopped halfway down the wooden staircase and then bent over to pan the area. She took special care not to make eye contact with her unwanted guest. Seconds passed and not a word. I sat still, waiting for whatever instructions followed.

"I don't want you sleeping on my sofa. Use that old cot over there," she said. "I don't want you burning my lights down here or using up my water. Use one of them rags over there and wash yourself in that laundry sink."

I didn't say a word.

"And don't you ever come up these stairs unless you are told to. If nobody's here, you keep yourself down here. I won't say it again."

For the time I was in that pit of a basement, Mrs. Eubanks must have reminded me of my place every other day. She never once looked at me directly or solicited a response from me.

Most mornings I woke up with one or two roach carcasses stuck on my back or arm. One morning soon after my arrival, I rose bright and early to hit the streets of D.C. in hopes of finding a job. Any job would do. On the bus I stood holding onto the overhead handrail, wearing one of the only two suits I owned, the beige Yves Saint Laurent three-piece. An elderly, gray-haired woman inconspicuously gestured with her finger that I should take note of my lapel. To my embarrassment, a small cockroach slowly made its way up towards my collar. I quickly brushed it off and tried to pretend it never happened. A moment later the old lady beckoned again, gesturing towards my shoulder. Another roach. Again I brushed it off and as soon as it hit the floor, another passenger smashed it under foot. The shame was too much. I quickly exited the bus.

Every morning I hoped and prayed that the good Christian Mrs. Eubanks would invite me up for breakfast. That invitation never came. I could only imagine sitting at the table enjoying a plate of grits, eggs and toast. I was glad the door was closed at the top of the stairs. That way I was spared suffering through the smell of whatever was cooking upstairs.

Finally, one night when my stomach was growling and I was weak from hunger I sneaked upstairs. I did not have a job yet and had very little money, certainly not enough to buy a meal. I knew the entire family was out.

I was painstakingly careful as I removed a pan from the cupboard. I took one egg from a bowl of what seemed like several dozen. I boiled the egg and ate it as fast as I could while being careful. Then I made sure I cleaned every trace of the privilege I was not supposed to enjoy and went back downstairs to my cave. I even took the shells with me.

A second after the family returned an hour or so later, Mrs. Eubanks clicked on the light and raced halfway down the stairs to her usual position. I was sitting upright in total darkness doing absolutely nothing but gathering my thoughts. The tirade began.

I could see that her teeth and the wrinkles on her face were accentuated by her yelling and her anger. An occasional droplet of spit flew from her mouth and down on me.

"Mister, didn't I tell you not to come up these stairs unless told," she yelled. "I see you stole some food from out my kitchen. I should take you and all your....your....your!" Her words trapped and hung up in all that anger. "And put you out that door right now! I don't care who the reverend is to you. I'll throw you out right now," she screamed

She ran back up the stairs and slammed the door behind her.

All this foolishness for one damn egg! If I had made an omelet or a sandwich she wouldn't have hesitated to throw me out the door. I was so terrified that I had this jabbing pain in my gut. I knew at any moment she would return with her husband and ask me to leave, but she didn't. And I didn't repeat that mistake again.

A couple of times I bought a cheap burger from McDonald's, but it cut deeply into my meager monetary stash. Meanwhile, Mrs. Eubanks seemed to believe God called her to save my soul from the wilds of Satan, but in particular, from the Catholics. No less than four times weekly, regardless of my plans or lack of interest in the Eubanks's church, I had to attend service with them. Sometime finger sandwiches, cookies and other delectables were served following a church function. I loaded my pockets up with unwrapped tuna sandwiches, cheeses and boiled eggs. Often I took enough food to last for several meals. The color or smell of an item might be slightly off by the time I ate it, but nothing could stop me from devouring it. At other times I spent part of my day scouring publications on the lookout for social events that served refreshments. In a city that was 80 percent black and had a church every few blocks, I could count on several social events weekly where they served everything from snacks to elaborate southern dinners. Still, there were truly days when I had no idea where my next meal was going to come from. One thing I knew for certain, there would not be a feast for me at the Eubanks' Christian home.

I decided to contact Father George Stallworth, who was then pastor of St. Annes Catholic Church in far Southeast Washington, D.C. Prior to this meeting we had several conversations during my turbulent times with the church in Alabama. Father Stallworth had plans to move quickly up the hierarchy of the Catholic Church. He wanted to employ what was called a black theology, which gives an afro-centric flavor to the liturgy. He was well respected among black clergy and the National Office of Black Catholics. He told me in a telephone conversation when I was in Alabama that getting involved in my case was a "powder keg," which would only hamper his efforts.

But I decided to attend his church one Sunday and reach out to him. Following a rousing charismatic mass that closely resembled a southern Baptist church revival, I was invited to the rectory for lunch. A priest, who introduced himself as Father Powell, soon joined us. Father Stallworth began asking questions of a personal sexual nature.

"You sure are a *big* boy!" Father commented, as his eyes scanned me from head to toe. "I'll bet with what you are working with, the ladies *love* you," he chuckled.

I left abruptly.

I lived in the Eubanks' basement for nearly two months. Finally, I landed a position as a lifeguard and swimming instructor with the YMCA in Bethesda, Maryland I took two buses and traveled nearly two hours to get to work. Mrs. Eubanks insisted that I give her my entire salary for rent and additional money to cover back rent.

"Mrs. Eubanks, I need to save some money so I can move out," I explained.

We agreed to speak again about the money in a couple of weeks or so.

I arrived at the Eubanks' just before dark one Friday. I found all of my belongings packed and sitting outside near the front porch. I figured they had just finished a major cleaning downstairs and set out my stuff so it would not be in the way. I walked in as usual through the front door, greeting Mrs. Eubanks, who pivoted and walked back toward the kitchen. The thuggish son mumbled over and over, "This ain't right, man. This ain't right."

The oldest son, who always espoused the virtues of Christianity, walked up to me and said, "You have to go."

It still did not sink in. "Go where?" I asked.

"I don't care, but you got to get out. Now leave." he yelled.

"Where am I supposed to go?' I said, my voice cracking, tears streaming down my cheeks.

"Just get your stuff and get out," he yelled.

Through my tears, I screamed, "You all don't have to put me in the streets like this."

The oldest brother raised his fist as if he was preparing to strike me.

"This ain't right, ya'll," the youngest son continued repeating. "This ain't right."

I turned and headed out the door. The "Christian" son gave me a sharp push from behind, as I stumbled down the stairs. I sat on the last step. I could hardly see through my tears. Finally, I stood and started gathering as many of my belongings as I could carry. I walked several blocks down the street to the bus stop carrying my black footlocker, bags of clothes and shoes. I returned to get the rest of my things and walked back to the bus stop as I stumbled, occasionally dropping items from overstuffed bags. The youngest boy ran out to help me, taking some of the items from my grasp.

"I heard you say you have no money," he shamefully said in a soft tone. "Here is a dime, maybe you can call somebody."

But there was no one for me to call.

"Sorry 'bout all this, man. Take it easy," he said, adding more of my things to the small pile at the bus stop before walking back towards the house.

The only person I could think to call was Terry Raspberry, the man who hired me to work at the YMCA. When he heard my story, he asked one question: "Where are you?"

Within an hour, he drove up to the corner where I was waiting. He took me to his house on upper Connecticut Avenue in Northwest Washington. His community of shiny new cars and beautiful high-rise apartment buildings was light years from what I was used to. Aside from going home with a fellow seminarian on Thanksgiving, I had never spent the night in the home of a white person. In truth, I had never entered the front door of a white person's home.

Terry had his son sleep in another room and put fresh linen on his son's bed for me. But I insisted on making a pallet by the door of the room and sleeping on the floor.

"You can remain here as long as you need," Terry said.

But his wife and I had never met and it was obvious I made her uncomfortable. She seemed to look at me from the corner of her eyes. Our initial greeting was our first and last time addressing each other directly.

CHAPTER 13: HOW LOVELY IS THY DWELLING PLACE

The next day at work I told Terry the YMCA's early morning masters swimmers required my assistance and that I had found a place to sleep and live close to the "Y." In actuality, I was sleeping in a cluster of shrubbery across the parking lot from the building. At the time, I didn't have a blanket or anything to shield me from the night air. So I walked from the YMCA to the Chevy Chase Inn, which was about three miles away and near the D.C. line. I waited patiently for the cleaning lady to enter one of the rooms. Then I ran from the wooded area and grabbed a blanket and bathroom tissues off the cleaning cart.

After a couple of weeks passed, Terry asked me to open the "Y" each morning. I eagerly agreed, knowing that having a key meant I could find a place to sleep inside the building, away from the inclement weather. For the next few weeks, I slept in the tiny broom closet. Amid the buckets, splintery push brooms and mops, there was no room for me to stretch my 6'6" frame out completely on the cold, gray cement floor.

One night after the "Y" had closed shortly after 11 p.m., Terry stopped by and found the closet door next the water fountain slightly ajar. He pushed the door open as it bumped against my feet, startling me awake.

"Len, what are you doing here?" he asked, as he turned the light on. "How long have you been sleeping in here?"

"A few weeks, maybe more. I'm not sure," I responded, while covering my eyes from the light.

"You said you found a place to stay," he said. "I didn't expect to find you living in the Y."

"I thought what better place to sleep since I must be here at the crack of dawn anyway," I said.

"You can stay here a few more nights but then you have to make other living arrangements," he said.

Terry later explained that if something happened to me in the building after hours, the "Y" could be held libel. He didn't want to take that chance.

By week's end I was back on the streets, living off the kindness of strangers in downtown D.C. I resorted to stealing food and provisions, sleeping in thickets adjacent to the Bethesda-Chevy Chase YMCA. There were occasions when the few worldly possessions I owned were hidden in a wooded area far away in -Southeast Washington or in the basement of a building being renovated off DuPont Circle.

Dear's precious Bible was among my belongings. I carefully wrapped the Bible in plastic and in her old white towel and placed it in a protective cloth case in hopes of sheltering it from the elements. Dear never knew that I was homeless or the peril of her Bible.

I found it rather relaxing being perched in the lifeguard's tower, attending to the swimmers and sun worshippers after a long morning of teaching Polliwogs, Fish and Minnow classes. I was good at this teaching and protecting and thought of it as possibly the only thing I had expertise in. Those swimmers who braved the early mornings and the cool temperatures were predictable and adhered to their daily routines and rituals.

Decades have passed and I still recall which swimmers kicked harder with one foot than the other, which ones lifted their heads too high out of the water while breathing; which of my five- year-olds had potential and which ones needed a little extra love and security in order to convince them to jump into the shallow end of the pool. More importantly, I remember the day I was sitting poolside when a young female bather completed her swim before coming over to introduce herself. I observed her for weeks wearing a full black latex swimsuit that crossed in the back and a too small white rubber swim cap. The way she dashed across the deck, eyes straight ahead led me to believe she was either shy or extremely self-conscious. As it turned out, she was a bit of both.

One day as she was leaving the pool area, I noticed she was staring in my direction. I guess she decided after weeks of passing me every morning it was time for a formal introduction. She walked with purpose right over to the guard's tower. "Hello, I'm Cathy Carpousis," she said.

I later found out that Carpousis means watermelon in Greek, which supplied us with a few moments of light-hearted laughter every now and again. Cathy and I became best friends, lifelong friends, over and above the subtle objections of her boyfriend. On several occasions Cathy inquired about my living situation. For days I managed to deflect her concerns by saying, "I'm staying with friends across town."

She knew I was lying. Unexpectedly, she insisted that I move in with her boyfriend, John, and share his room in a group house across from the National Zoo in Washington.

I moved in a few days later. In the beginning he welcomed me, but his two roommates kept a cautious distance. I earned my stay by waking before the crack of dawn to help John deliver the early morning newspaper to about 200 subscribers. The Washington winters can be brutal and I was grossly unprepared. The fitful breeze cut straight through my thin, brown and red plaid overcoat. As I marched purposefully from door to door, I heard the crackling ice beneath my hole-riddled Converse sneakers. My numb fingers and toes felt as though they would fall off at any moment.

John's sparse room in the group house was located in the attic. I slept on an exercise mat covered by a sheet. I was grateful. Anything was better than huddling in a cluster of dried shrubbery or sleeping on an abandoned park bench. I remained in his house for several weeks until his nightmares got the best of him and me. In the beginning, his middle-of-the-night screams of torment were random. As time moved on, so did the frequency and recurrence of his screams. There were times he woke up hollering at the top of his voice. There didn't appear to be a regular pattern to his outbursts. All I knew was that he scared me out of what seemed like two years of growth. I couldn't remain in that situation so I decided it was time for me to leave.

John had already arranged for me to do odd jobs with him for a family named Capalby that lived off DuPont Circle, near the heart of downtown northwest Washington D.C. DuPont Circle was known for its upscale boutiques and restaurants located in the heart of Embassy Row. It was common to cross paths with diplomats representing different countries. DuPont Circle was also known for its concentration of Washington's elite gay community.

I spent my days poolside at the "Y" and my evenings and early mornings dry walling, painting, plumbing, and doing electrical jobs and more. I earned a scant $6,000 annually at the "Y," which was hardly enough to live on. One morning between classes, the director of the "Y" called me and a few other employees into the administrative office. In that office he led a brief ceremony honoring me for "my commitment to hard work in the aquatics program." To show the YMCA's level of appreciation, I was awarded a whopping five cents raise on the hour, which meant I earned an additional 40 cents a day or $2 a week. At the time, any amount, large or small, would help ease my difficulties.

At times, I walked through Georgetown, asking perspective renters the price of available housing. During down time, I made my way to the center of the city, where I begged for coins from strangers and passersby.

There were things I feared more than death: Loneliness, isolation and being irrelevant. I often looked in the mirror and hardly recognized the person peering through the looking glass. Staring back at me was the reflection of just a fraction of the man I once knew. The face in the mirror was vaguely familiar, like seeing an old friend the years had not been kind to. My face was gaunt and my hair was unkempt.

I only took showers on the days I worked at the "Y." By all accounts, the YMCA was my lifeline. For nearly one year, I managed to keep my secret away from those I loved. As far as they were concerned, I spent every night in a vacant apartment off DuPont Circle in D.C. Some nights this was true, but other nights I was just one of many poised in the free Thursday night soup lines. Months later, when I was finally free of D.C. streets, I instinctively found myself wearing a coat and tie with a briefcase in hand, queued in line for that same free soup, standing with smelly beggars reeking of urine with their filthy matted hair and fingernails. In Washington, there was no place that welcomed them or should I say, that welcomed us. I had slowly slid out of a culture of three-piece suits and people considered socially acceptable, into a class of others looked at as discards and rejects.

"Your eyes are too clear and teeth too straight. Why don't you get a job." one passerby exclaimed, as I extended a hand for his spare change. Why would he say such a thing? He didn't know my story and surely didn't care enough to inquire.

On the other hand, an elderly blind man near the Old Riggs Bank on F Street in downtown Washington shared his favorite panhandling spot with me. You could hear him bellowing out familiar gospel tunes from more than a block away. Onlookers gathered around, but few were willing to part with a portion of their precious earnings. The gentleman told me that in his younger days he sang for the President. I don't recall which president, but either way it didn't matter. He had a wonderful baritone and tenor voice that was fit for royalty.

When my day of panhandling ended, I gazed down at the sparse collection of pennies, dimes, gum wrappers and nickels collected in his perspiration stained cap. I could use the extra money, but I figured he could use it more. Whenever I showed up at that spot unexpected, he always welcomed me to join him. One day I came a little early and there he sat, on the stool in the nearby liquor store, caressing a half pint of whiskey. That was the last time we shared that corner or a visit. My departure didn't rise from a position of being judgmental; just seeing him perched on that wooden bar stool, caressing that bottle like a freshly cut diamond, reminded me of what could happen to a man, any man.

The next day I decided to try a different tactic, one that was certain to bring me some much-needed income. My clothes were stored at the "Y" and a little of my wardrobe was in a deserted basement flat. I put on the only suit I owned and headed for the bustling roundabout at DuPont Circle. There I stood, styling and profiling in hopes of catching a wondering eye of some lonely older ladies. There were no takers. After standing there for hours, I returned to the apartment, dejected, broke and hungry.

The Capalbys told me I could use a bottom floor apartment until all four dwellings in their building were completely remodeled. I was only allowed to stay the night when I put in a full day's work renovating the above quarters. My nights on the streets were suddenly reduced. I slept on an old blue sleeping bag that was given to me by a friend. The apartment was freezing! Ice gathered near the bottom of the basement door leading to the outside. When I opened my mouth, I saw my breath float through the chilled air. Tiny beads of ice water collected on my mustache. Still, I was glad to have a place off the streets, though temporary.

The pharmacist at Schwartz Drug Store on the corner of R Street and Connecticut Avenue, a few blocks from the apartment, knew my predicament and gave me Pepperidge Farm cookies or other treats to curve my hunger pangs. For nearly six months I toiled well into the night, getting those four apartments ready to be rented. Other workers came, completed their work and left the job, but I was loyal and steadfast. The need for food and shelter will chain a man to a place and a situation. But then came the day that I cut and laid the final kitchen counter top and I was asked to vacate my first floor apartment. I had been sleeping on that cold floor for such a long time that I honestly believed I had a right to that dingy flat. However, that right only existed in *my* head.

CHAPTER 14: LIFELINES

I was determined to formulate a plan that would take me off the streets and far away from panhandling. Cathy and I both shared an interest in theology and she understood my financial difficulties. She and another person had already secured a house in Chevy Chase, Maryland. They needed a third person, so I was invited to join them. I moved in the day after I left the DuPont Circle apartment. My job at the "Y" was a short walk and a quick bus ride away. Life was beginning to look a little brighter.

A precocious kindergartener in my morning YMCA swim class stole my heart the very first day of the new classes. Leslie Minna was brash, abrasive, and fearless with a loving heart as big as her smile. Her mother was an attorney and her father was a director of cancer research at the Bethesda Naval Medical Center. When my birthday rolled around, she insisted her mother make me a light green pistachio cake. I ate the entire cake in one afternoon, not because I was hungry, but because it was so good. Leslie wanted me to come to their home for family events, large and small. The Minnas became my family in the Washington area. Lynn, the mother, had substantial real estate holdings in the area and at times hired me to do odd jobs such as painting and lawn work. Over the years I taught their two daughters to drive and I babysat the girls on weekends when Lynn and her husband went out of town. They trusted me without boundaries and their trust helped heal my heart.

For years after the Minnas sold their Bethesda, Maryland home and moved to Texas, I kept their house key on my key ring. Any negative racial residue towards white people in general, was seriously diluted by my relationship with the Minnas. They were my constant reminder that white people were capable of extraordinary benevolence.

Sometimes something that seems so insignificant at that moment can cause a major shift in your life. It happened to me one day when a young Washington Post Metro reporter named Neil Henry stopped by the "Y" looking for a story centering on kids from wealthy Bethesda families who opted out of working during the summer to spend leisurely days lying around the pool. The director introduced him to me since he figured I knew most of the kids at the YMCA. Neil exhausted the entire morning darting from person to person, finally concluding there was no real story of interest. I was sitting out in front of the building on the stone wall about to have lunch, which consisted of one of those pre-fabricated tuna sandwiches wrapped in clear, clinging foil.

"Didn't find what you were looking for?" I asked, breaking my sandwich in half, giving part to him. He seemed surprised at the offer. Oddly enough, I have always shared what little I had at the time, so sharing my sandwich with this young reporter was not so unusual.

"Nah, this isn't going to work," he replied, not hesitating to take the sandwich and scoff it down.

Aside from the groundskeepers and the cleaning crew, I was one of only two blacks who came in contact with the membership.

"So, what's your story?" he asked. "I detect a slight southern accent in the way you pronounce some words."

I gave him a little information, including mentioning that I had been in the seminary. When my break ended, Neil asked permission to stop by my house later.

That evening he came over with a photographer and asked to hear about my brief stay in the seminary. For more than an hour, I relived and recounted incidents I wanted so desperately to forget. He took my journal that covered both seminary and subsequent days, which consisted of more than 300 handwritten pages.

I was stunned to see myself on the front page of the Washington Post Metro section before the week had ended. Calls poured in to the "Y" for the next couple of days. Some members expressed their support, while others showed displeasure that I had aired Catholic dirty laundry in a major newspaper. Local television crew came by the "Y" to sit poolside and interview me. I was a hero to many and probably a villain to even more. I painted a picture of rampant homosexuality and recounted anecdotes that probably fed rumors of pedophilia in the seminary and priesthood. My words were met with skepticism at best sometimes. To some, I was just an outright liar.

The article described that despite specific orders from Frank Mucello, who was in charge of all future priests from my Birmingham diocese and who forbade me to attend the Louisville Parish, I increasingly frequented the all-black parish in Louisville headed by Father Edward H. Branch, a critic of race relations in the church.

"With his background, the seminary just couldn't suit his needs," Branch said. "He is an effective believer, not an intellectual. At St. Meinrad, students are trained to deal with large white suburban parishes. So from that point of view, we're dealing with racism."

"The attitude of people in authority is let's see if he works? Let's see if he conforms, if he is a white priest with colored skin."

Branch said, "The biggest problem with the Catholic Church in the U.S. is that it has swallowed that melting pot thing hook, line, and sinker. The Italians, Irish, Germans and all have cultural slants in their rituals, everybody except the black folk. We didn't have the black clergy to interpret all this."

Father Branch described me as "injudiciously aggressive, serious, black, six foot five and intimidating."

Parish council member Robert Coar said, "His dismissal shocked our congregation. Attendance has been falling ever since," Coar said. "The diocese is always talking about the need for black priests. Leonard had it all going for him. Everybody here loves him and encouraged him. I think it was pure prejudice," Coar said. "The Diocese really doesn't want black clergy."

After the article ran, I was working poolside one morning when I received a call from a man identifying himself as a member from the Brothers of Christ Christian Church in Camp Springs, Maryland. I was unfamiliar with the organization.

"Mr. Cooper, my name is John Flowers and I, along with other members of our congregation, read the article about you in the Post," he said. "We believe that based on that story alone, you were grossly mistreated. There are people who would like to correct this wrong by considering you as a possible recipient of a scholarship we offer for ministerial training, regardless to affiliation," he said.

"You mean you would offer a scholarship, even if I am Catholic and my intention is to remain Catholic and maybe even return to the seminary someday?" I asked.

"Yes Mr. Cooper, your being Catholic does not play a role in our decision making."

"Perhaps we can meet and discuss this further," he offered.

Days later I met the gentleman in a luxurious Washington, D.C. restaurant, where he surprised me with an offer of a full scholarship to the Howard University- Catholic University Theological Consortium. I felt things were starting to turn around. Since I always hoped to finish school, I notified him a few days later that I would accept his offer.

CHAPTER 15: MY LAST GASP

For the next couple of years, I attended classes at both Howard and Catholic Universities as a part-time student of divinity and theology. Early on, my Catholic instructors and some of the students commented unfavorably about the article that ran in the Post about my time in the seminary. For sure, enough time had passed for the story in the paper to be forgotten, so I thought. The instructor asked for us to introduce ourselves and share something about our religious affiliations. I was surprised when one of the students recognized my name and freely shared that information with the rest of the class. During discussions the students often expressed anger or mild disdain for me.

"I remember that story," one student exclaimed. "You are the one who alleged that the priesthood is full of gays and child molesters."

I ignored the comments as the murmuring continued.

"Yeah, I remember that article," another said. "So you are that guy," he said.

"If you despise and detest the church so much, why are you here?" a different student angrily said.

At times, their pointed questions reminded me of my days in seminary. But I was not concerned about their displeasure with me. During the break in the lecture, a Benedictine monk followed me outside to my usual spot. He introduced himself as Brother Abraham.

"I remember reading the story. A lot of people were upset with you. It must not have been easy and I thought you were pretty brave," he said. Brother Abraham was dressed identical to the monks of St. Meinrad in long black cassock, sandals and a wide black leather belt.

"There was something pure and honest in the way the story was told," he said.

"Well brother Abraham, you see where all this has gotten me," I replied. "The church wants nothing to do with me and maybe you should stay clear as well."

"When that story came out, there was a big discussion in my monastery," he continued. "Mr. Cooper, you do have friends and based on some of the sentiments expressed in my monastery, I do believe I can help you get reinstated into a program."

"Are you serious," I said with excitement. "I would do most anything to get back into the program."

"Even if it meant leaving Washington?" he asked.

I was still passionate about becoming a priest and I was willing to do whatever was required.

"Give me a few days to work things out," he said. "I'll invite you to the monastery to meet the abbot and have dinner with a few fellow monks."

This also meant in little time he would need to find a bishop that was willing to take a chance on sponsoring me. The gravity of my dismissal still weighed heavily on my mind. Already I was imagining my triumphant entry to the Birmingham diocese, where my parish would once again embrace and be proud of me.

A few days passed. Finally, it was time for me to meet with the priests at the monastery. I was elated that there was a glimmer of hope I could return to the seminary. I arrived early and used the time to calm myself and gather my wits about me. I walked around the surrounding community to pass the time. Upon entering the door, I waited patiently near the vestibule, which was adorned with beautiful wood carved crown molding and dark antique furniture. None of this mattered. My only focus was to do whatever was required to get back on track to becoming a priest.

The monk emerged from a room in the corridor directly in front of me.

"Len, what in the hell did you do?" he asked in a gruff whispering tone, covering his mouth.

I was surprised and stunned by his question.

"There isn't one single bishop in the country that is willing to give you the least consideration as a sponsor to the priesthood, not even on probation."

I was angry, hurt, dejected, but mostly saddened by the thought of being routinely labeled and reminded that I was some kind of terrible, confused man. Not a single bishop in the United States was willing to give me a second chance? Maybe I *was* the confused enigmatic person with "special concerns" they made me out to be.

Nothing had changed. I was hoping the time tempered with a modicum of understanding would ease some of the restrictions placed on me. I decided not to remain for dinner. My appetite had faded.

"I'm going to leave. Thank you for trying," I said.

At that moment it became painfully clear: My desire to become a priest would never be realized.

I sank into a depression. Then a friend brought me a moment of comfort by telling me about Bishop Eugene A. Marino, a black bishop from the Washington Archdiocese, who was celebrating mass that weekend at St. Benedict the Moor Catholic Church on the opposite side of town. Surely this black bishop would lend his help or at least a sympathetic ear.

I had tried to meet with Jean Jaudeau, the Pope's apostolic delegate, who had an office among the embassies on Massachusetts Avenue in D.C. I made numerous calls to his office, but none were returned.

I even joined the Pope's choir during his visit to D.C. in 1978, in hopes of having a brief audience with the Vicar of Rome to state my case. I never got within 20 yards of him.

I arrived at the back entrance of St. Benedict's to find it packed and a few parishioners standing on their tiptoes to see over the throng gathered at the door. I wasn't going to be able to get near the bishop. In my head I imagined sitting with him while he listened empathetically to my story. I knew if I had the chance to tell my side, he would be sensitive to my plight and gladly be my champion.

As the bishop completed the benediction and started the procession from the church, I waited patiently for the crowd to clear while he shook the hands of the last remaining stragglers. Finally, he was alone.

"Father forgive me, I am hoping that I can have less than a minute of your time?" I said while extending my hand. He nodded his head in suspicious approval.

"Father, I was a seminarian from the diocese of North Alabama, studying at St. Meinrad's. I believe I was unfairly removed from the program....."

The bishop interrupted. "What is your name?" He stared at me with a look of anger and confusion.

"My name is Leonard Lanier Cooper."

As I spoke, he beckoned for the priest standing guard to stand even closer to him. Smiling and waving, he leaned forward and whispered his admonishment in my ear. "I know who you are and all I have to say is that you never try to contact me again. Do you understand, Mr. Cooper?"

The priest standing guard subtlety directed me towards the exit.

No, I didn't understand any of this. He was one of our own and if he, a black bishop didn't or wouldn't look out for me, then who would? I felt like a part of me died that day. I thought for certain the bishop, being one of the few black bishops in the world, would take a personal interest in the possible unfair treatment of one of the few black seminarians. I suppose he was Catholic first and being black was of less importance.

I ran from the church grounds as fast as my legs could carry me. I raced down the subway escalator and found a secluded cement bench to sit on at the far end of the platform. There, no one would see me crying.

The brief moment with the bishop was a defining one, marking the end of a dream and the beginning of an acceptance for me. No matter what I did or how hard I tried, there was no way I would ever be permitted to return to the priesthood program.

That week, I resumed my course work at Catholic and Howard universities. During a lecture at Catholic University on mysticism, I realized I was not listening. The priest's lips were moving, but I did not hear a word. My attention was far from the lecture and my mind even farther. Everything seemed to move in slow motion. My thoughts of church, religion, priesthood and school spun around and around like a whirlwind inside my head. Finally one day, I suddenly shot up from my seat, excused myself from the classroom, and leaving my books, pens and notepad atop the desk, I walked out and I never went back.

That day marked the end of my march to the priesthood. Even now, when I reflect on this period, it is difficult to determine which started first, me losing faith in God or God's loss of faith in me. I so badly wanted to believe in God and wanted all that I had learned about him to be true. At times, I convinced myself that all the doubt in me was a phase and in time it would pass, but it didn't. Amid all the doubt and uncertainty, still I tried to hold firm to my belief in God, and read the Bible as frequent as before, but both eroded in time. I abandoned Catholicism soon after walking out of my class at the Catholic University. "Why should I be a part of an organization that didn't want me?" I asked myself. The more I read the scriptures the more contradictory the Bible seemed. I had many questions and no satisfactory answers. I needed something much more than regurgitated Bible verses or empty promises of blind faith. There had to be more!

I asked my questions to any minister who would listen. There were those who said I was an instrument of the devil in my unrelenting quest for Biblical explanations.

"These questions are coming straight from the devil," one minister told me. "Satan is working through you and has you all confused now."

But I didn't believe that. So I dismissed such claims and continued my inquiries.

At some point between 1980 and 81, my life became void of prayers and biblical debates. I had no more interest in God or the Word. For me, the change was gradual. I cannot remember when the questioning stopped and my doubts began, or when my total detachment from anything having to do with religion ended. I do remember that in the early 80's I was invited to attend mass at my old parish during a trip home to Alabama. I took communion that Sunday, not knowing it would be the last time I participated in the ritual I once loved with all my heart. The same altar where I received my first communion would also be the place where I received my last.

CHAPTER 16: ASKED AND ANSWERED

I always had my doubts about the sincerity of organized churches, but this was the first time I questioned my longstanding belief in God. This was much more difficult than the days I spent wrestling with my doubts about priesthood. Now, I was doubting the existence of God.

In my new state of mind, I traced the seeds of uncertainty about God to my earlier life, beginning with all the unanswered childish prayers. Begging for God's intercession when my father was hitting my mother only seemed to make matters worse. God did not answer. I read in the Scripture that if you have the faith the size of a mustard seed, you also possess the strength to move mountains. Yet, in my life, no mountains moved. Part of the problem for me, as I saw it, was that I took God at His word. Now the time came for me to put away those childish things.

Not only did I entertain the question of God's existence, I also concluded, I probably never really believed. I rationalized this by noting that at no point in my life have I ever heard the voice of God. As a child down in Alabama, God never spoke to my heart. Now as an adult, I could not feel His presence.

For years, I forced myself to go to church and read the Scriptures. At this point, the more I read and listened to sermons the less they spoke to me. Then one day, I stopped trying. I gave my personal Bible away and discontinued all religious affiliations.

I grew comfortable with the idea of separating myself from all things having to do with church and God. For some reason during this time, it was in the back of my mind to make an effort to make things right with Father Mucello, my former priesthood vocational director. I promised myself on my next visit home, I would stop by the rectory and at least try to have a civil conversation with him.

On many occasions my parish priest described Mucello as a "whiny little queer." Mucello wreaked havoc in my life throughout my entire priestly adventure. As providence would have it, months after leaving the theology program at Howard and Catholic universities, I was stepping off the bus in Georgetown and physically bumped into Mucello and a young man. The young man was tall, extremely effeminate and skinny, wearing a black shirt with lace sleeves. If he wasn't gay, he was doing one heck of a job pretending.

"Len," Mucello said, clearly startled to see me. He didn't bother introducing me to his companion.

"Father! What on earth are you doing here?"

"I'm in town on church business and I'm staying at a nearby rectory. You must stop by for a chat."

As he spoke, his friend paced nervously. When he stopped, he had his back towards me. Mucello squirmed uncomfortably, which was very rare. It was obvious I had seen too much. I found the whole scene rather amusing. In times past I would have tried to get as much information as I could regarding Mucello' s visit to D.C. and for certain I would have tried to find out the nature of his relationship with his companion. But I was out of the priesthood program for good and at this point none of that mattered to me. I agreed to visit him at the rectory later that afternoon.

I arrived at the Annunciation Catholic Church in D.C. a little after sundown. I agreed to meet with him, not to make a vain attempt to re-enter the priesthood program, but because I was tired of fighting and I just wanted to make peace.

Father Mucello was waiting for me in a side office. As before, we exchanged insincere pleasantries, both being well aware that for years we only tolerated each other.

"Father, it wasn't so long ago that I had the upmost respect for you and loved you as if you were family," I said.

I wasn't surprised when he offered only silence while gazing out the window. For a moment, I entertained the idea of forcing a discussion about the young companion I saw him with earlier. I wanted to confront him in hopes of forcing them to tell the truth. Monsignor told me Muscello was gay, but that was not the issue. I was just tired of all the lies and deceit. I had traveled this road so many times with priests in the past. There was no point.

"I give you my word. You won't have any further trouble from me," I said.

Still, there was silence.

I stood and turned to walk out the door. I heard him utter over and over again, "Leonard, you can't hurt me. You can't hurt me."

"Goodbye Father," I said, as I left the room.

Our paths never crossed again.

CHAPTER 17: JERUSALEM

I thought the meeting with Mucello would have a profound emotional effect on me as in prior encounters. But this time, there was nothing. There was no critical analysis, no afterthoughts or emotional deliberations. Nothing. The moment came and passed, as if it never happened. The next morning, my life continued on the same path as the day before. I returned to my 5:30 a.m. perch at the Bethesda Chevy Chase YMCA pool. My thoughts traveled to many places, but none came to rest on Mucello. I was calm and finally at peace.

One morning while guarding the early bird swimmers, I decided to peruse the local community newspaper. I came across an ad for an audition for a singing position with the Washington Concert Singers and the National Choral Society. I thought, "I can do this. After all, I was often called upon to sing for visiting dignitaries in the seminary."

The ad also made it clear that only serious musicians would be considered and reading music was mandatory. I didn't know a crescendo from a quarter note but I knew I had to at least try.

I took two buses to get to the church where auditions were being held. I had just made it through the door when Maestro Francisco de Araujo asked me to join him at the piano. The conductor was a long, wiry, white-haired man of about 40. He was stern and serious about his music. There were about 50 regular choral members sitting quietly on the metal risers.

To my surprise, he started playing, "What a Friend We Have in Jesus." I knew this song from my childhood. He played high scales and lower notes. I nailed them all.

"What's your name, son?" he asked. "You have one of the purest, natural bass voices I have ever heard. Please join us."

I did not know then but my audition was the beginning of a union that would last for more than 30 years. And at least five years passed before Maestro Araujo realized I could not read music. I memorized the entire Handel's Messiah score, the Verdi's "Te Deum," Brahms's "Requiem," Rutter's "Requiem" and "The Many Moods of Christmas." The Maestro was impressed with how easily I committed to memory very difficult pieces of music.

Shortly after joining the chorale, we were invited to sing a concert entitled, "A Spiritual Jubilee of Love." The concert tour was going to take us to Amman, Cairo and Jerusalem. The program was in honor of the Egyptian and Israeli war dead. We rehearsed for nearly a year. Hundreds of people paid to join us on this spiritual pilgrimage. I had never been a part of anything on such a grand scale and so spectacular.

Meanwhile, I began pursuing another dream. Since my days back in Saint Meinrad Seminary, I dreamt of publishing at least one story in a major magazine or newspaper. After arriving in Washington, I began sending articles I had written to the Washington Post newspaper, only to have them rejected. I didn't give up. I wrote an unsolicited article about the tour and submitted it. My stack of rejection letters had grown to nearly two inches thick. Each letter explained that I did not satisfy the editorial needs of that publication. Still, I believed if I got just one story published in a major newspaper, I would consider myself a successful writer.

Two days prior to our departure for the concert tour, the maestro called the group together.   We sat patiently waiting hours for him. He walked in with a grim face and announced, "The tour has been cancelled. We can salvage it if members agree to fund a portion of the cost of the trip."

I thought this was outrageous but kept my comments to myself.

A female friend I was extremely fond of had come from Alabama to go on the tour also. Now she insisted that she and I still go. She had booked her own travel and so she put that money towards travel for the two of us to go to Israel on our own.

Neither of us had ever left the U.S. No longer a man given to introspection, I viewed my visit to the land of the Bible as nothing more than an exotic excursion. In my constricted world, Israel had little relevance and was relegated to faded memories of my childhood Bible classes.

I was surprised to find early in the flight that Israeli mothers traveling alone plopped their young babies in my lap, as they excused themselves. They left sleeping children nestling close to my pounding heart, sometimes for what seemed like hours. Out of the corner of my eyes, I kept a close watch over the gathering of ultra-religious Jewish men, adorned in their prayer tallits (shawls), holding their prayer books, swaying back and forth, side to side in the rear of the plane. I didn't get any time to sleep. Israelis seized every opportunity to practice their broken English on me or share stories about the hardship of living in the Middle East, though they would never consider living any place else.

My travel companion sitting beside me was amazed at the openness of strangers. I had never witnessed such adoration and dedication to a country. This love for a land was as foreign to me as the Hebrew words permeating my ears.

After the plane landed we were instructed in English to deplane and wait for shuttle buses to the main terminal. As I stood on the tarmac with 300 other passengers, I caught a hint of jasmine wafting on the autumn breeze. I experienced an overwhelming feeling of calm, peace and completeness even though Israeli soldiers stood as security guards near the plane and bus we were about to board. Both male and female military personnel had rifles and machine guns standing at the ready.

Twelve hours had passed since leaving New York and for the first time in my life the color of my skin appeared to be irrelevant. I did not know I was falling in love or that this was the start of a life-long journey that would bring me back to Israel time and time again. But I knew that a "nigra" boy from Alabama was experiencing a sense of well-being he had never experienced in his life, not even in his native land. I was 25 years old and living in a country known as "The Land of Plenty," but not once had I felt valued in American society. From my first visit, in Israel I stood among strangers with nothing visibly in common with me, yet I seemed to know these people well. I was more than smitten. From that day forward I was determined to focus on doing whatever was necessary to make this troubled land my home.

Shortly after our arrival in Tel Aviv, Vernita, my traveling companion, insisted we take a quick walk on the beach before the sun went down. We checked into the

Dan Hotel and headed for the boardwalk. I had known Vernita since my second year of high school. Back then, I loved her from a distance, but was too shy to let my intentions be known. I waited for her at the back gate of the school just to get a simple "hello." Now we were two friends comfortable with one another because we knew each other's beginnings and we were mature enough to explore the possibility of an intimate relationship.

We walked hand in hand along the scorching whites sands as the sea swallowed the fiery orange and yellow sun right at the horizon. Though I loved Vernita, she was convinced I lived in hopes that someday a bishop would reconsider and sponsor me to return to my seminary studies. Vernita and I had decided not to have intercourse until she was sure I was going to be the man she spent the rest of her life with and there were no residual desires on my part to become a priest.

There were times when I was certain I was done with the church and there were other moments when I was trapped in the thoughts and recollections of the dream I missed. Vernita said I had a sadness and longing in my eyes whenever we discussed my time in seminary. Still, I loved her deeply. At the beach, we sat on a towel with her head resting on my shoulder. The moment was perfect to me and I could have sat in silence that way forever. But Vernita wanted to talk. We found the perfect secluded area. The sound of the roaring waves crashed against the rocks. We sat in stillness until her words pierced the silence.

"I have been seeing someone else," she whispered.

I knew immediately that what she really meant was she was doing with another person what I could not do until the priesthood question had been resolved.

"I don't understand. How could you do this? If you wanted to see someone else, why would you keep seeing me?" I choked on my tears, unable to speak.

She did not answer. I stopped crying enough to say, "I've been faithful and true to you from the start. I have not as much as held hands with another woman."

"Being faithful is not a part of this relationship," she replied.

I was puzzled. We had discussed our commitment to each other and agreed we would not date anyone else. But by her comment, it was apparent she had decided to renege on this but had forgotten to tell me.

I wanted to get away from her so badly, but at the same time I wanted her to reconsider what she was saying. I was confused by her decision and by our relationship. Here we were, stuck together, thousands of miles from home on a trip she suggested we take together. People in our tour group made early comments about how we were such a perfect couple. I didn't want that image to change so we remained civil for the sake of appearances and she agreed.

But Vernita handled the awkward game much better than me. She was able to laugh and play along with the others while I found myself at times sitting alone moping.

In spite of my despair with this love, I slipped deeper and deeper in love with Israel. I concentrated on becoming as acquainted with this land as I could in little more than a week. Once I even ventured off from the tour group in a futile effort to find a job. For nine days we did the typical touristy stuff, swam in the Sea of Galilee, climbed Masada, took a mud bath in the Dead Sea and spent five full days in Jerusalem. Vernita was having a grand ole time hanging out with the others and spending minimal time with me. We ate together and shared the same room, but there was little interaction or conversation between us.

Without a doubt, Jerusalem and Israel made an inexplicable impression on me. Once the tour was done and I returned to the U.S., I felt like a jilted suitor, longing to capture unrequited love. But it was the country, not Vernita that I longed for.

CHAPTER 18: THE YMCA

As much fulfillment and joy as I gained from working at the Bethesda-Chevy Chase YMCA, I knew the time to leave was rapidly approaching. I kept thinking about the three articles I wrote back in seminary and how they gave me an insatiable desire to write. I figured with any luck maybe I'd get something published. At times, in the middle of a disagreement I left the house I shared and found myself sitting in the dark on the concrete steps in the park, scribbling notes on a pad with the only light coming from the tiny bulbs embedded in the walkway.

Life in the house with friends had become unbearable. I didn't mind too much when girlfriends and boyfriends stayed overnight or on weekends. But over time those nightly visits became weekly and monthly stayovers. The added houseguests did not pay for their stays or bring additional food.

I tolerated the extra freeloaders until one night I came home and found Cathy nearly in tears because her boyfriend had taken the television from her room and thrown it down the stairs. I figured a man this far out of control would eventually hit her or me. There were already too many negatives going on in my life; I didn't need the added burden of being a referee in my own home. So I left.

Cathy's boyfriend and I had done some odd jobs for a couple who lived in a townhouse in the Georgetown neighborhood of Washington. Attached to their luxurious home was a tiny garage apartment. The man once said to me, "You would be an ideal tenant. I hope you give some thought to moving in." I balked at their initial offer; hoping things would get better at home.

But now, I took the offer.

My new tiny apartment was in the middle of bustling Georgetown. I had a small living room and an even smaller kitchen. The cooking area wasn't big enough for a table, so I did much of my dining on the living room floor. The bathroom was off the kitchen with a shower. The group house I left behind in Chevy Chase was at least eight times the size of my new place. But it didn't matter. This space was mine and mine alone. Georgetown was nearly 800 miles from Birmingham. Most of the time it seemed like another lifetime when I was at the mercy of a racist southland. Georgetown, nestled on the northern bank of the curvaceous Potomac River in Northwest Washington, was one of the wealthiest sections of the nation's capital, with picturesque hills scattered with million dollar homes. Georgetown was once a black community until it surrendered to gentrification following World War II. In the heart of Georgetown is the Jerusalem Baptist Church, the only black establishment in the area. Before and after services are the only times blacks in great numbers walk the residential streets in this predominantly white community.

I was still working at the YMCA. My rent was around $200 a month, leaving me approximately $184 per month for all other living expenses. The additional odd jobs kept me off the streets and from stealing food. I was comfortable working with the membership and staff at the "Y," who I grew personally close to over time. I was invited to their homes for Seders and brunches, even asked to sing at a few weddings. I wasn't making much money, but I was rich in friendships that I would maintain over many years.

One day I was standing poolside when this teenage girl asked me, "Why is a 28-year-old man still working as a lifeguard?"

I couldn't think of an answer. I was embarrassed and wore my shortcomings like raw emotional trophies. At that moment in my life, I had chalked up multiple failures. I had failed in the priesthood, failed at the university, failed at becoming a dentist, failed to gain the love and admiration of my father. Failure loomed large in my life at the time. That little girl reminded me of one more unfulfilled dream. During my break, I scribbled my resignation on a piece of paper.

CHAPTER 19: THE WASHINGTON POST TO JERUSALEM

Two weeks later I was unemployed and painting, spackling and doing other odd jobs, barely enough to sustain me. Much of my life I had been told to get that perfect job, "It's not always what you know, but who you know." For me, that perfect job was writing for a leading newspaper and I knew no one in the field. But I had a plan.

For days I donned my beige, three-piece suit and made my way to the Washington Post lobby, where I stood with my hand extended to anyone who would take it. I was hoping to make the acquaintance of someone who would help me with my future as a Washington Post staff writer.

"My name is Len Cooper," I said to strangers. "I am a very hard worker and I am looking for a sponsor who could help me in getting a position, any position in the writers' department."

Today, I am embarrassed thinking about how foolish I must have appeared. I never knew any of the names of the people entering the building. Some stopped, only to realize my intent and then walked briskly away. This humiliation went on for weeks. Finally, a tall gentleman with a rich Spanish accent seemed to take an interest in me.

His name was Juan Sardi. As fate would have it, he was the manager of production personnel, which was in no way affiliated with the newsroom. He invited me up to his seventh floor office. He asked questions regarding my mechanical aptitude, my physical stamina and my flexibility in working odd hours. Finally, he gave me a written exam that consisted of simple math and reading. I had no problem scoring well above the norm.

"Would you be interested in working in a journeyman trainee program down in the pressroom?" he asked.

I had no idea what that was, but when he told me if I completed the training program successfully I would start at a salary of nearly $40,000 annually. I agreed to the terms with no further questions.

Within two weeks, I was stuck in the dungeons of the Post, breathing ink mist and wallowing in black filth until the early morning hours. I continued submitting articles to the newsroom --and the editors continued to reject them. At night, once those steal monsters fired up, I pushed tiny yellow sponge-like earplugs deep into my ear canals to try to silence the roar. Still, my ears rang for days.

I sat on the wooden bench near my assigned area, staring down at my permanently ink-stained palms. I was in hell. At the completion of my shift, I often blew my nose and found the tissue filled with black clumps of mucous. I decided to wear a double canister gas mask with face protection built in and in addition to wearing gloves. Each night I coated my hands with a substance that wouldn't allow the ink to adhere to the skin. My co-workers said these actions were all they needed to confirm that I was "gay," a label I wore in the Washington Post pressroom for years. I wasn't bothered by their comments regarding my sexuality. It seemed anyone who didn't use profanity or have an interest in sports or was just a little different was considered gay. No, this labeling had no effect on me.

Among the men and women journeymen, there were those who chased the dream of becoming low-level drug dealers and those who dreamed of becoming barbers, club owners and photographers. Some of them had been stuck in that roaring, inky hell for nearly 20 years. My unfulfilled dreams of becoming a writer were on the brink of joining the abandoned aspirations of other pressmen. I often compare my 10 years in the pressroom to that of a prison work release program. During the day, I was free to assume the semblance of a normal life, but at night I returned to the steel, concrete and filth of my captivity. Year after year I grew weary of the rudeness of many of my co-workers--the testicle grabbers, the chronic farters, and a constant volley of foolish verbal exchanges. Through it all, I was grateful for the money that changed my life and the life of my parents in Alabama. My lifestyle didn't require the nearly $1,000 I was earning every two weeks, so I regularly sent money back home to Dear.

I finally had no financial worries. My first check was spent entirely on new clothes and a beautiful brass, Westminster table clock with chimes. I admired for years those clocks in the window of Continental Jewelers in downtown D.C. My friend Cathy gave me a large, shiny stainless steel skillet that I hung from the ceiling in my kitchen as a reminder that I would never be hungry or have to beg again. Never. Aside from working nights in that pressroom, everything was good.

I became well acquainted with many of Georgetown's posh restaurants and clothing stores, where I shopped and dined frequently. Some shopkeepers even knew me by my first name. My friends were impressed with my familiarity to this exclusive area and I poked my chest out, beaming with pride. Why not? I had paid my dues. In addition to the fancy clothes and expensive haircuts, I graduated from the slew of cheap sample colognes I brought with me years earlier from Alabama.

One day when I stopped in at Neiman Marcus to replace those colognes, a beautiful woman with caramel skin and short wavy black hair assisted me. She sprayed several fragrances in the air and I poked my head into each misty cloud. I actually pretended to be conflicted in my choice in order to spend more time with her. She didn't seem to mind as long as no other customers were waiting.

I asked her to make the selection for me. To my astonishment, without hesitation she chose Lagerfeld. I had never heard of that particular brand. But it didn't matter to me as long as she was still smiling. By now other customers were lingering in the area waiting to be assisted. I leaned slightly forward towards the counter to get a look at her nametag, which read "Glenda Moore."

"Ms. Moore, I don't know you and chances are I will never have this opportunity again, but would you consider having dinner with me?" I asked.

To my surprise, with little deliberation she said, "Yes," and scribbled her number on a piece of paper. That Saturday, we met for dinner in Georgetown. She parked her car near my apartment. The American Café was about four blocks from where I lived and the weather was perfect, so we decided to walk.

Dinner was pleasant and I must have said all the right things because we returned, walking arm in arm, taking the longer route. We stood by her car under the streetlight in front of what was known as the ABSCAM House. I remember that this house was known to some people because back in the '80s it was used to nab several U.S. Senators in a government sting operation.

A police cruiser with two officers rolled by as we stood in the street near her car. One of the officers was speaking on the two-way.

"Get in the car," I told Glenda.

She got in the driver's seat and I hopped into the car on the passenger's side. I knew this script too well. "In a few minutes those officers are going to return with reinforcements," I said.

Glenda looked at me like I was a little crazy, paranoid. "Come on, Len, you're over-reacting," she said.

In the middle of her protest and scolding, we heard blaring sirens and saw flashing lights.

"What the...!" Glenda was shocked into speechlessness as police cars screeched to a halt in front and behind her car. "They can't just roll up like this!" she shouted, while reaching for the door handle to exit the car.

"Keep your hands still and on the steering wheel," I said, calmly, with both of my hands resting on the dash.

In seconds police surrounded the car with pistols drawn. Several officers stood back from the car as two others cautiously approached, one on each side.

"Glenda. Whatever you do, don't make any sudden moves or do anything to piss these guys off," I whispered.

She seemed angry and annoyed by the police but she followed my instructions. I saw the fear in her eyes. This scene was commonplace for me, a part of my life.

"Those are a nice pair of beige pants you are wearing," said one of the officers, his eyes fixed on Glenda's ass while she exited her car.

She glanced toward me but kept her rage in check as the officer opened the rear door of the patrol car, placed his hand atop her head as she sat down in the back seat. Another officer placed handcuffs on me before directing me to the rear of another patrol car. By now there were no less than five cop cars and a swelling crowd of onlookers. My next-door neighbor, who was a friend, seemed to come out of nowhere.

"Len, I am so sorry," he said. "Whatever you are being accused of, I know you didn't do it." Our eyes were fixed on each other as the officer slammed the door shut. But there was nothing he could say or do to make things better.

"You fit the profile of suspects who robbed a party two blocks away," one officer explained to me.

"Listen, I used my American Express Card to pay for dinner less than an hour ago and the receipt is in my wallet," I said, speaking evenly and slowly.

He didn't bother to check my story. The police car I was in roared up the street, stopping a few blocks from where I lived and near the entrance of a home where other policemen stood waiting out front. One at a time, Glenda and I were paraded out in to the middle of the street with blinding patrol car spotlights in our eyes. Guests from the party were called to the street to identify us. They took one looked at my date and cleared her of the alleged crime immediately, but they were not as kind with me.

Several guests came to the street as I stood there. I could see them talking to the officer but could not make out any faces of the residents due to the bright lights.

Finally, the officer removed the handcuffs and returned me to the police car where Glenda sat waiting.

"Your friend is cleared but these people aren't so sure about you," he said. "You are still under investigation. Do not leave the area over the next few days."

My neighbor who knew me said people on my street suspected I was a drug dealer and as they stood under the bright street lights that night, they were certain they had witnessed a big bust.

Shortly after this incident, I was walking home at night and a few paces in front of me was a young white woman. She was visibly frightened. She glanced slightly to her left then to her right. She was too afraid to look back behind her.

"Madam, please don't be frightened," I said, talking to her back. "You cannot possibly be any safer than you are right now with me standing near you. I mean you no harm."

I felt her fear and uneasiness dissolve in the night air. A friend told me once that a few of my neighbors voiced their concerns to him regarding having a black man living in their midst. I made it a point not to give my neighbors validation of their suspicions and concerns.

Following my nightshift in the Washington Post pressroom, I ran home through the city streets as part of my daily exercise regiment, instead of wasting precious minutes trying to hail a taxi that in most cases would not stop anyway. One night after a run, I stood outside a 7-Eleven convenience store in Georgetown sharing a brief conversation with Pat Ewing, a Georgetown Hoyas basketball star. We exchanged small talk for about 10 minutes or so. It was very late, so I shook his hand and wished him continued success. Then I completed the run to my home, which was only a couple of blocks away. As I turned the corner, a marked police car slowed down, the officers casing each step I made. I pretended not to notice them, hoping not to draw undue attention. I stood in front of my house, winded and trying to catch my breath.

"Don't move!" one of the officers commanded.

By this time, I had plenty of practice at how to prevent such scenes from escalating into full confrontation. Both policemen, one black, one white, had their guns drawn, pointed in a downward position.

"Keep your hands where I can see them." the black officer commanded.

I complied. I was wearing sneakers with low cut socks, skimpy nylon runner's shorts and a matching runner's shirt. My keys and driver's license were stored in my wristband. There was no place to hide a concealed weapon. The officers accompanied me into my house, demanding that I produce a letter or utility bill with a name or address matching the license I presented. I showed them the mail stacked on a table just inside the door.

"Nice house," one of them uttered.

"Mr. Cooper, by law I have to ask if you wish to file a formal complaint regarding this matter," he stated.

"Good day, officer," I replied, closing the door behind them.

While these incidents of racism are forever etched in my memory, I was given a fair shake by most of the ordinary residents of Georgetown but not by the police. Besides, a boy who grew up in Alabama during the civil rights movement knows there is racism everywhere, not just in Georgetown. For instance, a friend asked me to do construction work on her property. I didn't need the money, but she and her family had helped me out of so many scrapes during financially lean times that I decided to do this for them as a favor. In order to finish a job I needed to make a quick run to a local hardware store in Maryland. While perusing the paints and paintbrushes, two plain-clothes policemen approached me from both sides.

"Do not move!" one yelled.

I froze.

"Put your hands behind your back," an officer commanded as I looked over my shoulder at the two men standing behind me.

"Please be quiet and come with us," he said.

"Am I under arrest? Please tell me what is it you think I did?" I asked my voice raised.

I was handcuffed and paraded out of the store pass onlookers and curiosity seekers to the waiting squad car. There was no fear, just another repeat of a bad movie I had seen already and frankly, I was getting tired of it. There had been an attempted bank robbery three blocks away and once again I was the likely suspect. I had an officer on each side of me, gripping my arm as we entered the bank. As soon as I stumbled through the double glass door, a middle-aged, white woman said loudly, "Take those things off him. He looks nothing like the man that was here or the description we gave you. Now let him go!"

Hard to imagine a would-be bank robber stopping by the local hardware store to peruse the selection of semi-glosses, flats and baseboard trimmings. I left the bank without saying a word. There was no apology from the Maryland police officers for this humiliating mistake. I'm not sure why I even entertained the idea that the two officers might apologize. I've never known policemen to express any concern for my well-being or apologize, even following such an egregious mistake. I never knew if the hardware owner called the police or if the store was part of their patrol beat. Either way, once again I was insulted and humiliated. I decided not to ever shop at that store again.

The fact that I had to alter my natural behavior separated me from white men, free to go wherever they wanted and to act however the felt like behaving--within the law, of course. As a black man, I could not experience such freedom. Not in Birmingham. Not in Washington, D.C., or its surrounding suburbs.

Back at the Washington Post, I was painfully aware of every hour, every second I spent in that god-awful pressroom. My off days were often Tuesday and Wednesday. It was rare for me to spend a full evening with family and friends on weekends. I left evening events early in order to report to work on time for the night run. Whether friends came by for holiday dinner or if I wanted to spend precious moments with my family, at nine o'clock sharp I had to be at my post, standing next to the press, the oily, loud monster.

There was always the risk of losing fingers, hands and even your life, if you made one simple mistake. At times, my eyes fixated on the glittering, spinning steel cylinder and I wondered how it might feel to have my limbs crushed paper thin up to my elbows. Often, I was accused of being overly careful and concerned, but I didn't care what the other operators thought of me.

I wasn't going to get maimed in that greasy, filthy hole no matter how much money they paid me.

Nearly a full year passed and I continued submitting my articles to the fifth floor newsroom only to have them rejected. I was still singing with the choral society, although working nights made it difficult to make engagements. Following one Tuesday night rehearsal, Maestro Francisco de Araujo asked, "Would you like to travel to Israel and stay expense-free for six months?"

"Frank! Are you serious," I raised my voice with the excitement. "I've been dreaming about going back to Israel for years!"

It had been two years since the choral society had cancelled our Middle East concert tour. Nevertheless, I was still moved by the trip my friend and I had taken to Israel. This time the maestro was going to Israel to perform two theater productions called the *Passion Play of Jerusalem* and the *Nativity Play of Bethlehem*. The *Passion Play* would be performed outdoors on the slopes of the Mount of Olives and the *Nativity Play* would be in the Shepherd's Field near Bethlehem. We were asked to contribute over $1,000 to cover the airfare; everyone in the organization agreed. I paid half and convinced the maestro I would pay the balance upon my return to the U.S. I wasn't taking any chances on investing in this project and running the risk of something going wrong and me losing the *full* amount.

The trip was a dream-come-true, if I could only convince the Post to allow me to take an extended leave of absence while still on my probationary period. Everyone I knew advised me not to ask since I had only been with the company a short while. But I asked and to my surprise, the leave was granted. My only problem was that I had very little money saved, certainly not enough to live off of for six months. Still, I was determined. I had an opportunity to return to the land I loved and to get the hell out of that damned pressroom for six months. I was going to make it happen by any means.

As it turned out, a friend sharing my tiny apartment assumed all financial responsibilities until I returned. My landlady had no problem with her new temporary tenant. The Post agreed to grant my six-month leave request and leave was renewable should I need additional time.

In the El Al airport lounge I met nearly a dozen other travelers to Jerusalem, recruited by Araujo for the plays in Israel. The morning of my departure I had a tooth extracted so I wasn't much in the mood for small talk. I slept during most of the flight to Tel Aviv. A van was waiting to ferry us to Jerusalem to join with another group Araujo invited to be a part of his production. Many of them were students from Seventh Day Adventist schools from across the country and they had arrived weeks prior to us. Once again, I slept most of the 45-minute ride from Ben Gurion Airport to Jerusalem. I felt an inexplicable peace and calm.

We arrived at the house shortly after dark. The house was actually a five-story building made of off-white Jerusalem stone. Those who were already situated helped us with finding our quarters and getting acclimated in what was called the "Passion Play House." I was one of the oldest residents of the group at 28 years old. All total, there were about 30 actors, most of them religious. I was the only one who would be considered a heathen and ungodly.

At this point in my life, I had no religious affiliation and absolutely no interest in their little Bible and fellowship meetings. By now I was completely done with the God thing and for sure He was done with me. I was more than ready to spiritually fend for myself. I was visibly absent from prayer meetings and Saturday morning worship services.

Our routine became making our way up the slopes of the Mount of Olives overlooking the golden Dome of the Rock and the Old City of Jerusalem just after sunrise every morning. For hours we dug out a portion of the mountainside in preparation for staging "The Passion Play of Jerusalem." The million-dollar production consisted of livestock, Roman soldiers dressed in authentic uniforms riding horses, and an elaborate set. I played the part of Simon the Cyrene, an African who helped Jesus carry the cross to Golgotha. All day we hammered, dug trenches and painted in the sweltering heat. After dinner we rehearsed our parts well into the night.

After being in Jerusalem for a few weeks, I must have made an impression on one of the Israeli dancers named Ruti, who had been hired to work with our theater company. During rehearsal, her eyes trailed every move I made. She seemed to dance with greater conviction and passion when she knew I was looking on. My limited Hebrew vocabulary was matched by the few English phrases Ruti managed to string together. She was free-spirited, tall with long thick curly black and brown hair.

Eventually we met for romantic late night interludes of kissing and petting. During one kiss, she held me by both shoulders, forcefully pushing me away. She kissed me quickly and said "OK." She embraced me tightly and said, "OK!" Then she grabbed both breasts firmly with her hands and said "No!" with a quick sucking sound, which meant emphatically "No!" She looked down toward her private area, shaking her head, making that sucking noise with her eyes drilled in to mine, to make certain I understood sex was totally out of the question. The line was drawn. I never tried to persuade her to change her mind. I found Ruti extremely alluring, but my respect for her overruled any lustful desires I harbored.

Once I was sitting with her on a fallen stone column amid the rubble of an ancient Roman temple just outside Jerusalem. Ruti instructed me not to move as she disappeared behind a rock wall.

"Len, you here. I go," she said while pointing in a downward motion towards a stone slab. I understood that she wanted me to remain seated and not follow. I had no idea what she was up to. Maybe she had to use the bathroom. I sat and waited for a couple of minutes. Suddenly, she jumped from behind the partition, stark naked, performing a traditional Arabic dance. She encouraged me to clap my hands in time with her movements. There was no music as the rhythm of my heart kept a steady beat. I will never forget the sunlight glistening off her dark, even-tone olive skin, her untamed wiry hair swirling around and around with those 2000-year-old walls serving as a backdrop.

Though brief, I enjoyed the time spent with Ruti camping out in the ruins of Ein Karem near the Jerusalem forest and at other ancient sites elsewhere throughout the region. There were times when we met in the wee hours of the night just to kiss and embrace. Neither of us had money to frequent bars nor falafel stands. Our precious spare time was spent walking for hours on steamy days and misty nights. She and I must have covered every inch of the hills and slopes of Jerusalem by foot, at least it seemed that way. I just knew this tall, crazy, dancing bohemian was going to make my six months in the land of milk and honey all the more magical.

The night before opening, all the props were assembled. There were no more lines or scenes to rehearse. The Baptist House, a Christian congregation in downtown Jerusalem, gave us a party in appreciation for our bringing to Israel our massive production of the life of Jesus. Everyone, except one person, was darting about the house getting dressed in their finest before the bus arrived to take us to the party. Kevin, the lone actor that remained behind, hated me only half as much as I hated him. To me he was the pious demon in charge of housekeeping . I always remembered him by an intrusive comment he made: "The question of God's existence is the most popular topic in hell."

The night of the party he was sick to the point of throwing up and not able to leave his bed. Initially, he got no pity or sympathy from me. I despised him. As everyone piled onto the bus, I hung back to see which of his many friends would offer to stay behind to assist him. No one did. And so I stayed.

The bus drove off without anyone noticing that the two of us were left behind. I returned to his room and asked him, "Where are your friends now? Where are they?"

He was lying under the sheets with only his face, white as a ghost, sticking out.

"Tell me where all those good, God-fearing friends of yours are when you need them," I said.

He looked at me, wheezing and coughing.

"You Christians make me sick," I continued. "Isn't this a sight for sore eyes--the heathen charged to look after the saint?"

At first he didn't respond, as if he didn't hear me.

For the next few hours I waited on him hand and foot, even going out to find ginger ale. In Israel, the Jews sold 7-Up and the Arabs sold ginger ale. Or maybe it was the other way around; I can't remember. On this day, I was Kevin's nursemaid. I had a heck of a time trying to find ginger ale, the beverage I had been taught soothed upset stomachs. I never found any. I made tea for him and cooled his brow by dabbing it occasionally with a damp cloth. After that night, he and I became friends and remain so even to this day.

The show opened in early August of 1982. You could see the blaring spotlights as far as downtown Jerusalem, which was a couple of kilometers away. We performed before a packed house of dignitaries, tourists and locals dressed in minks, suits and blue jeans. The set was elaborate and the costumes were true to the period the actors portrayed. Nevertheless, before weeks' end, the audience dwindled to a handful.

To Frank Araujo, the director, the three-hour performance was played out in full costumes, lights, and animals, no matter how many people were in the audience. Once only two people were in the audience and still the show was presented in its entirety, full blast.

After each nightly show, one male had to stay behind to stand guard over the equipment. When I was asked, I refused. How was I to stop a would-be thief if someone wanted to take anything from the set? How would I notify anyone for help? We were also asked to sell tickets on the street corners of Jerusalem and I refused this task as well. The Jewish population saw us as proselytizers, trying to convert Jews to Christians. It was against the law to do missionary work in Israel and I did not want to risk being asked to leave the country.

Shortly after this, I was summoned to the office for a late night meeting

I entered this upstairs office and found the director waiting for me, along with his assistant Greg, who played the role of Jesus in the play. I took a seat as instructed. There was no small talk or exchanges of pleasantries.

"You have to perform all tasks assigned to you, whether you agree with them or not--or you can leave the house," said Araujo.

"Do you think I need you here to play the role of Simon?" he continued. "I can find anybody to fill your spot."

I was adamant. "I'm not going to stand on the street corner in downtown Jerusalem and sell tickets. Nor am I going to camp out alone at night on the site to protect equipment," I said.

"Leonard, you have 48 hours to leave the house," he shouted. "I will have the driver take you to the airport to make sure you get on that plane. Good night Leonard!"

A few cast members were waiting outside the door as I exited. Several of them embraced me. A few cried openly. I wanted to cry so badly, but I held my tears in check as I was coming undone inside. I returned to my room and lay atop my unmade bed as it began to sink in that in a couple of days, I would leave this place that I loved so much. A couple of tears rolled down the side of my face while I stared up at the ceiling. I sank deeper and deeper into depression as I recounted all the things I was going to miss the people in and out of the house, the scenery, the language I didn't understand but loved to hear, the smell of jasmine, and there was Ruti. The pain in my heart was multiplied. I regretted not yielding to Frank's demands.

The day before I departed was spent saying good-bye to Israeli friends I grew to love and just walking around town with Ruti. When she cried all I could do was hold her close to my breaking heart. The night before I left, I asked the director to revisit his decision to expel me from the house, but he said his decision was final. The next morning I was chauffeured to the airport and my passport was returned to me. My plan to live in Israel for six months had been reduced to two months.

The plane touched down in Washington in the middle of a steamy August day. If only I had kept my mouth shut and followed whatever orders were handed down, as all the others in the house did, none of this would have happened, I thought. I sat on the curb near my Georgetown apartment. I pulled from my pocket photographs of Ruti and a wad of pictures I had taken of friends in the Passion Play House. I even dug deep inside my luggage to find a half bottle of body lotion I bought in Jerusalem. I rubbed the pink, creamy liquid in my palms and covered my face with it, tears streaming down as the familiar aroma hit my nostrils.

I was desperate to recapture and relive just a moment of my time in Israel. I thought maybe if I called Frank and begged for forgiveness, he would accept me back into the house in Jerusalem. But my thoughts were foolish dreams. Even if all were forgiven, where would I get the money to make a journey that normally takes months of planning?

I lugged my bags to my little garage apartment only to find the locks changed. I was turned away by the friend I temporarily surrendered it to two months prior. She later told me she was under the impression I was not returning to the U.S and if I did, I would find another apartment. Didn't recall ever having that conversation. Once again, I had no place to live.

Jessie and Jerry, the owners of the garage apartment, lived in a luxurious townhouse next door. They were my last and only hope. I dragged my bags up the brick staircase and rapped on the door, using the large metal knocker. Jerry and Jessie welcomed me into their home. I would remain there for the next two and a half years. Jessie was still working in adult and continuing education in her Pennsylvania Avenue office not far from the White House. She was always the voice of calm and reason. I was out of cash and desperately needed her counsel. It was a nice day so I decided to walk to her office in hopes that she would have time to see me.

The walk from Georgetown to where she worked took all of 45 minutes. To my surprise, she wasn't busy.

"We can talk as long as you need," she said. For the next hour, I gave my summary of my two months in Israel. Not once did she interrupt me.

At times, I sobbed, unable to speak, though I kept muttering. When I finished, she said, "Maybe you should return to Israel." To her it was obvious my time there was incomplete.

I had never given serious thought to the idea of going back to Jerusalem until that moment. I left her office with a sense of urgency and returned to my old garage apartment. My friend wasn't there, so Jerry gave me the key to enter.

I was surprised to find many of my belongings were still there. Somehow during an earlier conversation the friend living in my apartment got the idea I was not returning to live there, so she started making arrangements to redo the apartment. I figured this meant my belongings had to go. Now I made a pile of all my stuff, most of which was stored in the closet. The only things I owned worth any real value were a gold ring from my seminary days and some jewelry I was given from my first trip to Israel.

This was not the time for sentimentality. Everything had to be liquidated. I took my only assets to a jeweler in Georgetown who saw behind the mask as I made a vain attempt to hide my desperation. He wouldn't budge in his price, less than a quarter of what was originally paid for the items. I didn't have nearly enough money for the trip to Israel. Then I remembered acquiring a Trans World Airline credit card that I had never used.

After parting with all my valuable worldly goods and paying off a few past due bills, I had $20 remaining in one hand and in the other a round-trip, 30-day ticket to Israel. This meant I had approximately 66 cents a day to cover all my expenses. My lack of funds, lodging and food did not concern me. At the time, there was a travel rule that required me to wait 20 days before leaving the country again. To pass the time, I tried unsuccessfully to find work doing odd jobs hoping to make some added cash. Much of my time was spent with friends or in my upstairs room in Jesse's and Jerry's Georgetown townhouse. I was aware of every painful tick of the clock.

The morning of my flight, I shoved my clothes, cooking utensils and whatever else I had that I thought I might need into a large, green army duffle bag. I laced my used sleeping bag around the large green military sack. I was ready to go when I received a call from the airline informing me my flight was delayed by several hours. When time came for me to finally leave for the airport, I chose to take a leisurely stroll down Wisconsin Avenue. It was my plan to take the bus, or walk to the subway. I stood on the corner in front of the Georgetown Inn, shouldering my bag as I sported a large black felt cowboy hat. In a moment, a beautiful black stretch limo pulled up in front of me and before I could say a word, the driver exited, opening the rear door for me. It was obvious I was mistaken for a guest at the luxurious hotel.

"Where to?" the driver asked. Little did he know there would be no tip waiting for him at the end of the line.

I was whisked to the airport in elegant fashion with hardly a dime to call my own. Most people wouldn't imagine traveling to a foreign country, thousands of miles away with just $20. But I didn't have any such inhibitions.

The flight was rather uneventful except for the fact that a lovely flight attendant made sure that my time aboard the plane was as enjoyable as possible. The plane was nearly half full. After a quick dinner, the lights were dimmed as we flew into the nighttime.

"Do you want to change seats to the rear of the Jumbo Jet?" the attendant asked. "You will have more leg room back there and you can lie across several seats, if you like."

I took her up on her offer and made my way down the sparsely lit aisle. After taking my seat, she returned with a blanket and pillow. We engaged in casual conversation each time she returned to her station.

Upon my arrival in Tel Aviv my first order of business was to return to Jerusalem. I stood near a curb just outside the airport with my pointing finger aiming downward, as the Israelis do when signaling for a ride. The first approaching car came to a sudden stop.

"Olechet lerushalyem?" This was my way in broken Hebrew of asking, "Are you going to Jerusalem?"

"Kin," said the driver, as I loaded my pack on the back seat and climbed in.

In less than 40 minutes I was back in the heart of Jerusalem.

The flight attendant supplied me with plenty of airplane food and bags of peanuts and pretzels, at least enough to last for a couple of meals. Still, I needed a place to sleep for the night. I didn't dare return to the group house, although I desperately wanted to. While walking down Ben Yehuda, which was the main street in the city center, I recalled a thicket of rosemary and other shrubs not far from the house that I thought might make good sleeping quarters for the evening. The walk was a kilometer or so down King George Street, which is lined with restaurants and small shops until you get to Keren Hayesod Avenue, which is primarily residential.

I crossed the Liberty Bell Park, whose stone walkways are lined with flowers and aloe vera plants, and walked north to the intersection headed towards Beit Lechem Road. Near the intersection, across from the community referred to as the German Colony, was the mound of shrubbery. Settling in for the night atop the sparse grass and heavy shrubs conjured memories of time spent on the streets of Washington, D.C. Unlike Washington, this situation was a choice in which I had full control. Sleeping outdoors didn't bother me. Perhaps living on the streets in some small way prepared me for this or at least made it bearable. The ground wasn't terribly comfortable and the cool nights made it difficult to sleep at times. Still I was happy to be in Jerusalem, even under less than desirable conditions. I spread my blanket on the lumpy incline behind the shrubbery and used my bag as a pillow. Exhausted, I was asleep within a half hour.

The next morning I emerged from my makeshift lair, making futile attempts to wipe the sleep from my eyes. I was still tired. The sloping earth and prickly grass beneath me kept me from being comfortable during the night. I made my way to the YMCA across from the famed King David Hotel to see if I could take a shower and use the facility. A rather overweight Arab door keeper sitting near the entrance leading to the men's locker room allowed me to wash and change and told me

I could come back any time to use the shower. I returned almost daily to wash away the sweat and dirt from my skin as well as to wash socks and underwear in a secluded basin.

After attending to my morning personals the first day, I gathered my goods and began my short trek to the Passion Play House, hoping I stood a chance of being welcomed. The major financier of the production was informed that I was in the area and demanded to see me. I was excited with anticipation. I was called in to the small upstairs office. Instead of being welcomed, as I had hoped, the financier told me, "You owe us half of the fare for your initial flight over. And I want the payment now!"

I refused and once again, I was escorted from the house, but not before the financier said, "Don't ever set foot on this property again for any reason."

If I wanted to visit many of the friends I maintained in that house, we met at the nearby bus stop across the street. Later that day I heard that the performance had closed soon after the first curtain. It was pointless for me to hang about where I wasn't wanted. So I decided to start my trek to the North Country.

For soldiers and civilians, hitchhiking in Israel has always been an integral part of getting around. In all the times I depended on Israeli and Arab strangers for a lift, I rarely waited for more than a couple of minutes.

The first stop in my journey was the jagged mountains of the Judean Desert, about halfway between Jerusalem and Jericho. I spent much of my time there exploring caves and canyons and just trapping up and down ancient Roman roads. The Bedouins, nomads who wander the desert with livestock and sleep in black cloth tents, were extremely kind to me and I was surprised to find that some of them knew a little English. I filled myself daily with pita bread and fiery hot tea. I was extremely grateful for whatever food or drink people shared with me.

I slept out in the open in the desert, which brought unexpected minor challenges. As the night progressed, the air got damp and cooler, cutting through my thin sleeping bag. I got very little sleep. Some of the sounds the animals made were foreign to me.

I was awakened as the sun peaked over the Jordan Mountains east of the Dead Sea. I continued my trek in to Jericho, where local merchants gave me fruit and bread. I didn't ask for it; I suppose they were being hospitable. For the next couple of days I continued my uneventful journey north to Tiberius and Galilee. I actually drank water from the Sea of Galilee. Standing in this sacred sea where Christians believe Jesus walked on water, I remembered fishing with my father in Alabama and having to drink from a fishing hole called Lake Purdy, just south of Birmingham. We were out of water and he told me to drink from the lake, but not too much. I reckoned the same rule applied to the Sea of Galilee.

I continued north to the Lebanese border, then eastward to the sea caves or Rosh HaNikra. Without money for a ticket, I could only see a portion of the beautiful blue coastal water caves. I saw pictures in the display case near the entrance, showing photos of what a person might see inside if they purchased a tour ticket. But I had been there before as a tourist on my very first trip to Israel.

Fortunately, I still had some of the snacks given to me by the flight attendant. I continued southward now, walking, riding and resting whenever I saw fit. I was in no hurry and had no special place to be. The countryside was adorned with olive groves that boast of thousand-year-old trees. The seaside was splendid with its crystal blue waters splashing against the ancient Roman columns scattered about the shore. My nostrils took in every bit of the many aromas, jasmine, rosemary and lilac.

Just before nightfall one evening I made it all the way down to Tel Aviv, which was my last stop before returning to Jerusalem. I decided to make camp on an isolated portion of the beach just a ways up from the hotels and boardwalk. I gathered paper from a nearby trash receptacle and dried twigs that had been collected near the water's edge and made a fire. I used boiled seawater to prepare instant rice, using very little of the water because I knew if I ingested too much I could become ill. It was a tasteless yet filling meal, which was all that mattered.

As I was about to settle in for the evening, a young Israeli woman out walking her Jack Russell Terrier noticed me resting against the large duffle bag. She walked over and introduced herself as Sema Kuby. I don't remember the yapping little mutt's name. Her English was advanced for an Israeli.

For the next half hour or so she sat with me in the dim light emanating from the distant hotel. She fired question after question about my recent journey.

"Do you plan to sleep on the ground all the time you are in Israel?" she said while cradling her dog in her lap. "It is a little bit strange that you are in a country that is not your home, you don't know how to speak the language and you are not afraid," she continued, unable to lose the Hebrew guttural sounds in the back of her throat in the pronunciation of some words.

"I feel safer here than I do back home," I replied, as my eyes panned the surroundings. "I've been up and down the country and never had any safety concerns."

"Aren't you afraid of a bomb or that a terrorist may kill you?" she said leaning forward making swooping hand gestures. "Everyone in America and Europe is afraid to come to Israel."

"Sema, there are more people killed in Washington, DC in one year than the number of people killed in all of Israel, even with the wars," I said. "No, I am not the least bit afraid to be here and yes, even if I am sleeping on the ground."

Even as I was explaining this to her, I was also pondering why I was not afraid. Why I felt so safe and at home in Israel. I could have explained that as a black child growing up in the South in America, I had experienced terror because I knew what it was like to be hated and despised and to have my life considered of no value. I knew what it was like to be mistaken time and again for other black men who looked nothing like you, but who were being hunted for committing a crime. No, in Israel I did not experience any of this. Instead, people gave me bread and watched out for me so that I could take private showers in public places. Here, my life was valued much more than it was in what was supposed to be my home.

I could have said all of this-and more, but instead I simply explained that I was not afraid for my safety, even if I was sleeping on the ground, under the sky. We continued our exchange for another hour before she continued on her way and I settled in for a night's sleep.

The Tel Aviv central bus station was a short walk away and I knew it was most active in the morning and that it would be easy to hitch a ride from there back to Jerusalem. I had been in Israel for a week and still had the original $20 I had when I arrived. I was sitting at the bus stop when I spotted several actors walking towards the Passion Play House. A few came over to wish me well. Some of them expressed again their dismay that I was barred from visiting them at the apartment building.

Jerusalem's schools were not in session in observance of the holidays, so I decided to make camp in the local schoolyard. I didn't make a fire for fear of attracting the local authorities, who were extremely suspicious of any strangers, especially those without a fixed residence. I unfurled my ratty blue sleeping bag in the sandbox and attempted to roll myself up in it for protection from the Jerusalem chill and night dampness. I was developing a cough and scratchy throat, but it didn't seem too serious. Early in the evening, a light icy rain fell. The towering eucalyptus tree didn't offer much protection from the elements. And my little sleeping bag was not designed to stave off inclement weather.

Before morning, my nose and throat were aflame and it seemed that every muscle and bone ached. Once again, those snacks from the plane came in handy. The schoolyard sandbox remained my home for two more days and nights. The Jerusalem heat returned by the third day and I began to feel much better. I packed up my things and made my way over the brick wall to the neighboring streets.

Later, when I had recovered, I returned to the schoolyard to remove any and all traces that I had ever been there. I rested outside the Passion Play House for a moment, sitting on the ground and leaning against a wall. For some inexplicable reason I began lamenting over my situation. I sat on that ground and leaned against that wall for a couple of hours. A seven-year-old girl on the opposite side of the road was taking out the garbage when she noticed me. She crossed the street and started speaking to me.

"I'm sorry, but I don't understand what you are saying," I replied over and over. But she was persistent in trying to communicate with me, smiling, waving her hands, speaking loud Hebrew then slower Hebrew, but it was pointless. Finally, she grabbed my hand and led me across the street to her home. I had met one of her brothers earlier, but this was my first time seeing her. When we finally made it up the stairs to their second floor apartment, I found her entire family was crammed into the small living room. Family and friends sitting on the black leather sofa scooted to the side, making room for me. I joined them in eating dates, nuts and cakes and in drinking mouth-scalding Turkish tea, which sat on the small table before us.

"You are a guest in our country and should not have to sleep on the ground," her middle brother said.

Meanwhile, their mother was changing the linen on one of the beds in the bedroom shared by two sons.

"I cannot accept your generosity," I said more than once. But they ignored my objections, so eventually I stopped offering them and agreed to stay under one condition: That I make a place on the floor so the brothers would not have to give up the comforts of their room. The father was clear that I was welcome in the Halevy household, but I needed to be out every morning when he left for work and could not return until he came home.

Yet after spending a couple days with the family and sharing the Shabbat dinner, this rule was lifted and I was free to come and go as I pleased.

After a few days had passed, I was completely recovered from my ailments. The family's generosity was sincere and free but I felt as though I was taking advantage of their kindness, so I left.

I returned to my various makeshift camps around West Jerusalem, choosing my location depending upon what part of town I was in at nightfall. It was always difficult to get a good night's rest, so following my morning shower at the local YMCA, I spent a couple of hours napping, sprawled out on the Y's front lawn.

The remainder of my time in Israel was spent visiting the Halevy family daily and enjoying a few moments with my Ruti, the Israeli dancer with the production. Neither of us had money, so the hours were spent visiting her friends or just hanging out in the park. We continued until Ruti suffered pains of conscience, feeling that our 'friendly' relationship was somehow wrong because her boyfriend was serving in the Israeli Army in Lebanon. I didn't try to change her mind. After all, we were doing lots of kissing all the while her heart belonged to another. Soon after my departure, I received a letter from one of Ruti close friends saying Ruti married the soldier and settled on a kibbutz up in the north. I was happy for her.

The Halevy's became my family in every sense of the word. No matter where I was or what I was doing, I was expected to be at their dinner table every Friday night at sundown for singing, prayers and dinner. I was included in trips to the Dead Sea, the beach in Tel Aviv and shopping excursions. I had never known people to be so unconditionally kind, especially to a stranger.

My months' stay in Israel was coming to a close. This time there were no tears but the sadness rolled in like a dark cloud. I was leaving my new family. I knew once I returned home and to my job at the Washington Post, most, if not all, of my vacation time would be spent in Jerusalem.

And this is exactly what happened. Over the years, I have returned as often as possible, sometimes twice in a year. In all this time, I've been unable to articulate just what it is that makes me love Jerusalem so totally. I can't explain the emptiness and longing I feel every second that I am away.

On the last day of my visit, the Halevy's and friends showered me with hugs, kisses and sweets. I was numb, speechless.

To this day, I speak with the Halevy's often and sometimes daily. When the oldest son completed his military duties in 1988, I gave him a trip to the U.S. as a token of our friendship and gratitude. This was his first time flying in an airplane and his first time out of Israel, other than the time he spent in Lebanon during the Israeli-PLO war. When their daughter Yafit, who was the little girl who had led me across the street to her family, completed her military duties in 1996, I gave her a trip to the U.S. as well. To this day, the Halevy's remain my example of goodness and unconditional love. They inspire me and keep me grounded. Speaking with the Halevy's is like calling home to get caught up on the latest wedding, bar or bat Mitzvahs, or just talk up the day-to-day events.

Upon my return to Washington the Ulin's invited me to move into their Georgetown home, since their little garage apartment they rented to me before going to Israel was no longer available. I was a little apprehensive, but grateful. I was given full run of the house, food and the use of the car. I was in desperate need of cash so I made an appointment with the personnel office of the Washington Post to make a request to terminate my six-month leave a few weeks early. The request was granted and I returned to the pressroom the following week.

To my surprise, I was assigned to work in the southeast Washington plant rather than the pressroom where I worked before. The new location was twice the distance from my house. Pressroom work hours started at 9 p.m. but ended at 4 a.m., an hour before the buses started running, I used the bus service to get to work but I had to walk or take a taxi home unless I waited an hour until public transportation was available.

The first day at the plant I was assigned a locker, a work crew and a press. Once the press was prepared for the night's run, we all stood around bantering. My crew usually talked about sports or sex. On my first night, it was sex. The only thing that made the presses seem tamer, their roar seem muffled, was if I concentrated on writing an article.

At times, I could not find peace inside or outside of the pressroom. For months I depended on the D.C. Metro bus and subway to get me to work and on my legs to get me home. The walk from the Post building in southeast D.C. took more than an hour. I strolled across the grounds of the U.S. Capitol and across the National Mall near the Washington Monument, down Pennsylvania Avenue, pass the White House and on into Georgetown. Most nights after completing my shift, I found a place on the wall near the Library of Congress or sat in the nearby park and waited an hour for the buses to start morning runs.

On my regular day off, Lynn Minna, who I met when I was working at the YMCA, invited me to join her for lunch. In-between doing odd jobs for her and working with her and her daughters on swimming techniques, we became good friends. On this day, as I was walking her back to her office she made a detour to the nearest ATM machine. She withdrew a thousand dollars and placed it in my hand.

"I want you to accept this," she said.

I knew to simply say "Thank you." She didn't want any gratuitous gestures or promises to repay.

Lynn and her family became an anchor in my life during these turbulent times. As I mentioned before, not only did she give me unfettered access to her home and left her young daughters in my care, the Minnas were the first whites I met in my life who showed me unconditional love, kindness and respect. If I had any adverse racial residue from growing up in a racist South, the Minnas presence in my life ran counter to all I believed to be true about most whites.

Several months after I had returned to my press operator's job, the foreman called me into the office and asked if I had an interest in returning to the northwest facility. I jumped at the opportunity. I didn't even bother to clean out my locker to take anything with me. Please understand, both of these places were hellholes. The northwest pressroom just happened to be closer to my home and put me just five floors under the illusive newsroom, closer to my dreams. In the pressroom at night, I continued writing. I must have submitted a dozen articles, but none of them were accepted. Nevertheless, I continued writing articles on my little beige, eight-line display Tandy computer and the newsroom continued rejecting them.

Jessie, my friend from whom I had rented the small Georgetown garage apartment, also worked as the Director of Continuing Education for Presidents Carter and Reagan. I asked her to critique my writings and she gladly did. It was a big mistake on my part because I was not prepared for the honest critique that followed. When she handed the papers back to me, I was astounded at the amount of red ink. Whether my feelings were hurt or not was completely irrelevant to her. Every few days or so I made my way downstairs to her bedroom, where I sat while she ripped apart me and my writings. No one had ever been so critical of my work. But receiving so many rejections had made me so embarrassed that I hardly shared my writing with anyone.

Before Jessie's critique, my writing lacked style and my writing skills were abysmal. After each of her critiques, I saw that my copy was so problematic that nothing could be salvaged outside of a complete rewrite. Jessie had no qualms in reminding me just how lacking in technique my writing was. As weeks, then months, passed, the best I could ever get out of her was, "Your writing is improving, but not nearly enough yet for publication."

I tried everything from reading self-improvement books on writing to listing the journalists she frequently read in the Washington Post and New York Times and then trying to mimic their literary styles.

Finally, one evening she said, "Not bad," referring to a piece I gave her on some topic I can't even recall today.

I was feeling completely inadequate as a potential future journalist. I noticed one day that Jessie and her husband were reading David Habersham's *The Powers That Be*. I raced out and purchased the book, reading it in its entirety in a couple of days. It was a rather scathing summary of the U.S. news business and was particularly hard on the Post. One night Donald Graham was in the pressroom and I asked him to comment on some of Habersham's claims. Don was standing in the isle between the rows of presses before they came roaring to life. He was talking with a group of operators dressed in blue ink stained uniforms. Don always meandered among the workers and presses wearing a white shirt with the sleeves rolled up. When the conversation dragged, this was the opportunity to poise a couple of lingering questions from my readings.

"Hey Don. I just finished reading Habersham's book and he seemed to come down pretty hard on the news print industry," I said. "He talked about your father's death and some questionable dealings in the early days of the Post. Is any of that true?"

Looking around at the other operators, who were not involved in our conversation, Don returned his attention to me. "Coop, remember some writers take liberties with facts and events in their work," he said in his calm nasal voice.

I wanted to ask him if that was the case in all of the news print industry, including at his newspaper. But he had been gracious in our brief exchange; there was no need to push his patience and generosity.

Over my years in the pressroom, there were times when I ran into Don outside of the paper. I was proud when he said hello to me by referring to me as "Coop." We were in no way considered friends. We had brief exchanges, not ever lasting more than a few minutes.

I don't recall ever speaking to Don directly about my desire to write for the company. It wasn't a secret I was trying to get my articles in the paper. People in the pressroom were aware of my failed attempts. Some even got a big laugh out of it at my expense, but I kept submitting my stories. Then there came a time when I was working days for a brief while and Don stopped by and in the middle of our chat, he asked with a wide smile, "Coop! How's the writing going?" I was shocked because he and I never discussed my writing.

"Haven't had any success to speak of," I said. "But I'm hopeful."

A few days passed when Don returned to the pressroom for a visit.

"Put your street shoes on Coop and come with me," he said, as I looked to the crew chief for approval to leave. "I want to introduce you to some folk on the 5th floor," he said.

I was stunned. Even a lowly press operator knew what it meant to be seen walking with the publisher of one of the most powerful newspapers in the world. I raced to my locker and slipped into my sneakers and grabbed a folder containing current writing projects. I took a long look in the mirror to make certain I didn't have print ink smeared across my face and paper dust in my hair. My ink stained press operator's uniform added to my nervousness, but there was no time to change into a clean pair of pants and shirt. My embarrassment had to wait. I didn't want to keep Don or this opportunity waiting longer than what was necessary. I returned to the pressroom floor where Don stood waiting with the day foreman.

"You're all set Coop?" Don said.

"I think so," I replied.

I hated the way other employees in the Washington Post looked on me and other pressmen with disdain at times. Sometimes during lunch, we left traces of black ink on a chair or table in the cafeteria. Employees from other departments ridiculed us after finding black stains on their clothes or belongings. There were times I wanted so badly not to be associated with that damn pressroom. For once I wanted to be able to wear a nice suit or white shirt to work. Instead, I felt confined to that hellhole in the basement and required to wear that blue uniform covered in filth. But on this day, for just a moment, I was transformed from being a press operator to a man worthy of being in the company of the publisher of the Washington Post. To walk those hallowed halls with Donald Graham meant people took notice. I needed so desperately to have it affirmed that my existence mattered. At the time, I didn't really know whether he wanted to dash my hopes of becoming a writer once and for good, or if he truly wanted to give me a shot at fulfilling my dream. Either way, the door to contributing to the paper was left ajar and the next move could very well be mine. I was nowhere near ready.

Don asked the day foremen to excuse me from my duties for a few minutes. He and I took the main lobby elevator up to the fifth floor. I was embarrassed when I realized I was leaving tracks of black ink on the newsroom's gray carpet. But I walked proudly too, because I was with the owner's son. Those cub reporters, copy aides and researchers eyes scanned me from top to bottom as if they detested the fact that I was in the newsroom. I was ashamed as we weaved our way through the room and pass the sounds of clicking computer keyboards. Finally, we made it to the office of Tom Wilkerson, the assistant managing editor of the paper. Don introduced me and left the office to mingle with writers out in the newsroom.

Wilkerson clearly talked to me only because Don had asked him to. He almost grunted his questions and fidgeted with papers while I answered. Wilkerson's piercing stare could have burned a hole in Don's back as he left the office. Every few minutes he either checked his watch or looked towards the newsroom anticipating Don's return.

"Do you have any prior writing experience?" Wilkerson asked.

"None," I said. "But I have some writing samples."

"Can I see them?"

"They are pretty raw and not ready for review,' I warned.

He insisted, anyway. So I handed him the two articles I had typed out to be reviewed and edited by Jessie.

He read the first couple of lines and shoved the papers back to me without a word. Ben Bradlee, the editor, stuck his head in the office, growling off instructions to Wilkerson about something. At least Wilkerson introduced us. Ben spoke to me and was gone.

"Did you attend college?" he asked.

"I studied at the University of Alabama in Birmingham," I replied.

Wilkerson grunted while nodding his head and still looking out into the newsroom. I was expecting a follow-up question, but there was silence. I must have been in

Wilkerson's office all of 5 minutes. Wilkerson shot up from his chair as we saw Don coming, weaving his way through the rows of reporters working at their cubicles.

"Mr. Cooper, I hope everything works out for you," Wilkerson said, ushering me away from his office before Don had a chance to say a word.

I extended my hand to Wilkerson. "Thank you for taking the time to talk to me." He shook my hand and that was it.

Don and I maneuvered through the writers who sat in open cubicles throughout the huge newsroom with towering stacks of newspapers and periodicals. I felt outside of my intellectual element. Whether my perception was grounded in reality or not, as we wandered pass each desk, I imagined the reporter probably graduating top of his or her class from a prestigious East Coast university. All I had was the University of Alabama in Birmingham and not even a degree from there. Yes, I was way outside of my intellectual and educational element.

My brief stroll with Don ended at the District Weekly desk. Post reporters often spoke in protest of how it was beneath them to contribute articles to the weeklies. Don introduced me to Jan Wilson, the editor of the District Weekly, and to several other staffers and freelancers.

"Jan, this is Len Cooper from the pressroom. I know this is a little unusual, but I have a little time and wanted to introduce him to some of the people up here," he said. Once again I was left on my own as Don vanished amid the maze of waist-high cubicles and busy journalists. As Jan Wilson and I exchanged small talk, Neil Henry, the reporter who had written the story about me some years earlier, headed over to greet me.

"Len Cooper, what are you doing here?" he asked.

"I've been working downstairs on the presses for over two years," I said, surprised he remembered me.

"You've been down there for *two years*? So what brings you up here?"

"Just making the rounds with Don. Maybe I will get a shot at getting a story in the paper one day," I said.

"If I can help you in any way, just stop by," he said, pointing at his desk.

He seemed in a bit of a rush, but did manage to tell Jan Wilson that I was a decent guy. Jan never asked me a question about my writing experience or my interest in journalism. I suppose since I was down in the pressroom, she assumed I had no experience as a writer. Maybe Don mentioned to her my desire to write.

"Do you have a story idea to pitch? Can you type?" she asked.

I told her I could type and that I had a story in mind, but in actuality I had nothing. The only thing that saved me was the fact that she wanted the story idea in writing. She asked someone from the newsroom systems department to give me a crash course on the use of Raytheon computers.

"You have about a half hour to come up with a story that I will consider," she said.

There were no computer terminals available in the District Weekly section. The woman from newsroom systems escorted me to the sports section and introduced me to the editor, George Solomon. While I poured over back issues of the District Weekly, trying to get a fix on the types of stories she might accept, a senior sports writer named Shirley Povich (father of TV host Maury Povich) stopped by for a brief chat.

He was extremely personable and gracious and thought it was something remarkable to have a uniformed press operator sitting at a terminal in the newsroom. I truly appreciated his company and inquisitiveness, but his timing could not have been worse.

"What are you working on?" Mr. Povich asked.

"Nothing. That's the problem," I said.

Mr. Povich had a face deeply chiseled by wrinkles.

"Write about what you know, or profile a friend who's doing interesting things," he advised.

Immediately, I called a friend who owned a wool and knitting shop off DuPont Circle near the heart of downtown D.C. I had spent many hours with him swapping tales while sitting near the fireplace in his little row house shop. Now I sat at the Raytheon computer, hammering out a query that could either catapult my journey as a writer or bring it to a tragic end. I must have re-read that single paragraph a thousand times. I was well past my 30-minute deadline. After an hour or so, I finally mustered up enough nerve to hit the send button, marking the beginning of the waiting game. Just a few minutes had passed when I looked up to see Jan looking for me. I braced myself for the worse. In no time she was standing over me, staring downward at the printout in her hand, never cracking a smile.

"Have the copy ready by five," she ordered and walked away as quickly as she had appeared. I had roughly two hours to complete the story. I returned to Mr. Povich and thanked him profusely for the advice. He smiled and nodded his approval.

I spent the rest of that day interviewing Charles Higginbotham of The Woolgatherer and some of his friends. I didn't need to go to his shop to get a sense of the atmosphere. I knew his store well. The next day, a Post photographer was assigned to do the artwork for my very first Washington Post story.

It was a warm story that began, "An Old English sheepdog nestles in a corner, a red-brick fireplace and antique furniture combine to create the atmosphere of an 18th century home at The Woolgatherer, Inc. That's part of what places this establishment near DuPont Circle a cut above most yarn shops.

Rows of brilliantly colored yarn line the walls of the shop like three-dimensional wallpaper. Baskets of knitting accessories surround a yarn wheel set in the middle of the room."

I recalled that the owner, a native of Indiana, had once been a dress buyer in a Florida store, but that he had fallen in love with Washington when he had visited 15 years ago. He had also fallen in love with knitting.

I described the yarns and quoted a customer and employees. I quoted Charles Higginbotham: "Knitting is more than a trade. It's 'therapeutic'."

I thought my ending was lovely: "Whenever I'm on a plane, train or bus, I never have to worry about people bothering me. They see a man knitting and I guess they assume I must be deranged or doing it for some sort of mental therapy," said Higginbotham, who can often be seen by passers-by, sitting at his store's front window working diligently on a new creation.

"When I've knitted my last stitch and the time has come for me to lay down my needles, let it be said that Charles M. Higginbotham....had a great sense of humor and got through it all with a laugh. I hope my enjoyment of my profession will carry over to others who knit."

Following the acceptance of my first article, Jan asked me to come by the newsroom in case she had questions regarding the article. Over the next few days, she asked questions about my article, which meant I had more questions for Higginbotham. She assigned a desk for me near where she sat along with other freelancers. In time I claimed the area as my own by placing personal trinkets on the desk and pinning photos to the divider that separated the cubicles. I was angry when others used this area, but I reminded myself this space was not my personal work area and in truth I had no right to it. I never received an invitation to become a regular contributor to the District Weekly. I just started showing up daily and Jan didn't object.

For weeks, Jan sat on the piece, as I waited impatiently to see my very first byline. Meanwhile, my pressroom schedule returned to night duties and my misery was compounded once again. I worked 9 p.m. to 4 a.m., raced home to sleep maybe three hours, and then headed to the newsroom, where I remained until 4 o'clock in the afternoon. Working those long, arduous hours in the newsroom as a freelancer was the only way I could make sense of my time spent in the pressroom. In the newsroom I could wear a nice suit and tie, dine with people I only had contact with from a distance. These were extraneous benefits to writing, something I longed to do for years. I didn't mind working long hours as long as the newsroom validated my existence. In the beginning, much of my time was spent on the phone trying to find a story Jan would consider.

Then one day I was sitting at the desk in the District Weekly section when Jan told me I was needed to go out and cover an event hosted by the superintendent of schools.

'Go to the copy aide station and take whatever supplies you need," she instructed. "Take a taxi and keep all your receipts so you can be reimbursed for your expenses."

I was stunned. I had never had a job that reimbursed me for anything. It was amazing that something this small could make me feel important, but it did.

I arrived at the school, which was located in Northeast Washington and found a seat near the rear of the auditorium. I wrote feverishly, turning page after page of my reporter's notepad. I even directed the photographer on which shots I thought would be best for my article. My suggestions were ignored. At the conclusion of the presentation, I politely asked the superintendent for a minute of her time. In the taxi ride over I had compiled a list of questions that dealt with underperforming schools in the District and had nothing to do with the program she was hosting. But I didn't want to offend the superintendent and possibly blow my first opportunity as a freelancer, so I decided to stick to the story I was sent out to cover.

It was hard for me to believe *I* was posing questions to the superintendent of schools. It was exciting and exhilarating. At the conclusion of the interview, I taxied back to the newsroom and started writing the story, which wasn't due for several days. My day in the newsroom was winding down. I decided to continue working on the story while on the presses that night, but first I needed to go home for a couple of hours of sleep.

The story featuring the superintendent ran a few days later. I stood before that thunderous GOSS 1940's press as the sparkling cylinders turned faster and faster, the sound becoming more and more deafening and finally, there it was, "by L. Lanier Cooper, Special to The Washington Post." Not sure why I initially chose to use the name L. Lanier Cooper as a byline. I must have read that little, insignificant story a thousand times. I tucked away a copy in the recesses of my wallet and whipped it out in full view with the least encouragement. I collected copies of the Post that day and mailed the entire paper to friends and family everywhere. My mother was so proud. She, too, carried her clips of my story and proudly displayed them before her friends and co-workers at the post office and five and dime store. As a writer, all I ever wanted to do was to have one article published in a major newspaper. That dream was fulfilled Wednesday, June 8, 1983.

I often ask myself was it worth it to work those 16-hour days, year after year, just to get a story in the weekly section of the paper? It was a steep price to pay for a small parcel of success, but, yes, it was well worth the sacrifice to me.

Don Graham once told me that I was the first person at the Washington Post to write articles by day and print them while working as a pressman.

On that night in 1983, I only told a few coworkers about my first article being published. As it turned out, most of my fellow journeymen were supportive, while others tried to mask their disdain for me through a vain show of interest. It didn't matter to me whether they approved or disapproved. I was ecstatic!

The story of the Woolgatherer ran that same summer. Sometimes I had multiple stories in the same edition. But life was still bitter sweet because I couldn't shake that albatross called the pressroom.

My life at the Washington Post was truly a dichotomy. By day I spent time defending my stories and positions before some of the brightest minds in the news industry. The newsroom was my lifeline and saving grace.

Because of my work in the newsroom, I was introduced to a side of life I had only seen from a distance. Suddenly, my two closest friends were an editorial writer who worked for Meg Greenfield, a legendary editorial editor and writer at the Post, and an investigative reporter working for Bob Woodward, one of two famous journalists who broke the Watergate scandal that led to the resignation of President Nixon. Both men trusted and confided in me with sensitive information regarding their professional and personal lives.

After more than a year of working long hours, day and night at the Post, I decided in the spring of 1984 that it was time for a much needed vacation. For me there was only one place on the planet to get recharged, renewed and redeemed: Beautiful Israel! This would be my first return trip to Israel since the days of my hitchhiking around the country and being rescued by the Halevy family.

The flight over and subsequent ride to Jerusalem was uneventful. This time I was invited to stay in a group house with three Israeli women. I had become close friends with the owner of the apartment during my days living in the Passion Play House, which was just around the corner.

I was no longer a tourist. Instead of sightseeing and exploring, I enjoyed long visits with new friends. I sat with them for hours drinking coffee and eating cakes and fruits in the city center. At night I joined friends for delectable dinners in small cafes in Tel Aviv and on Shabbat (the Sabbath). When many shops closed at sunset, we traveled to the West Bank to eat Arab cuisine. This was back when Israelis frequented Bethlehem, East Jerusalem and Jericho on Shabbat.

In late August many of us trekked over to near the Damascus Gate to buy hot fresh pita bread or join Palestinians in large white tents to watch bad movies and get our fill of honey sweet watermelon. Yafit's brother, Uzi, who was a teen at the time, invited some of his friends to join him on a candlelight night tour of Hezekiah's Tunnel. This was a wonder that most tourists were completely oblivious of. Just after sundown, the group arrived at my door.

Hezekiah's Tunnel was dug underneath the City of David in Jerusalem before 701 BC during the reign of Hezekiah in Israel. The tunnel is referenced in the Bible, II Kings. The walk to the Old City wall was less than 45 minutes. We descended down a couple of flights of rugged stone steps, which led to a small pool. Near the pool was a crevice, which led to the opening of the tunnel. It was pitch black when I stepped into the freezing water, about knee deep. The cave was about 533 meters long and at some points I had to turn sideways in order to keep moving through its narrow walls. Some of the candles were extinguished when we carelessly splashed water, so it was dark. My heart raced with every step.

I was overjoyed when we finally made it to the end. But the exit was gated with a huge metal lock. My heart felt like it was lodged in my throat. I was terrified at the thought of wading through the water in the darkness once again. Uzi and his friends laughed and teased each other every other step of the way. I kept silent. They had walked this tunnel most of their lives. The water and darkness was too much for me. As before, while spelunking, I again imagined there might be a shift in the earth or a rockslide, or just some natural disaster that would keep us trapped and never found. In my vision, it had rained outside and the water rose in the tunnel, drowning us all.

I kept both hands planted against the stone walls on each side of me. I slid my feet on the bottom of the three feet deep water so that I would not lose my footing. Now we were in total darkness. We emerged from the tunnel after about a half hour.

"I never saw anybody so scared." Uzi said of me, as they all laughed.

I joined in the laughter too. We returned to Uzi's house for dessert and drinks. All and all, that night was a wonderful gift I will cherish forever.

The following evening, one of the ladies in the house where I was staying invited me to a rooftop party at a home on Emik Rafaim. Over the years Emik Rafaim had evolved into a street with a vibrant nightlife and some of the finest restaurants in all of Israel. There were establishments serving middle-eastern and Arabic foods as well as American and Far East cuisine.

During my early days in Jerusalem, the street was kin to sleepy hollow, lined with a few hardware stores and novelty shops pedaling colorful trash pails, mops, brooms and what have you.

But now Emik Rafaim was the place to be.

A block from the apartment building we heard the beat of the music. The terrace where the party was being held was decorated with sparkling lights and beautiful plants. The dance floor was full of revelers. One Israeli woman continued dancing even when the music stopped. All eyes were on her as her full, flowery summer dress spun with every turn, afloat in the springtime breeze. Her long wiry red hair spun and kept time with the thumping beat of the drums. I was mesmerized just as every other man in attendance. To my astonishment, she whirled over to where I was sitting with friends, grabbed both of my hands and pulled me from my seat. I was smitten when her eyes caught mine. She told me her name was Dina. We spent the rest of the evening on into the early morning hours dancing and singing songs I didn't know words to.

Dina invited me to remain with her for the few days I was in Israel. I graciously accepted. We spent evenings dining with friends or visiting the homes of her acquaintances. But most times we canceled whatever was planned for the evening to remain in her home. In one of our conversations, I expressed interest in returning to Jerusalem permanently.

"Why don't you consider moving in with me, if you decide to relocate?" Dina offered.

I was awed by her generosity. Having a place to live was a major obstacle to my returning to the one place that felt like home to me.

My months' vacation in Israel came to a rapid conclusion and I headed back to Washington to resume a life I dreaded, one replete with conflicts. Though joyous, my time in Israel only dampened my spirit at home and strengthened my longing to make a permanent move to Jerusalem. Few friends and relatives understood my attraction to a place they termed "a volatile region of the world."

Whether I was on leave or in the newsroom, there was rarely a moment when I was not working on a story or cultivating a future source for an article. As a press-operating journeyman, my job consisted of working nights preparing the newspaper, which often carried my stories, for the morning newsstand. In the morning I scrubbed my hands clean, wore a suit and tie and carried a handsome leather briefcase. During my 15 years as a pressman with the Post, two men lost fingers and one lost a hand. Shortly before I was hired, another man lost both arms up to the elbow. At times, I envisioned myself tangled in those churning presses and being dismembered.

But for me, the pressroom was my only path to gaining a shot at a job in the newsroom. I was trapped. The Post newsroom was chocked full with reporters and aides with degrees from Ivy League schools or people who had worked previously at some reputable daily newspaper. I had neither the desired degree nor the experience. I was reliable and came up with most of my District Weekly stories, but it wasn't enough. At age 31, I was too old for the summer internship program and too inexperienced to become a staff writer. The weekly stories I covered and wrote were good stories, but most reporters in the newsroom saw the weekly as a journalistic and professional dead-end. No one in the Post newsroom voluntarily contributed to the weeklies.

I didn't share their sentiments and neither did several other gifted freelance writers. We were honored and treated the opportunity as such. I would have been more than grateful and satisfied to spend years at the Post's District Weekly, if at some point it would have freed me from that pressroom. I needed to do something drastic and bold that would yield stories fit for one of the daily sections of the newspaper.

I decided to withdraw the few dollars I had saved in the Post credit union and return to Jerusalem. I had hoped to return sooner, but it had been nine months since my last visit. I didn't have as much money as I would like to have had and it would have been nice to have accumulated more leave time, but I figured conditions would never be perfect for my departure. The yearning to return was too strong and encompassing. It was time to go.

I was delighted the Post pressroom once again granted me an indefinite leave of absence. I had already determined if my leave request was rejected, I was prepared to resign. I thought for sure I had seen those monstrous 1940 Goss presses for the last time. I envisioned writing stories from Israel not only for the Post but for other publications thirsting for copy from the region.

Much of the time before I left for Israel was spent finishing up projects and sharing time with friends I had made in the newsroom. Columnists like William Raspberry, Dorothy Gilliam and Courtland Milloy stopped by my area to express their support and well wishes. Throughout the day I moved from the copy aides' stations to Photography, Sports and Style, saying farewell to co-workers I had grown to respect and admire.

I arrived in Tel Aviv just before dark on the evening of January 18, 1985. Waiting for me in the crowd was Dina, the tall, redhead Israeli who invited me to move in if I relocated to Israel. She waved frantically, wearing multicolored gloves with the fingers cut out. She hugged me tightly and kissed me passionately and with parted lips. Eventually, Dina abandoned the idea that she and I would make a life together, but allowed me to remain in her home until I earned enough money and found my own place to live.

I was in Israel to fulfill a dream of making a life there, including pursuing my desire to be a journalist. I was told that Israel had nearly 2,000 staff reporters from all over the world and a slew of freelancers. I was facing impossible odds to get my articles into print, especially since I was not affiliated with a reputable news agency. I decided my niche would not be economics, the government and the war effort, since scores of journalists were clamoring to cover such stories. I limited my interests to the effects these issues had on the everyday citizen.

As a courtesy, I checked in almost daily with Linda, Rivka and Rapi Horowitz, the director of the Beit Agron (the government press office). For some reason, they took an immediate shine to me, pointing me in the direction of possible story ideas.

"I admire the fact that you are making a bold attempt as a freelancer to write stories about the day-to-day lives of the people of Israel," Rapi told me.

Much of my time in the evening was spent trying to file stories with the Washington Post. Many correspondents used telex machines to file their stories when they were away or out of the office. Year's back I had purchased a little Tandy laptop with an eight-line black and white screen. I used brown, hard rubber acoustic cups that fit over the telephone receiver to transmit copy. Most times it was a challenge. In retrospect, it didn't matter too much if it transmitted or not, the Post had a reporter on the ground in Jerusalem and certainly they weren't going to accept a story from me. That didn't stop me from trying. There were times when I submitted an idea to publications only to have it rejected then appear in the same newspaper with someone else's byline. But as a freelancer I had no recourse.

Months passed without me having any success getting published. Every day without deviation, I contributed much of my time either interviewing people, researching or perusing periodicals in search of a venue that would consider my writings. Every story idea, query and submission fell off into the journalistic abyss, often without as much as an acknowledgment of receipt. I even tried writing for smaller papers that could not afford a fulltime correspondent. Still, there was no encouragement.

One night I was visiting a friend's home in Tel Aviv. The daughter of Ben Gurion, the first prime minister of Israel, was in attendance as well. The conversation became rather heated and emotional when several guests concluded, "Israel will sell weapons to anyone." One guest even cited incidents where former Israeli soldiers sold their military weapon to Palestinians.

"Why are you so surprised that former Israeli soldiers would sell their weapons to the very people who are trying to kill them?" one guest asked.

"Our government has been selling weapons to the highest bidder for years. We even sell them to the government of South Africa to kill their own people."

This was in 1985, during the height of the apartheid crackdowns in South Africa. I listened intently and decided such a claim warranted closer scrutiny.

I decided to do a little research to find out if Israel was indeed selling weapons to the South African government. After speaking with authorities in the Department of Strategic Studies in Tel Aviv, I arranged a meeting with government officials in Jerusalem. I waited for 45 minutes in a small office not far from the Knesset. Two men dressed in military uniforms sat down at the table across from me. Though it was common for high officials in the Israeli government to field questions from reporters at any time, I was surprised that one of the men was Yitzah Rabin, who was serving as Israel's Minister of Defense at the time. I didn't recognize the other man.

"The only thing we export to South Africa is Jaffa oranges," Rabin said, denying that Israel sold weaponry to South Africa and all the while wearing a smirk on his face.

It was a brief interview. Unfortunately, there was no story.

I cultivated an extensive pool of sources and leads to stories that never went anywhere. Many of them found their way to print, but I certainly wasn't the one who wrote them. There was no way for me to prove that my ideas and stories were being funneled to staffers on the ground. Anyway, I wasn't willing to risk alienating myself from what little access I had to the foreign press corps by hurling such accusations. But I had strong suspicions.

Unable to find a single news outlet willing to give any of my story ideas serious consideration, I sold off a few of my personal possessions. I found a spot on Ben Yehuda in the city center, which is a popular pedestrian area. I placed on a towel batteries, pencils and paper and other items bearing a U.S. logo. Israelis love anything that bears an American trademark. In less than 15 minutes, I had an additional 100 Israel shekels, around 25 U.S. dollars.

The day was warm and agreeable, so I decided to walk the long way home pass Brechat Hasultan, the Sultan's Pool just outside the walls of the Old City. In centuries past, this deep impression in the ground surrounded by boulders, was used as the site for burning animal carcasses used for ceremonial sacrifices as well as the burning of bodies after prisoners were crucified. As I strolled past there were throngs of people and television trucks blocking the entrance. I saw a friend who worked as a cameraman for the local TV station. He raced towards me, kissing me in the traditional way people greeted one another.

"What are you doing down here?" he asked.

I explained I was heading home after spending some time downtown. "What's going on?" I asked.

He said the singer Ofra Haza was filming a TV special. My heart raced. Three years before, I had seen a picture of her plastered to the wall of a bus stop. She was the top Israeli performer. But I didn't care about any of that; her beauty alone was enough to draw me in. I was lost in my thoughts when my friend's voice interrupted. "Do you want to meet her?" he asked. And before I could reply, he had me by the arm, pulling me towards a gentleman standing not far from us.

He introduced me as a New York Times reporter and said that I wanted to interview Ofra for a possible story. I didn't have a chance to correct him. The gentleman opened a small door leading to a room and pushed me in. The door immediately closed behind me. There she sat, wearing a long white slip and her midnight black hair full of enormous pink and blue rollers.

"Ms. Haza, please forgive me for this intrusion. I am not a reporter with the New York Times and I am not here to do a story," I explained.

"Sit down and just talk to me," she said in English, with a slight Israeli accent.

For the next 10 minutes or so we talked about her music and her childhood. She seemed genuinely engaged in the conversation. After finishing her make-up it was time for her to slip into the long blue dress hanging from the back of the door.

"Ms. Haza, it was truly a pleasure to meet you," I said.

"You're not leaving are you?" she said. "Wait outside. I'll be out in a minute."

Immerging from the room, she instructed her manager, the man who pushed me into her room, to allow me to accompany her to the back of the facility. Instead of going directly to the stage from the dressing area she exited the rear door and approached from the side aisle. Supporters mobbed her as she made her way to the platform. Once on the stage, she posed so I could take a few pictures. "Take one of us together," she said. I handed the camera to one of the stagehands.

She sang a few songs as I stood to the side of the stage watching. When she was done, she walked over to me and we exchanged numbers. After that, a couple of times a month I received calls from Benzalel Aloni, her manager, inviting me to join them when she was entertaining Israeli troops or making appearances, primarily in Jerusalem. Her world was high energy, high profile and always on the move, running from one engagement to the next. I found this lifestyle unsustainable, a world away from what I was accustomed.

Once Benzalel and Ofra invited me to join them on the set of a video shoot. During the course of the telephone conversation, Benzalel played for me a new song he and Ofra were arranging. He played the beat on a petrol can, which the Yemenites use for drums. Ofra was on the phone with me humming along. I was honored they wanted me to be there for the filming of the video, but I respectfully declined the invitation. I had begun to feel more and more like a groupie and I wasn't comfortable with that. I was 30 years old, not some star struck teen chasing after an allusive idol. Since our first encounter in her dressing room, it was rare to have a private conversation with her. Even during telephone calls, there were always others vying for her attention in the background.

As time passed, I accepted fewer and fewer engagements that involved meeting them in various places between Jerusalem and Tel Aviv. In time, the calls tapered off.

For the next 15 years, I collected all of her music and followed her career closely in the news and on entertainment programs. Eventually, she moved to New York City and then to Los Angeles. Disney animations never interests me, but when I learned Ofra sang a score in the Prince of Egypt and landed a small speaking roll, I did go to see it. By all accounts, Ofra singing was reaching new heights in the U.S.

In early 2000, I received a call from Uzi in Jerusalem.

"Hey Len, did you hear what happened?" he said.

"No." I replied. "Is everybody ok?" I asked.

"Yeah, yeah," he rushed to respond. "Ofra Haza is dead. She died today here in the hospital."

At first I could not believe what I was hearing. My heart felt like a lead weight in my chest.

"She checked herself in and die soon after of AIDS," Uzi said.

Although it had been years since the brief time I spent with her, she was an important part of the tapestry I created which made Israel magical for me. Now she was gone. She was 42.

A friend who remained in Israel after the Passion Play closed landed an on-air television job for CBN at the Jerusalem Capital Studio. He remembered that night of the cast party, when he fell ill and I stayed behind to take care of him, even though I didn't particularly like him or his bad attitude. Still, I was there for him when he needed someone and he was grateful. We met one night at a local restaurant along with the CBN Jerusalem bureau chief, Andrew Green. After a brief interview and chat, Green decided to give me a chance at writing for TV news. I knew nothing about TV news and to compound the problem, I had nothing interesting to report.

The best source for contacts and information in Jerusalem always started with Rapi, Rivka and Linda in the press office. They could arrange interviews with the Prime Minister himself, if they deemed your inquiries legitimate. One morning at the press office Rapi cornered me and in his raspy voice said, "Finding lots of good stuff to write about in Israel?"

"Maybe that's my problem, what I am writing is too positive about Israel," I said. We both laughed. Then he made a request I found to be a little strange.

"When you have some time to kill take a ride out to the old Tiberius Road, just north of the old town of Jericho on the West Bank, and see what you can find."

Jericho was a pretty far haul based on little to no information as to what I was looking for, but I trusted Rapi. He told me to report back to him if I found anything of interest in the area.

The next morning, I rose early to catch the first bus from the central bus station in East Jerusalem to Jericho. The station in East Jerusalem is located at the foot of Golgotha, the place of the skull, which Christians believe is referenced in the Bible. This is one of several sites where many believe Christ was crucified. The bus ride was rather colorful and deserving of an article in itself. In front of me a young boy was trying to keep his goat calm by pulling it closer and rubbing his head and ears. There were several lambs and goats on the bus and a crate of cackling chickens, all accompanied by their owners. It is not unheard of and somewhat expected in the West Bank that on public transportation you could share a seat with a chicken, goat or lamb. Other than these few pleasant, humorous distractions, the trip was uneventful. The bus let me off near the city center in Jericho, which consisted of a small roundabout surrounded by vegetable stands, variety stores and repair shops. It was congested to say the least. For the first time I saw several black faces amid the crowd, some of them shoppers and others just mingling. I walked over to a young black man and asked, "Do you speak English?" I'm not sure why I was surprised when he answered me in English with hardly a noticeable accent.

"I'm Yasser," he said. He was of average height and build, but what caught my eye was the fact that he was so dark you could hardly distinguish where his blackened face ended and his hairline began.

I had traveled to Jericho on numerous occasions, but I had never noticed any blacks living there. On this day, however, there were several blacks moving around carts of fresh fruits and vegetables. I even saw entire black families that appeared to be out and about, conducting their morning rituals. Yasser told me there were two communities of blacks living just outside of town on the old Roman road to Tiberius, north of Jericho.

"You are welcome to come to the village for coffee if you wish," said Yassar.

"Sure," I replied with excitement. "That would be great!"

Yassar motioned to a young man of about 20 years and asked him to provide transportation. The ride lasted for all of two minutes.

"Is this it?" I asked, as we exited the car and Yasser pointed towards the mountain in the distance. I knew this area well. In past years I frequented the Mount of Temptation restaurant with Israeli friends in the evenings. I never ventured towards the mountain in my previous visits. In front of the restaurant was a little Black boy of about 12 years, tending to a camel. The boy was dressed in all white from the white keffiyeh on his head to the long snow-white cassock covering the full length of his thin frame. Yasser muttered something to the boy in Arabic, handing me the reins. The boy gave the camel a light tap with a rod as it knelt down on all fours.

"Climb and be easy and calm," Yasser said to me. "He knows where to take you and I'll see you in a few minutes." I figured this meant Yasser would be right behind me on another camel.

I wasn't too enthusiastic about taking a camel ride to some unknown place. Sporting my cowboy hat and backpack, I rocked and jerked from side to side as the beast clumsily made its way up the mountain side. For the next 20 minutes or so that spitting camel and I were one. We trekked through rugged, stony mountainside, banana orchards and lose sand. The camel and I arrived atop a hill near a stone house where several men and women stood outside. They were all black except for one. The lone white female, was the bride and to my journalistic fortune, I had stumbled upon the wedding rehearsal. It was rather odd to see Yasser waiting for me in the middle of the group. He had driven a cab up the mountainside.

"Did you enjoy your ride?" he asked, before translating to all the others in attendance. The group laughed at me, but I thought it was rather funny as well. Yasser commanded the camel to kneel as I climbed down. As it turned out, it was all a light-hearted joke. The camel was the boy's livelihood for tourist willing to pay for a photo or short ride. The boy, who owned the camel, lived in this village, so the camel was accustomed to making the walk up and down the mountainside.

While he was making his introduction my attention turned to a rather shy, attractive Arab woman whose head was covered in a golden lace scarf with tiny dazzling stones. I nodded as she smiled at me. Before I could get a word out, several men seized me and pushed me into a secluded area in the back of the house. I could not understand one word amid all the shouting and yelling. What in the hell had I done?

Yasser rushed to my rescue.

"Mr. Len Cooper you are to never, never speak with the women here!" he shouted. "Never! Never! If you wish to speak to the females, you must speak with the father, brother or uncle and they will speak for you!" he continued shouting and flailing his hands and arms. "Never look at the females directly. Do you understand!" he shouted again.

"Yes! Yes! I understand." I quickly replied. I was a little shaken by all the yelling and screaming, but not frightened.

Following this brief encounter, I still wanted to meet her but I chose instead to respect their customs. One by one, Yasser escorted me before each man in the house for a proper introduction. The groom was about a foot shorter than the bride and sported a thick black, caterpillar-like mustache. He was as round as he was tall. His face resembled that of a black Asian. We men sat in the corner and drank coffee and then I puffed a few times from a large brass multi-tubed nargile that set in the middle of our group. Yasser walked over to me and when I turned, the groom was extending a hand to greet me. He vigorously shook my hand while uttering something in Arabic, which Yasser translated. It appeared I was invited to the wedding the following day. I asked the groom's permission to film the event. He was delighted. The groom also insisted that his cousin give me a ride off the mountainside. I was happy I did not have to ride that camel back down the hill and I knew I did not want to miss that wedding.

I walked quickly back to the heart of Jericho to get the next bus back to Jerusalem. The walk to the bus stop took more than an hour. Near the stop there was a restaurant with a group of Arab men sitting at tables drinking hot mint tea and playing backgammon.

I passed several small outdoor shops that had tables and chairs sitting out front and most of the people were eating hummus and pita bread. It had been a while since I enjoyed a meal in Jericho, but I was faced with limited time to get back to Jerusalem. Whenever I walked pass a group of young or old Arab men they stared until I was nearly out of sight. I was an obvious stranger, but I believe they wanted to see if I was going to visit one of their neighbors or friends, which would give them an excuse to meet me and learn more about me.

Tall, lean crepe myrtle trees lined the road like sentries in beautiful pink regalia. I was fortunate and pleased to find out the wait for the next bus to East Jerusalem was less than a half hour. This gave me a half-day to gather background information and pitch the story idea to Andrew. The bus came to a stop near the city center. I climbed aboard and took my seat next to passengers already on board. The ride was about thirty-five minutes and stopped at the station near the heart of Palestinian East Jerusalem. I exited the bus and began my walk across town to the Jewish side of the city. To my surprise and dismay, there was no information about the blacks of Jericho in the library and archive of the American Cultural Center, the Hebrew University Givat Ram or the T.V. Library. But I was happy that the story was an easy sell to Andrew. He assigned a team, which consisted of a producer, a soundman and cameraman to be at my disposal. I asked each member of the crew if they had any inhibition about working out on the West Bank and everyone said no.

Early the following morning, I raced over to the Beit Agron to see Rapi, hoping he, Rivka and Linda could get me a bit of information in regards to the blacks in Jericho. I was about to film and write in detail a story about people whom I had no knowledge. Again, I found no one had any information. It seemed people were aware of the black presence in Jericho, but no one was curious enough to do any substantive research on them.   Rapi encouraged me to continue with the story and promised that by the end of the day they would have a name of a professor to assist me. I met my crew in front of the TV studio and soon we were on the road to Jericho.

We arrived in what appeared to be a small makeshift mosque shortly after noon. The wedding party was happy to have the film crew making a fuss over the celebration. For a moment, in the midst of the poverty and despair, the camera and microphones made them feel like celebrities before their neighbors. The wedding was held in a small, dingy gray room, with about 20 or 30 people in attendance. Many of the men wore suits with the coats and pants unmatched, as if they had been fished from a Goodwill bin. The ladies wore business casual dresses, but covered their heads with lacey scarves with colorful shiny threads running through them. The men and women took turns whooping, clapping and dancing about the cement floor, but never together. The camera crew left just before dark, but I remained. Yassar, his cousin Najal and Mr. Moukmoud and I sat in the dark in front of one of the dry mud huts in silence. A middle-aged lady emerged from the hut bearing hot tea and sweets. The conversation and translation stalled briefly, but we each knew that we were savoring the close of a very good day.

The darkness was full and a few stars peeked through the sparse clouds as I made my way down the rugged hillside for the long walk back to Jericho. Maybe I had missed the last bus to Jerusalem and maybe there were no more taxis for the evening. It didn't matter. I certainly was not afraid, not at all frightened, like I would have been as a boy in a strange white neighborhood in Birmingham. The day was full, I had a heart full of joy and for a moment all was well with the world, even on the West Bank of the Jordan River.

As it turned out, the small group of blacks I saw in the village center the day before were only a fraction of the number that resided on the hillside not so far up the road. More than 1,000 blacks of Nubian heritage lived in dire poverty on the outskirts of Jericho, less than a couple of kilometers north of the ancient ruins. The sandy slopes of the Judean Mountains served as a backdrop for the villages of Nuwayma to the right and Ein-Duke (spring rooster) to the left. Some of the families made their homes in the brown and gray abandoned mud and straw hovels left over from the 1948 Palestinian refugee camps. According to residents of Nuwayma, many of the blacks once lived in the Judean caves and later under burlap tents as the desert Bedouins have done for centuries. In 1980, electricity was finally introduced to the villages. In 1985, while I was there filming, I learned that only one home in the entire community had a television. During the summer months, as nightfall approached, the children herded the animals inside to keep them from wandering off while the family slept outdoors on raised platforms built of wood, petroleum barrels and colorful hand-made quilts. The blacks of Jericho made their living by working the fields in the Jordan Valley. They earned an average of $50 for working a 72-hour week. Should they need food to feed their families, the landowners permitted them to take food from the fields with the understanding the difference was deducted from their meager wages. Those families fortunate enough to rent land could owe as much as half of their crop to the owners at harvest time. The children of these communities attended school in the United Nations Relief Associate (UNRA) system. They usually completed just two years of high school and then most of them returned to the fields to work alongside their parents.

During the spring and summer season you find one distinguishable thing about Ein-Duke and Nuwayma: Directly in front of each tiny house is a single plot of emerald green grass. The lawn is usually not more than ten feet long and ten feet wide. This plush area is reserved for receiving guests or a place for family and friends to gather following a visit to the mosque. I found people socializing there, talking about their day or sharing a simple meal, usually consisting of eggs, vegetables and on rare occasions, meat.

After returning to Jerusalem the night of the wedding, I savored my time spent on the mountainside with newly acquired friends. But I had work to do. It was important to the story that I get some background information or quotes from an authority on the topic of a Nubian presence among the Palestinians. There was no one to interview. The Beir Zeit University, Bethlehem University and the Hebrew University on Mount Scopus had nothing in their libraries and archives. Even the sources I heavily depended on at the Beit Agron came up short. I turned my attention to historians employed by the Rockefeller Museum in East Jerusalem, the Israeli

Museum and independent historians. The hypothesis they pieced together was that during the 1,000-year existence of Nubia (that area of northeast Africa west of the Red Sea which formerly encompassed Egypt and the Sudan), several battles were fought between the Nubian Kingdom and the Assyrian Empire in and around the area known as historical Palestine. It was customary during this time for conquerors to take slaves from the conquered country. Some historians believe a few of the Nubian slaves managed to escape from their captors and settled in the Jordan Valley. In a long distance call to Dr. Charles Copher of the Interdenominational Theological Center in Atlanta, he said he believed the origin of these black people dated back further than any of the more popular opinions. Dr. Copher said that he and other noted biblical historians believe these blacks are descendants of the original inhabitants of the Jordan Valley. He said he also believes that the small community of Sudanese, who have lived in the Old City of Jerusalem (the Prison Gate) for centuries, is of the same lineage. When I asked one black resident of Nuwaywa about their lineage, he said in English, "We are the descendants of the Canaanites."

Some other historians have concluded they were descendants of slaves belonging to rich Arab landowners in the Jordan Valley. I worked feverously on the story in order to meet a weekend deadline. This was my first television news story. The broadcast on the Middle East Television news network had a viewing audience in Israel, parts of Lebanon and Jordan. I worked on that story day and night for a week. As soon as I was done with the writing, I handed it over to the anchor for final approval.

A week after the wedding my story was on the air.

The network did not air it in Jerusalem, but it did in Tel Aviv. I never understood this. When I asked about it, I was told that Jerusalem was outside of the network's viewing area.

I settled for watching the recording in one of the editing booths. I watched my three-minute story over and over again. It was disappointing to see that so much footage was edited, but what bothered me most was that the news anchor received the praise and accolades for my work. But I soon let go of my anger because I was happy that such an important story finally made it on TV and that I was finally making money, which meant a burden was lifted off of me.

This was just the first of many stories. I remained with the network for six months, submitting stories on the Hebrew Israelites (the blacks who left the U.S., back in the early 70s, claiming Israeli heritage). I also did several pieces on the Ethiopian community in Israel.

Pat Robertson, who owns the Christian Broadcast Network and made an unsuccessful bid for the presidency of the United States, had an unscheduled visit to tour the station and meet the staff. All employees, whether they worked full or part time were expected to be there. I had no particular interest in meeting him so I was conspicuously absent when he toured the station.

After that, I was never called again.

In the U.S., women saw me as just one of many, a nothing-special black man at that. But in Israel, I suppose the women saw my nearly two meter (a bit more than 6 feet 6 inches tall) black frame as a novelty. All the attention worked wonders on my damaged and fragile ego. There was even a time in Israel when I enjoyed the company of several different women, though it was rarely a physical relationship. Mostly, we talked, shared stories, danced, traveled, drank coffee and ate cake.

One evening several journalists and I decided to go dancing at a Jerusalem disco, following our daily tours into Lebanon. The Psycho Club was in the city center and walking distance from where I lived. On this night I was on the dance floor when I noticed an Israeli woman dancing seductively alone in the middle of the room. I had met her before briefly on Ben Yehuda, the main pedestrian street in the city center, and I knew she was a physician. As she danced, she knew she was the object of the fantasies and affections of all the guys. But she sashayed over to me and extended her hands to invite me to join her for a dance.

She was wearing a full-body black spandex suit that gripped every twist of her curvaceous frame. Her hair was pulled back in a single blond braid that ran the length of her back down to her waist. As her body slowly gyrated she purposefully extended her rear, followed by her pelvis thrusting forward. With her eyes partially closed, her moist tongue caressed her luscious lips. Our eyes were inseparable. With every twist and turn that braid softly whipped my head, neck, back and shoulders. I trembled with pleasure and anticipation. When the music stopped and I staggered back to the bar, my buddies congratulated me on just how lucky I was. They were unable to mask their envy as I basked in their admiration. Our eyes followed her every wink, every titillating movement until the early morning hours. As time approached for us to leave, my friend Alain, the French radio reporter, asked if I needed a ride home. Before a word parted my lips, the physician interrupted saying, "He doesn't need a ride. He's going home with me."

I died and ascended to heaven. What had I done to be so lucky? In the car, she raced from street to street and through all the flashing traffic lights. The light in a main intersection turned red as we approached.

"This light holds forever," she said in exasperation. "Kiss me," she commanded, moving closer, her eyes closed. It seemed like the closer we came to her part of town, the more red lights stopped us. We didn't mind. We kissed and touched one another like fresh lovers at every stoplight. When we finally made it to her first floor flat, she couldn't wait to separate from that black cat suit. We didn't make it to the bedroom. We lay on a large thick white rug on the floor with white pillows against the wall. When we finished, I fell back with my eyes closed, ready for a brief night's sleep.

"What are you doing?" she asked.

"I'm sorry," I replied, thinking maybe she didn't want us sleeping on her living room floor. "Where is the bedroom?"

She giggled. "You can't stay here tonight," she said, gathering up my clothes and shoving them into my chest. The next thing I knew I was standing outside her door half dressed. Then the front porch area went black, as she turned the lights out. Could I have possibly been that bad as a partner? Days following our adventure, I called her and she was always too busy to talk. I sometimes left messages for her to call me, but she never did. Her careless disregard for me totally threw me off, made me temporarily feel worthless, humiliated. I felt as if I had satisfied her misguided sexual fantasy and then discarded, not worthy of a proper goodnight, just put out on the curb like a bag of trash. After a week or two of being ignored by this woman I hardly knew, I promised myself I would never use a female for my recreation or a one-night stand unless my intentions were clear and both parties were in agreement. To this day, I've maintained that promise.

During those rare down moments when I wasn't interviewing or researching a potential story, I spent leisurely hours enjoying friends and making new acquaintances. One of my favorite pastimes was sitting at the Atari Café on Ben Yehuda Street near Zion Square. This was the city center and the place to be in the evenings before and after the close of Shabbat. For hours we watched all sorts of people walk pass. Looking back, I realize there were times when our comments toward the less fortunate and the religious fanatics were not very kind. Still, these were some of the most memorable times of my life. The sun bearing down on me, the smell of falafel and fresh jasmine made for a relaxing respite. The company of good friends and thousands of strangers walking up and down the stone pedestrian mall, looking for bargains or a delectable meal added to my many simple pleasures.

One day I even shared a sandwich and coffee with Moses. This particular Moses was about 45 years old with long, wiry white hair and a beard and mustache. He was dressed in a long white robe, carrying a staff and briefcase.

"I realized I was Moses incarnate about two years ago,' he said. "I had come to Israel as a tourist and during my visit I received His calling."

It is common in Jerusalem to meet several Moses, John the Baptists, Elijahs and many other biblical characters. This condition is referred to as Jerusalem Syndrome. There is also a clinic in Israel whose function is to treat this temporary religious psychotic phenomenon. For some inexplicable reason seemingly normal people come to Jerusalem and during their stay they experience some sort of religious awakening. I wasn't bothered by this one bit. It was part of what makes Jerusalem the city that it is, full of mystery and conflict. It is virtually impossible to spend time in such a place with so many competing religions and races and not come away without an emotional connection. Maybe there is some truth to the Israeli saying, "God gave the world ten wonders; he gave Jerusalem nine of them."

My days in Jerusalem ended pretty much the way they started, with a leisurely stroll down Ben Yehuda pedestrian mall, which runs from King George Street down to Zion Square (Kikar Zion). The walk is lined with buildings erected during the British mandate prior to 1948. Day and night, music fills the air: violins, harps and often the Hasidim positioned with their clarinets blaring out klezmer tunes.

One afternoon I was walking through Kikar Zion near where Ben Yehuda intersects with Jaffa Road. Due to the heavy concentration of Jewish shoppers and tourists, this area is a prime target for Arab car bombs and other explosive devices. This particular afternoon I was enjoying a wonderful falafel when I noticed a black woman dressed from head to toe in a black veil and robe. She appeared to be a nun of some sort, but not Catholic. It was rare to see blacks on the streets of Jerusalem until 1985 when Operation Moses and the airlift of Ethiopian Jews brought thousands of Ethiopians into Israel. At that time the Israeli learned the newly arrived Ethiopians hated being referred to as Falasha, which means stranger or wanderer. The Ethiopian Jewry view themselves as neither strangers nor wanderers. They believe they always had a kinship with Jews in the Diaspora and live in hopes of reuniting with other tribes in Jerusalem.

Unable to contain my curiosity, I approached the woman in black and introduced myself. Her name was Sister Miriam and to my surprise she spoke functional English. Through her scattered words and hand gestures, I was directed to accompany her to the Mount of Paradise Ethiopian Orthodox Church. We walked to the building, which was situated off Ethiopia and HaNavi'em streets, just east of Zion Square. The church was circular and made of Jerusalem stone, as are most buildings in Israel. Instead of entering, we headed down to Jaffa Road towards the district government offices. Then we walked along the Old City wall towards Jaffa Gate.

Many types of stones make up the ancient wall of Jerusalem, some spanning several millenniums. Some of the newer stones date back 400 years to the Ottoman Empire. Those stones with borders called Herodian stones are believed to date back to the time of Christ and King Herod.

Upon entering the gate, to the left is a small, protected area where two graves are located. It is said that this is where the two original architects of the ancient city are buried. All around in the shadow of the Citadel, also known as King David's Tower, are Palestinian merchants selling touristic trinkets, hats, sandals and hand-pressed fresh juices in brilliant colors. Little has changed inside the Old City over the past couple of thousand years.

The woman and I made our way down through the tiny stone streets to the Church of the Holy Sepulcher, the church originally built by the mother of Emperor Constantine in 330 A.D. in the Christian Quarter. To the right of the main wooden door, standing nearly two stories high was a tiny entrance that was rather nondescript. I had to bow to enter to keep from bumping my head. Inside were two small chapels with white plaster and cement crumbling from the ceilings and the walls. The smoke of ancient incense clouded the room. Ornate traditional Ethiopian paintings surrounded me as I ascended up a wrought iron staircase so narrow worshippers and tourists could only travel in one direction at a time. An elderly monk, who said nothing and was sitting in an old wooden chair, watched me place a few coins in the metal donation plate in the upstairs chapel. He was eager to show me his ancient holy book. It was written in Ge'ez, the Ethiopian language of the Bible. The words were affixed to leaves made of 1,000-year-old goat parchment. I knew this from earlier research and writings I did at The Post on Ethiopian art.

We continued upward until we emerged on the roof of the Church of the Holy Sepulcher, over the site where Christians believe Christ was crucified, anointed, buried and resurrected. The heavy smell of disinfectant unsuccessfully masked the unmistakable scent of raw sewage. For a second I was delivered to the days of my youth in Alabama. One of the places we lived as a child was heavily infested with roaches and the toilets often backed up and overflowed. This odor was prevalent when we visited family members in rural Alabama, where all the homes had out-houses and my uncles bought lye and disinfectant by the drum full. I knew this odor well.

On the roof at the monastery, I was asked to sit on a stone wall surrounding a well while the nun scurried off for a moment behind a small wooden door that was barely hanging by its hinges.

Seconds later she returned with a young Ethiopian monk dressed in a long gray robe and black turban. His name was Solomon. He was a handsome fellow of about 24 years who stood nearly 6 feet tall with an even-toned complexion. His teeth were as white as ivory, which only accented his dazzling smile. He spoke English with a subtle British accent.

"You are welcome," he said, as he bowed and extended his hands as the sister made the introduction. "Please make yourself comfortable and join us."

The two spoke for a moment in their native tongue of Amharic.

I suppose Sister Miriam was providing him with what little information she knew about me. Finally, he turned to me and began giving what sounded like it might be the formal tourist spiel regarding Deir As-Sultan, the rooftop monastery. He gave me a general history of the place while pointing out significant walls and other structures. All the debris strewn about took me aback. I assumed that allowing the monastery to deteriorate this way showed a lack of discipline. The two dozen or so mud hovels exhibited severe water stains on the walls. The huts that had windows had cracked glass or windows half covered with newspapers and cardboard. The roofs were made of old, bent, rusty tin sheets.

Solomon escorted me to his personal quarters. All of his books and personal items were in order, but the wooden shelves were propped up by old discarded pieces of pipe or wood. The makeshift mattress or pad on the cot where he slept was lopsided and sunken in the middle.

Solomon never smiled, just as it was with the Ethiopian monks I noticed going about their business or just wandering near the sleeping quarters. Solomon and I left his room and walked back towards the courtyard. An Egyptian Coptic monk peered inside the gate across the way. When the Ethiopian monks and nuns saw him, my tour of the compound abruptly ended. I walked home that day, proud of my encounter with these African monks, yet at the same time ashamed and sad that of all the Christian communities in the Holy Sepulcher church, the Ethiopians were the worst represented and lived in abysmal conditions. Their little monastery was a mess and smelled horrible.

Solomon and I forged a friendship that brought me to the rooftop daily. I was impressed by the fact that he mastered not only the three languages of his country, but seven others as well. Day by day, bit-by-bit, he shared with me his history and the plight of the Ethiopian Church in Jerusalem. Solomon and I sat near the stone wall and I hung onto every syllable he spoke regarding Ethiopians' history in the Holy Land.

"Nearly 300 years ago under Ottoman rule all religions in Jerusalem paid homage to the Sultans, except our monks," he said in a quiet tone. "The sultan exacted harsh punishment against the monks by cutting them off from the mother church of Ethiopia, which left them unable to pay taxes. The sultan placed the Ethiopians under the Armenian charge," Solomon continued. "As the monks died, they were unable to get replacements from Ethiopia so the numbers dwindled in half from 100 to about 50 monks. The community was then ravaged by a plague causing further reduction in the monastery. The few remaining were unable to stop the greedy Christian neighbors from taking more land and Ethiopian

Church property," he said.

I supposed I finally gained his trust and the trust of the Ethiopian Monastic Community because one day, unexpectedly, Solomon said, "It's time for you to be introduced to Abune Athanasius, the patriarch of the Ethiopian Orthodox Church."

The Herodian stones and the 10th Century Crusader graffiti all over the church was a constant reminder that the monks and their rooftop monastery began thousands of years before I set foot in their modest sanctuaries.

The Monks of the Deir As-Sultan Monastery serve as spiritual representatives of the hundreds of Christian Ethiopians (Abyssinians) living in Jerusalem. It is believed that these Ethiopians are directly related to the Ethiopian eunuch that Philip baptized in the Book of Acts, Chapter 8; verses 26-40: Now an angel of the Lord said to Philip, "Go south to the road—the desert road—that goes down from Jerusalem to Gaza." So he started out, and on his way he met an Ethiopian eunuch, an important official in charge of all the treasury of the Kandake (which means "queen of the Ethiopians"). This man had gone to Jerusalem to worship, and on his way home was sitting in his chariot reading the Book of Isaiah the prophet.

The community of Ethiopian monks was banished from the interior of the Holy Sepulcher Church nearly 300 years ago by the Ottoman sultan and they have been living on the roof of the church in mud hovels since. The nuns were forced to build the mud huts by hand with dirt and water they brought from the Kidron Valley nearly a kilometer away. The Turkish ruler and religious groups occupying the church drew up a 200-year-old agreement, called the "Status Quo in the Holy Sites". This agreement is still strictly honored. It forbids cleaning, repairs or any changes in designated sacred areas unless agreed upon collectively by all tenants. Should this agreement be violated in any way, the offending party stands the risk of losing some or all of the property in question. All religious organizations represented within the Holy Sepulcher agreed that the Ethiopians were the major caretakers and tenants of this most sacred piece of property in all Christendom.

When Solomon introduced me to the patriarch of the church, he lowered his eyes and bowed his head reverently. I followed his lead. Abune Athanasius was a handsome man with a nearly full graying beard. Solomon believed the patriarch could persuade me to write an article about their 300-year-old plight. Athanasius appeared in a black cassock with a turban trimmed in gold atop his head. A man of advanced years, his face was free of all the markings of age. He was regal and stately. Athanasius, through the spoken translations of Solomon, reiterated everything I had gleaned from the months of conversations sitting around that stone well. His entourage of monks and nuns silently flanked him with their backs leaning against the stone wall.

"The other religions had the monks chained and dragged out of the church's sanctuary around 300 years ago," said Athanasius. "To this day, the Ethiopians are still not welcomed in the church and are seldom invited to participate in the religious events that take place within the Holy Sepulcher," he said.

Under the pretext of preventing the spread of the deadly plague, the Coptic Church burned their libraries of thousand-year-old manuscripts handwritten on beautifully designed parchment, according to Athanasius.

He paused in his explanations, deferring to Solomon to elaborate on historical details. The two continued by saying that even today in the old City of Jerusalem some of the Armenian Church's books are bound with covers made of parchment and covered with Ge'ez (the official language of the Ethiopian church) and Amharic script. Also, Ethiopian markings are found in the religious artifacts of the Greek, Latin and other denominations, ethnic groups and cultures.

The two explained to me that less than 30 Ethiopian monks resided in the rooftop monastery and the Egyptian Coptic church held the deed to their land. The monks had to do renovations and cleaning often in the dark so as not to be seen by other Christians living at the Holy Sepulcher. If they are found violating the Status quo of the Holy Land Sites, it could easily lead to their eviction. The Status quo of the Holy Land Sites preserved the division of ownership and responsibilities of sites holy to the major religions and current holders of the site. The monks said if they were forced to leave Deir As-Sultan Monastery, blacks would never again be represented in the sacred place.

The Status Quo of the Holy Land Sites has made life unbearable at times for the monks. Problems such as who has charge over the keys to the toilets or on what day a certain step is to be swept can lead to lengthy arbitration by the Israeli authorities. In the winter the temperature in Jerusalem often drops below freezing. The monks brave the cold in their 6 ft. by 6 ft. cubicles, often without water, heat, and lights. When plaster falls from the roof of their small chapel, days or weeks can pass before they receive permission from the other denominations to clean it up.

"Solomon, explain to the patriarch that it's not so simple to get stories published in the U.S. from abroad," I said. "Tell him I already put forth my best effort, but no newspaper seems interested. I apologize and promise to keep trying."

"Please try again. I beg you. The world needs to know about our situation and the conditions under which we live. If the building continues to deteriorate we will have to leave," the patriarch pleaded, his voice trembling with emotion.

"The only connection I have with a major newspaper is with the Washington Post," I told him. "For the story to receive serious consideration for publishing, I'd need to return to the U.S."

I said this knowing I had no intention of leaving Israel just to pitch a story, no matter the significance. Solomon translated and the people murmured to one another, loudly. No one needed to explain to me what they were saying. I saw their mood darken and their eyes stared at me with such intensity that I felt uncomfortable.

Then Solomon translated his Archbishop Athanasius' final argument.

"Mr. Cooper, if you don't help us, who will?" he said.

The Archbishop wanted me to return to the U.S. and do whatever I could to bring public attention to their plight. But Israel was my home now and I did not want to return to the U.S. at any point in the near future. What was waiting for me there? I did not want to return to that pressroom and assume a hellish life. No, I could not go back to Washington and argue on their behalf.

Still, as much as my intellect held onto this argument, my heart and conscious told me it was just a matter of time before I returned to Washington and did exactly what they asked. The pleas of the patriarch and the faces of those monks and nuns were etched into my memory. I was relieved when the Archbishop returned to the monastery, as I bid good day to Solomon and the other monks and nuns.

I continued my visits to the monastery in hopes that one day the newspapers might soften their position and publish this story. The following week the sisters prepared me a feast fit for royalty. All of the dishes served were traditional Ethiopian cuisine. During that summer of '85, I did manage to air the story on the Middle East Television News Network, which was a subsidiary of the Christian Broadcast Network. The story aired with little to no response, just as I expected. MTN had a viewing audience that consisted only of Israel, Egypt, Jordan and Lebanon and it was broadcast in English. I needed the strength of the U.S. news media to really effect change for those suffering monks and nuns. I had my own testimony as to how one story placed in the right publication yielded profound results. I needed the Washington Post.

I conducted business as usual in Jerusalem, traveling, writing television news and the occasional newspaper article, which was always rejected. No matter how I tried to forget, everywhere I turned I was haunted by the situation of the monks on the roof of the Holy Sepulcher. Winter was rapidly approaching and once again the monks would be exposed to the elements. I managed to convince myself that even if I did return to the Post, there was no guarantee the editorial staff would accept this article. After all, it had already been rejected once.

It became more and more difficult to face the Ethiopians in the Old City, knowing through all the pleading I was firm in my position to remain in Israel. It seemed as though at every turn during my daily walks through the city center I ran into one of the Ethiopian priests or nuns.

During one of my impromptu strolls through the Old City, I made a detour, which led me to the rear entrance of the Ethiopian Monastery. I rarely if ever used the back stone steps past the Coptic Compound, which leads to the monastery. I am not certain what happened that day. There were no tourists. No hustle and bustle. There was just a lone elderly monk, sitting in an old splintery chair near the well. He had both hands clasped together, resting atop the handle of his cane, and his head atop his hands as if to be carrying the troubles of the world. He looked straight through me with his sad, drooping eyes. I am amazed at times how some of the most effective arguments are made without a word being said.

"Damn!" I whispered to myself. It was time for me to **leave Israel.**

When November rolled around I finally returned to the U.S. My first month in Washington, D.C. was spent trying to land a position with a news organization. It didn't matter if it was print, radio or television. I was willing to accept any position that was available. I dreaded the idea of having to return to that dungeon called the Washington Post pressroom. But every attempt at employment in the media failed and I found myself again working the heavy GOSS presses in the basement of the Post. I had died and gone to hell for a second time.

I also returned to the newsroom during the day, which was my only solace for what I endured during the night hours. In the evenings, if I wasn't reading or writing during breaks, I spent time talking with the prostitutes outside. The Post happened to sit in their area of business and since my break was in the middle of the night, I had gotten to know some of these women. I had one close friend back in Alabama who worked as a prostitute to make extra money. Also, during my time on the streets in D.C., I occasionally struck up a conversation with women who worked the streets near the downtown area. I never had a problem with the way these women lived and I certainly was in no position to pass judgment on their choices. Most of them claimed to be students at one of the local universities or said they maintained some legitimate employment by day. I was surprised that many of the pressmen working with me believed them. Occasionally, these guys also hopped in their cars and bought the services offered by these women in the back alley.

A few months passed. Every day I asked myself how I could have done something so stupid, so thoughtless as returning to the U.S. after I had waited for years to live in Israel. I mustered up the nerve to pitch the story once more to the editor of the religion page. This time I did it in person. Again, my idea was rejected. I approached other editors and writers, but still there was little to no interests. I went to other religious and non-religious publications only to get rejected again and again. I felt hopeless. Maybe it was time for me to face the fact that I was the only person who saw merit in the Ethiopian monks and their rooftop monastery story. I had obsessed over the story for more than a year by this time and the memory of their plight was emotionally draining. As a freelancer, I continued contributing articles to the Post's District Weekly. But I believed it was past time to raise the ante by doing what seemed impossible: Writing for the daily newspaper.

Then something incredible happened. The recruiter in the newsroom approached me about joining the Post newsroom as a staff writer. It wasn't a firm job offer, but she was exploring the possibility. I was overjoyed until she said the position was as a staff writer for the Weekly with absolutely no chance of advancement. To agree to such egregious terms was journalistic suicide, as far as I was concerned. I would not consider even applying. It was insulting and degrading that I had spent time in Lebanon in very dangerous situations and had interviewed terrorists on the West Bank only to have the Post ask me to write about potholes and cats stuck in trees. Perhaps I was foolish and prideful not to pursue the offer, even if it meant working in the Weekly exclusively forever. I would have been free of that pressroom and all its danger and filth.

It didn't dawn on me until months later that this offer may have been the Post's way of giving me an additional foothold in the newsroom, freeing me from the presses. A temporary lapse in judgement may have cost me to miss the opportunity I had worked so hard and waited so long for. Surely, if I took the position and provided solid copy with good reporting to the editors, there was no way they could hold me back. But within days, the position vanished and was never filled or mentioned again.

Joel Garreau, who arrived each morning wearing cowboy boots and a cowboy hat atop his shocking red hair, was an editor of the Sunday's Outlook Section and was aware of my unorthodox route to breaking into journalism. While speaking and listening, he continually twisted and twirled the tip of his long mustache.

"I don't think there is a person in this entire building who works as hard as you do," he said to me one morning while sitting atop my desk. "I have to give it to you, you are ambitious and for one, I admire you for working those crazy hours day after day."

On another morning he chimed in on a conversation I was having with another freelancer regarding Martin Luther King, Jr. and how not all blacks in Alabama welcomed him or his ideas of equality with open arms.

I had barely finished talking when Joel said, "how about writing an article on coming of age in Alabama during the civil rights struggle."

I was overjoyed.

Two weeks later the article ran in the coveted space for any serious writer, the Sunday Outlook section, which at the time was read by 1.2 million people. I will never forget the headline:

Martin Luther King Jr.: One man's messiah was another's Satan in '60s Birmingham

Beneath the story was "Len Cooper is a Washington writer and a pressman at The Washington Post."

I was so proud!

I started the article describing that typical Birmingham, Alabama. Sunday morning in early 1963. I described how I was getting ready for Sunday school along with my mother, when all of a sudden the peace was disturbed by a huge explosion not far from our home. "When the dust finally settled, four young girls were dead and our lives were changed forever," the article said.

It continued by saying that Dr. King's message of hope and change was slow to take root among Birmingham's older Blacks, but the young residents were eager to join the movement. In time, the Blacks in Birmingham came to support the civil rights movement, unequivocally. Later, my parents talked about how foolish they were for doubting King and his intentions. When King was killed, they wept.

My article was picked up by the wire service and published in other newspapers across the country. I was up all night working the presses when the story ran. The next morning, I received congratulatory comments from everybody, including newsroom operators to Ben Bradlee, the editor of the paper. I received fan mail at home and in the newsroom. I basked in my newfound popularity. But in spite of all the pats on the back, firm handshakes and well-wishers during the day, in the evening it was time to run home to get some sleep to make the nightshift in the pressroom.

"Anybody could have written that story," one of the Weekly editors said, as she crumbled the article and pushed it in my chest. "Besides, you are thirty-something years old. Maybe it's time for you to shift your interests to a goal that's achievable before it's too late," she said, walking away.

I was hurt by her comments but pretended not to be. I forgot all the other congratulatory remarks, but this remark lingered in my head for days, weeks, even years. She could be right, I kept thinking. Maybe I should take her advice.

One of the newsroom operators named Marci, noticed me standing alone, looking dejected and sad from the editor's comment.

"I saw you standing over here by yourself. What happened? Why are you so sad?" Marci asked, resting her hand on my shoulder. "Did somebody say something to you?"

"It's nothing," I responded, trying to regain my composure. "There is one, there is always one," I said, shaking my head.

"Don't let these people get to you," Marci said. "Who was it, I'll straighten them out."

We both laughed.

My long days in the newsroom, meeting deadlines and calming temperamental copy editors, made the nights on the presses almost bearable. Many times I covered stories the staff writers and even interns refused to consider. I couldn't enjoy the luxury of turning down story assignments. "If I was asked to write about the sexual habits of the Japanese beetle and its effects on religion in the western world, I would do it, and do it with enthusiasm," I laughingly told a reporter one day.

Months passed as I continued the daily, around-the-clock grind. I was worn. It was time for a much needed break and for me, the only place where I could completely relax was Jerusalem.

Over the next few weeks, I made arrangements to schedule nearly a month off from the pressroom and made other plans for my trip. With everything set, that spring of 1986, I boarded a flight to Jerusalem. The flight was uneventful except for the beautiful dark complexioned Israeli female who sat beside me from London to Tel Aviv. In all my time in Israel I had never encountered a native Israeli with such dark skin. Aside from the Ethiopian Jewry, the Jews from Yemen were the darkest I had seen. This young woman had long coarse black hair and skin as dark as mine. Her English was almost as bad as my Hebrew, but we managed. She told me her family immigrated to Haifa, Israel many years ago from some northern province in Poland. As she talked, I wondered if dark-skinned Jews settled in Poland following their exile from Spain 500 years ago. I mentally archived some of her comments thinking that during Hitler's reign of terror in Poland and throughout Europe, blacks must have been sent to the death camps as well. I thought that possibly blacks that were not of Jewish ancestry were sent to the gas chambers or to concentration camps. I was curious but I had too many other stories to do before I'd have the time to investigate this. Anyway, the woman and I exchanged information with the understanding we would meet again in Haifa or she would call me while visiting friends in Jerusalem. But it didn't happen and we never saw one another again.

Upon my arrival in Jerusalem the first order of business was to drop off my things at a friend's home, where I was staying. Then I headed down to the Ethiopian compound in the Old City. The walk is one that I can do blindfolded. I made my way into the enclosed city, through the twist and turns, past the merchants selling blue and white Armenian dishes and other goods, past the large slabs of flat stones in the walkway that bore etchings of Roman games carved on the surface over 2,000 years ago. Occasionally in front of a shop or on a wall there were marks noting one of the 12 Stations of the Cross, indicating Christ's journey to his crucifixion. The air, as centuries before, was filled with the smells of Middle East spices and incense. I entered the Ethiopian compound from the rear and to my surprise there stood Solomon, concluding a tour. We kissed each other on both cheeks in traditional greetings.

"I am so sorry for not being able to tell your story in the U.S. press," I apologized through my embarrassment. "I give you my word I will keep trying as long as it takes," I said.

"The monks have been waiting for help for nearly 300 years," Solomon added. "A few more years won't matter."

Solomon expressed his confidence and that of Athanasius in my ability to get the article published some day. I was relieved by his kindness and understanding. We remained in the courtyard, sharing happenings since our last meeting. I left feeling good about seeing him and promising to stop by again before I returned to the U.S.

It was the spring of 1986. Over the next few days I visited friends all around Jerusalem and on the West Bank. I cannot articulate what being in Israel does for me. I feel complete in every respect while I am there. The closest I can come to describing how I feel is to say my soul feels hungry or yearns for something but nothing else will satisfy it except to visit Israel and Jerusalem. Then the moment comes when it is time for me to leave and it breaks my heart each and every time.

Back in Washington, I eagerly returned to the newsroom. As always, I was filled with optimism and excitement about the endless possibilities the day held for me if I continued writing. But there was the pressroom, lurking like a thief in the night, waiting to zap all the joy I gleaned from time spent working on news articles. During the day, I continued writing for the District Weekly, but I also cranked out many stories that got published in the daily paper, their subjects ranging from sports, to relationship problems to editorials and whatever topic I was assigned or found interesting. Each time my byline appeared, editors and staff writers from other sections congratulated me on a job well done and offered words of encouragement. In some way their praise and caring made it all worth the price I was paying each and every night in that abyss called the pressroom.

One day Henry Allen, a well-respected writer and editor who was editing one of my articles for Outlook, complimented me on my ability to tell a story and draw the reader into the scene. On this day, his words fell on deaf ears.

"I said that your writing and ability to take the reader to the scene through words is much better than most of the writers here," he repeated. "That should mean something to you."

I didn't even acknowledge his compliment.

"Much of my life I was told by my father, teachers and whites in my hometown that I wasn't shit and would never amount to a damn thing," I said in a normal tone, as my eyes moved from the gray carpet to his eyes and back down again. "The sad truth is there are times I believe it still. I don't want to feel this way and I have to tell myself time and time again that I am as deserving as the next person. But I have had this malady for a very long time and every now and then this particular demon rears its ugly head and there's not a damn thing I can do about it."

For a moment I was a 10-year-old boy again, back in Alabama cowering far underneath the bed with the dust balls, rat droppings and dried roach carcasses, waiting for yet another storm in my life to pass. What made my present storm different was that the feelings of inadequacy and self-loathing were being created and maintained by me and only existed in my head.

During my period of self-loathing, Henry asked me to write a first person account about my life as a seminarian and all the trials I encountered until I was dismissed from the program. His assignment was like ripping the scab off a wound that's barely healed. Yet, as painful as it was to dig up those dead memories, I agreed to write the story.

The article was printed on the front page of Sunday's Outlook section. As always, I was downstairs on the presses, waiting with excitement as the article rolled off. Sunday afternoon, both Catholic and non-Catholic friends called to tell me that me and my article were the topics of interest in pulpits and among congregants at churches in D.C.

It just so happened that the story was published the weekend the U.S. Council of Bishops was meeting in D.C. The Post's telephone circuits lit up all that Sunday and Monday. Then one night my phone rang and it was an assistant in the Outlook section calling.

"Len Cooper?" "Yes, this is Len," I said.

"Hi. Mr. Bradlee asked me to call to ask you if you would stay away from the newsroom for a couple of days."

I was surprised and for some seconds I was quiet. "Sure," I said. I wondered why but I didn't ask and no one offered an explanation. I presumed staying away from the newsroom had something to do with me not having a direct confrontation with the bishops. In truth, I never gave it much deliberation. Who was I to question the great Ben Bradlee?

After a couple of days passed, I returned to the newsroom. The newsroom operator told me that 10 Catholic bishops had paraded into the Post to meet with the editorial staff a couple of days prior to my return. I later learned the Post stood by their decision to print my article. Oddly enough, no one said a word to me regarding what was discussed in the meeting. It was almost like it never happened.

CHAPTER 20: MARRIAGE AND THE FAMILY

Gail Whitlow, a secretary for the Archbishop of Washington D.C, and I shared a mutual friend named Elaine Douglas, who frequented the Post's newsroom. Gail mentioned to Elaine that the Archbishop's office was abuzz the day after my story ran.

"The archbishop cancelled meetings and huddled with priests in his offices for a series of high level meetings. That guy who wrote that article is extremely brave to write that story about the church and seminary." Gail said, according to Elaine.

The two women talked for days about my piece, according to Elaine, who told Gail that she could introduce us, if she was interested. I suppose she was interested because one day Elaine gave me Gail's number. Gail and I spoke regularly for a month by phone before we decided to meet.

We agreed to meet for dinner at a moderately upscale restaurant called Chadwick's in far northwest Washington, D.C. I arrived 30 minutes early and she arrived 30 minutes late. I wasn't terribly bothered since I lived only a few blocks from the restaurant and she had to drive clear from the opposite side of town.

I stood to greet her when she arrived.

"I am so sorry I am late, but…"

I interrupted. "No need to explain. You've had to drive all the way from northeast. I am just happy you made it."

She sat down in the chair across the table from me. I thought she was so pretty, her long light-brown hair contrasting with her deeper dark brown eyes.

But there was an air of sadness about her. I attributed it to being a normal part of the struggle of trying to survive alone in D.C.

"It took a lot of courage and nerves for you to write such a scathing article about the Catholic Church and seminary," she said at one point in the evening.

I explained that to me there was nothing brave or courageous about any of this. "I just think parents should be better informed before shipping their sons and daughters off to study in such places," I said.

"Well, there's going to be some fallout from the Catholic Church because of your article," she warned, as she recounted some of the unflattering discussions about me in the Archbishop's office.

"Some people in my own Birmingham parish rejected me, so there isn't much more the church can do," I said.

Days after the article was published, the president of the Catholic University of America, Rev. David M. O'Connell, C.M., wrote a biting follow up in the Post that included this: "As a Catholic priest who was trained in a large seminary at the same time as Len Cooper, I was offended by the suggestion that such institutions were characterized by hatred, bigotry and rampant homosexuality. As a Christian, I was outraged that, in this day and age, after decades of struggle for civil rights and religious freedom, the major newspaper in a city that has a black majority and is largely non-Catholic, would further the cause of prejudice and misunderstanding by inciting further antipathy toward a religious denomination."

I knew there would be fallout from this article and it was no surprise that a written rebuttal from the church appeared in the same section as my article. For whatever reason, I hoped for understanding or maybe an indirect apology from the Church. Instead, I was accused of misrepresenting and grossly exaggerating my experiences as a seminarian.

I wrote a letter to Rev. O'Connell more than 20 years after this article ran. There are moments when I hear a story about priest molesting children and all the pain returns, as if it were yesterday. I got so angry at times when the church was not held accountable for their wayward priests. It was personal. My heart went out for all those victimized by the clergy.

When I wrote O'Connell I was at that point where for once I just needed to hear someone in authority within the church to say, "I am sorry about what happened to you." No one has and probably never will. I know that some hurts never heal and are always just under the surface, waiting to emerge again and again.

The good Reverend had retired from the presidential position at Catholic University several years earlier. He had trouble recalling his letter to the Post. He said that he had moved on with his life and suggested that I do the same. To me this sounded similar to the advice priests and church officials have offered victims of their unwanted advances and bad behavior. "Get over it and move on with your life." I wasn't surprised O'Connell showed no sympathy towards me. Since the day I was terminated as a seminarian, no priest or representative from the church has ever met with me to discuss my experiences. Not one. I wrote that letter with little or no expectations. It was just one of those moments when something I heard, read or saw opened that old wound once again. But just like times past, my heart ached, I shed a couple of tears, but the pain and disappointment eventually passed....until the next time.

Over the next few weeks, I was enraptured by Gail's conversations. I learned she had started college before her 16th birthday. She was a veracious reader and could talk for hours holding in-depth discussions on politics, travel, history, art and a host of other topics. She was enchanting and I was smitten.

We were married nearly two years later and in no time I was the father of a boy and girl. As the news spread my friends in the newsroom offered congratulations. Columnist William Raspberry, a known jokester, came to where I was sitting and expressed at length how happy he was for me. Then he said, "This is where it all begins. Look at all these pretty ladies in here and just think: For the rest of your life, all you can do is look."

Post staffers interrupted me continually, offering good wishes for my marriage.

"Yah mo!" said columnist Courtland Malloy. I never knew why he called me Yah mo, which is taken from "Yah Mo Be There" by the Doobie Brothers. "I'm happy for you man," he said, while vigorously shaking my hand.

Entering the pressroom, a worker raised his hand high to give me five and said, "Man I hear your bitch is a phat ass muthafucka!" I offered a fake smile of approval and begrudgingly gave him his props by fiving him and continued my way to the assigned press. In truth, there were some in the pressroom who were respectful and kind and I tended to gravitate toward those individuals.

In 1993 I had been in the pressroom for more than 12 years. I was writing less for the newspaper and doing personal research and collecting information on my family history in Alabama. I continued submitting occasional articles for publication in the Post without even setting foot in the newsroom for months at a time. Still, it was rare for me to have a story idea rejected by the Post editors.

I had submitted and published articles in the Post for nearly a decade and I was no closer to landing a staff position. The responsibility of taking care of a family no longer permitted me to spend 16-hour days and weekends at the paper. It was time for me to be completely honest with myself. I was a Washington Post pressman who submitted occasional articles to the paper for publication and that was the closest I was going to get to becoming a fulltime reporter. Maybe that Post editor was correct when she said that I was too old to pursue a career as a journalist, maybe I was wasting some of the best years of my life working day and night. For nearly a decade, I only had to consider myself in the consequences of spending much of my life in the Washington Post. It was time to grow up and be a responsible adult with a wife and kids depending on me. In the beginning, I wasn't ready to be a father or husband and I certainly wasn't ready to bid farewell to my dream of becoming a journalist. I felt as though the life I was accustomed to was being torn from my grasp. But in time my attitude changed. I settled in to my new life and was pretty good at fatherhood and being a loving and devoted husband.

We often rotated schedules in the pressroom. It was my turn to switch to days once more, which didn't allow much time for me to work the newsroom, anyway. One day another worker and I were assigned to install the color units on the press, each one weighing in excess of 100 pounds.

I steadied my end. He held his end by the metal handle. We slowly lowered the unit to affix the cylinders to the base of the press. Then my coworker's hands slipped and his end went crashing to the floor. Bam! I held firm to my end. I was leaning forward in a twisted position when it happened. Instantly, I felt a burning sensation on the right side of my back and a tingling sensation go down my legs. "This cannot be good," I thought.

"Sorry, sorry, sorry," the press operator apologized. "You, okay! You, okay!" he asked, while reaching out to me.

"I'll be fine," I said, walking away.

I continued working until the foreman came over 15 minutes later and insisted I see the Post's nurse. In the health office I laid down with a heating pad under my back for 30 minutes. I fell asleep. Before I left, the nurse instructed me to see a physician as soon as possible. I made the appointment for that same week.

The doctor prescribed lots of Advil and lower back massages. But month after month things grew worse. I developed chronic leg and groin pains. I stumbled without warning. After a year, I saw a neurosurgeon, who told me my situation wasn't going to get better without surgery. I hesitated at the idea of surgery until I started losing strength in my right leg. One day I was out front in my yard and fell without warning. I called the surgeon the very next day.

By all accounts, my lower back surgery was a success. While I was recuperating in my room on the day of the surgery with my wife by my side, the phone rang.

"Mr. Cooper, I am your occupational therapist and I have been assigned to work with you and try to sort through all this and get you back to work," she said.

Then after verifying my identity and exchanging a few niceties, she said, "Mr. Cooper, please tell me exactly what you were doing that caused the accident that supposedly led to your injury."

"Excuse me!" I curtly replied, taken aback by the word "supposedly."

"There are procedures for installing additional machinery on the presses and I need to be certain that those procedures were followed," she continued. "If there was something you did or didn't do, we can work through this, but we need to know the truth as to what caused the accident."

At the time of her call I was drugged out of my mind, but I was not stupid. "Look!" I snapped. "I will be home later today. Give me time to rest and we can discuss this further."

I hung up.

I received several calls from individuals hired to protect the Washington Post's interests. Soon after that first call, a person identifying himself as a representative from the Post's legal department called and asked for my account of what happened the day of the accident. I was still in pain, trying to recuperate, my back hurting most of the day. I was angry that the Post's vultures were circling.

"Look! I have no intention of suing the newspaper! All I want is to return to the company and work a job that pays comparable wages as what I earned in the pressroom," I said.

Yet the calls were unrelenting. The surgeon made it clear that my days as a press operator were over. I was happy at the thought of not returning to the pressroom but concerned over the fact that I had a family and no real job.

I was feeling pretty good after arriving home. I was in physical therapy for a couple of months and I was pleased with my recovery, except the pain in my left leg lingered. Over the next four years I was still with the company, but was out on workers compensation. Different occupational therapists were hired by the Post and assigned to assist me in finding work outside the company that didn't require heavy lifting. I was still an employee of the Washington Post until I was gainfully employed elsewhere. Although the therapist assisted me with possible job leads, I still had to go through the regular interviewing process.

One of the first jobs I interviewed for was a secretarial position for a retiring ophthalmologist in Rockville, Maryland. During the interview, he entered the room with urine stains on the front of his white pants. I wondered if the man was competent. It was hard to ignore, but I refocused on landing the position and I got it.

The doctor was trying to get a grant to research the effect of certain drugs to treat ailments they were not designed for. After he realized his application for the grant was going to be rejected, he decided to do his own unfunded research by administering the dosage to himself. Shortly afterwards he developed a white spot on the pupil of his eye, which obstructed his vision. As a result, he had to abandon his research.

"Would you consider returning half of the wages I paid you?" he asked, right after this.

I refused and he politely fired me. The job had lasted three weeks.

I still found time to write the occasional human-interest article between physical therapy sessions and meetings with lawyers and medical personnel. I heard that the Post had a new editor heading up the religion page. Seven years had passed since I gave my word to the Ethiopian monks in Jerusalem that I would help them by getting press exposure in the American newspapers. I placed a call to the new editor and pitched the story idea, but she wanted to see additional information. I raced to type out a query and shot it to her by email. To my surprise, she wanted to run with the story. I was ecstatic. I gathered all of my notes accumulated over the years and called Solomon in Jerusalem to update a few facts.

The day after this story was printed, Israel's Minister of Religious Affairs made an impromptu visit to the Ethiopian compound. He ordered an immediate investigation and repairs to the dilapidated structure. However, before the work started, the government in Ethiopia changed hands. Archbishop Athanasius was removed from his post and reportedly exiled to Kenya. I never heard from Solomon again. Many of the other residents I knew at the monastery were sent out on missions in Ethiopia and replaced by pro-government monks. It was time for another quick visit to Jerusalem to see the repairs first hand.

I took leave once again of my job at the Post and made arrangements to travel. When I arrived I dropped off my things at a friend's home and immediately made a quick visit to the press office, in case I needed my credentials. It was customary soon after my arrival in Jerusalem to spend my first hours in the Judean Desert. This time was no different. Other than a stiff lower back and some pain behind my left leg, I was fine. I climbed a small trail leading up the mountainside just off one of the many ancient Roman roads, which runs adjacent to the main highway connecting the Dead Sea to the south and Jericho to the north. My practice was to sit for what seemed like hours. The peace of the surroundings blended one minute into another. I sat serenely on a huge stone, overlooking the Wadi Qelt, which is a valley in the desert with a stream and plush green trees and grass in its base and rolling sand dunes and hills as far as the eyes can see. For me, this had been a place of enormous peace and tranquility. But apparently, others longed for the same respite. The Bedouins set up shop nearby and before you had a chance to exit your car, two or three children and adults pushed their hands inside your car window, trying to sell all kinds of beads, scarfs and trinkets. Once you started up the side of the mountain, several Bedouins surround you, peddling their mostly made-in-China goods. The presence of commerce had taken away the peace of my special place.

When I did feel serene, I felt the first tap on the shoulder. "Five shekels each," the man said, pushing his beaded necklaces and scarves towards me.

"Just a moment, as soon as I am done I will gladly take a look at your merchandise," I replied. Once again I closed my eyes and felt the warm desert winds blowing against the back of my neck.

"Two for eight shekels," the man said.

Once again, I replied, but this time with more annoyance in my voice. "I told you in a moment I will have a look. Now please!"

I moved a few feet to a different area. This time I could hear the winds whistling softly through the canyon below.

"I have nice things for you, specially made by hand," a voice said.

That did it! I rose to my feet and without another word I raced down the hillside to the car, got in and left.

My next stop was to visit the monks at their rooftop monastery in the Old City of Jerusalem. I entered the light brown stone compound, not surprised to see the windows and roofs had been replaced on all the huts. There were also new doors on the shacks and the bathroom fixtures were all new as well. Dark faces gazed at me. I did not recognize most of them, but there were several standing in a cluster I knew well. The few who remembered me rushed over and kissed me on the back of my hands and face in greetings. The welcome came to an abrupt end when a stern-faced monk walked straight pass them and planted himself directly in front of me. Without so much as a hello, he said, "Come with me."

I tagged along several paces behind him until we got to a small office. Waiting for me was a white Ethiopian nun who was in charge of all issues related to the press. She and I had met once before in years past. Athanasius did not trust her and she was not allowed in the compound under his leadership. She was born in Holland, but joined the Abyssinian church at some point. Now she was the historian and spokesperson for the Ethiopian monastic community.

"Sir, in the future please do not speak to anyone in the community or enter it without a formal escort or permission. Do you understand?" she spoke calmly, peering across her wire-frame glasses from underneath a traditional Ethiopian nun's black veil.

"I understand your position clearly," I said, leaving.

I was pleased to see the much-improved living conditions for the monks as I wandered from hut to hut gazing at all the new windows, roofs and doors. But clearly a lot had changed. Before, I never needed "permission" or a "formal escort" to enter the compound.

Most of the people now occupying the monastery had been sent there by the pro-Marxist government of Ethiopia. Every move I made seemed to be monitored by the watchful eyes of monks I'd never met or seen before. Some were even friendly with the Egyptian Coptic community adjacent to their compound. The Ethiopians had been at odds with the Coptics for centuries. Governed by century old laws, the Egyptian Coptics were the overseers of the Ethiopians and their property at the Holy Sepulcher in Jerusalem. I didn't want to cause added trouble for those few nuns and priests who remained after Athanasius's departure. I felt it was best that I sever ties with the community for their own good.

After that day, whenever I made a rare visit to Deir As-Sultan Monastery, I received the same treatment as any other tourist. It was almost as if my sacrifices over the years and all the time and effort invested on their behalf never happened. I left the compound never to return as a welcomed friend. I returned to visit my friends in Jerusalem for a few days before again leaving for Washington.

The Post's legal team and occupational therapists grew impatient with me not being able to find sustainable work. They formulated a projections chart that somehow calculated my earning potential over a period of years. They used the projections to determine how much I should be earning and reduced my worker's compensation by that amount. This meant that instead of being paid around $900 every couple of weeks; I was now receiving workers compensation checks for less than $200. I hired an attorney, but it took several weeks before my full compensation was reinstated. Meanwhile, the mortgage company started foreclosure proceedings on our home. I felt like less of a man because I was unable to fully provide for my family.

I was in pain for much of the four years following the surgery. Then during August of 1996 the hurting finally stopped, never to return again. My relationship with the production department in the Post was in shreds. I didn't care. I wanted out and this way was as good a way as any. I was still welcomed in the newsroom, and that was all that mattered to me. So after years of fighting intrusive lawyers and working odd jobs in private homes or on temporary assignments, in 1999, I decided to settle with the company and part ways. I was surprised I was allowed to keep my Post ID. In the end, I was given $145,000 and $35,000 of it went to my attorney. I was also required to sign a formal letter of resignation from the Washington Post.

No more breathing black ink mist! No more fear of losing a hand or entire limb in the presses! No more ignorant-ass conversations with people I was forced to talk to simply because we worked together. After more than 10 years on the presses and another seven years of litigation, I was finally free.

It was impossible for me to spend long hours writing articles in the Washington Post newsroom and have enough time to be a responsible husband and father. As months passed, I became a homebody and wrote less. I turned my attention to researching topics of interests I had catalogued in journals and held in the back of my mind for years. My thoughts strayed back to a trip to Israel in 1986 when I met that very dark-skinned Israeli whose family ancestry hailed from northern Poland. I had some knowledge of the Holocaust and I had a hunch that blacks in Europe were also victims of Hitler's murderous campaign. During one of my many visits to Jerusalem, I stopped by the

Yad Vashem Holocaust Memorial, where I posed this possibility to Yitzhak Mayes, the curator. To my surprise, he responded, "You couldn't be more mistaken. There are no records or recollections of events concerning black people in concentration camps in Europe."

There was no valid reason to doubt his word. As I was leaving, a woman I presumed was his secretary walked with me for a ways before turning to say, "Wait here for a moment."

She disappeared down the hall. A couple of minutes later she returned and presented me with a pamphlet entitled, "In the Shadow of the Towers." The small booklet gave a brief history of Johan Cosmo Nassy, who was an inmate in several death camps in Europe during World War II. Nassy was born in Suriname, but held a U.S. passport issued in San Francisco. He was an accomplished painter. The brochure had several photos of Nassy's art, where he captured a day in the life of other black inmates in Nazi concentration camps.

I had not written in almost a year. Still, I received the occasional call from an editor asking if I was working on anything. Black people dying in Hitler's death camps to me were worthy of investigation. The research I gathered was raw but still I shared it with an editor in the Post's Outlook section. By week's end, I was on the phone with the editorial assistant of the section asking if I could have the full article ready in a week. Once again I rang up huge telephone bills calling Germany and Israel and speaking with professors at Princeton and other universities. By the end of the following week, I submitted my article, which was followed by a call from the editor with the usual questions and comments.

The telephone rang continuously the Monday following the publication of my article entitled, "Aryan Nation, Germany's Cruel African Heritage."

For the next several weeks, I appeared on both local and national radio stations. The U.S. Holocaust Memorial Museum invited me as a guest lecturer on the subject of blacks in the Holocaust. The lecture was scheduled for the Rubinstein Theater but due to demand was relocated to the larger Meyerhoff. At the end of my lecture, the audience gave me a standing ovation.

My wife and two little children were seated in the first row. I could see by their smiles they were proud. My son, who was six at the time, raced up on the stage and hugged me as the applause continued. A knot formed in my throat, as I thanked the crowd. All I ever wanted to do as a writer was to get one article published in a major newspaper. At this point, I had lost count of how many articles I had published in my years at the Post. On that very special night at the U.S. Holocaust Memorial Museum, my worth-and in some ways my life-was affirmed. I was not one invisible little black boy on a dusty Alabama road. I was a man worthy of being heard, a man to be respected for the knowledge he possessed.

I was invited to speak at Dartmouth, the University of Maryland, Indiana State University and other colleges. Lecturing was not my forte, as I preferred the solitude of writing and to let others debate and discuss the merits of the topic. There were times I was anxious that I might forget a fact or lose my place when reading the text. I didn't want to embarrass my family or make a fool of myself. But as a teen in Alabama, I decided I would never give fear the upper hand or allow it to dictate anything in my life. So now, I followed this credo. Often, I picked up the telephone with the intent of cancelling an appearance, but each time my conviction to never let fear prevail won the debate.

By the time the fervor subsided from the article on blacks in the Holocaust, I had turned my attention to another longtime idea of mine, investigating whether or not slavery still existed in America in the 20th Century. My informal inquiry into this started back in the mid-80s. Now it was time to expand my investigation. First, I flew to Alabama to meet with the man I grew up hearing had been confined for years on a plantation in the Mississippi Delta.

I had other unfinished business in Alabama, too. One night my wife, kids and parents returned from an outing. I was in the house alone when I heard the car drive up. I went out to meet them and was headed back into the house when my father stopped me. I slid in the car on the passenger side.

"Len, I want to talk to you for a minute," he said.

I saw the look of embarrassment plastered on his face. He didn't need to say another word. I knew what was coming next.

"When you and your brothers were kids, I wasn't too good to ya'll and your momma."

I stopped him mid-sentence to spare him the agony.

"Daddy, I forgave you a long time ago. It means a lot to hear you say it, but it really isn't necessary," I said. "You've been great to Dear and you love the kids and Gail. There is no need to speak of this ever again."

I kissed him on his face as he sat looking straight ahead with teary eyes.

"I am so sorry for all of it, Len," he said.

I swore to myself that from that point forward the main focus of my story about him would be one of forgiveness and redemption. My father's words stayed with me for the balance of the evening and on into the night. He must have carried that heavy load for years and I prayed my reaction to his apology would finally bring him peace. It took a lot for him to say those simple words and for once I was proud to be my father's son.

The following morning, I called Cleveland, the man my grandfather said had been held in slavery for years in Mississippi.

Cleveland answered in a curt, sharp voice. I told him what I wanted. To my surprise, he hung up. I called back. His wife answered. I repeated my inquiry regarding her husband's captivity.

"Neither of us have anything to say to you," she said.

Before I could respond, she hung up.

For years after this, my Grandmother and Daddy-Yo tried to arrange a meeting in hopes Cleveland would agree to tell his story, but to no avail.

Daddy-Yo sent me to Bessemer, Alabama, to visit another one of his childhood friends, Booker T. Larken, who was familiar with the story. But he said that in all the years he had known Cleveland, he never talked about his time spent in the Delta.

"He is afraid and has always been afraid that those people who took him away will find him and take him back down to the Delta," said Larken. "White folk down there would have young colored boys staying with them and working for months and you wasn't allowed to talk to them. Then they disappeared."

Some of Daddy-Yo's friends recalled the same in Sumter County, where the boys were kept chained to trees or posts. Over the years I must have visited 20 families in Sumter County, talked with historians at five universities in Alabama and Mississippi, and visited probate offices, libraries and courthouses in several cities.

After a couple of weeks of fruitless long distance calls to historians at Ole Miss, Mississippi State University and The University of Alabama, I returned to Washington wondering if Daddy-Yo's recollections were jaded and obscured. I accumulated huge telephone bills, calling some of Cleveland's and my grandfather's elderly friends. They all were familiar with the incident but for unknown reasons were afraid or just wouldn't discuss it. Professors at the universities had warned me that elderly blacks, especially in the rural South, still maintained what is called "slave plantation mentality." Many of them see whites as overseers and live in fear of retribution should they do anything viewed as disrespectful.

When I wasn't attending to family matters or looking for gainful employment, I was reading books and periodicals on slavery or migrant workers, or on the telephone interviewing people. My search lasted for nearly three additional unproductive years. At times, I felt that Daddy-Yo's memories of slavery after the Emancipation Proclamation existed only in his head.

I grew despondent and was about to give up after nearly eight years of pursuing the topic, but my wife finally convinced me to spend one more day searching the files of the Library of Congress's Manuscript Division. Countless past visits had proven to be useless, but I promised to try again.

I placed a call to the librarian in that division. This time, I requested files that dealt with sharecropping, debt-labor, anything that vaguely resembled slavery in the South from 1921 to 1960. When I arrived a staff person rolled out a two-tier cart filled with gray cardboard file boxes. Many of the documents were of no interest to me. Finally, I came to a container loaded with copies of faded, handwritten notes. The box was labeled "Peonage."

As I read the notes, I cried. I read. I cried. I tried to mask my tears so I would not draw the curiosity of anyone nearby. But I could not hold in the agony. I wept for the mother from Harwell, Georgia, who in 1921 was forced to work the fields from dawn to dark with her five-month-old baby in a box at the end of the row. The cotton rows were so long the woman could not hear the infant crying when the baby fell from the wooden box that cradled her. Red fire ants ate through the baby's nostrils and ears and around her mouth. I wept for the white sheriff down in Livingston, Alabama, who was hung from a bridge for his efforts to free enslaved Negros in the 1920s.

I wept uncontrollably through one heart-wrenching letter after another, all nearly half a century old. I read about strangers who somehow seemed familiar to me.

The librarian came to my cubicle on two occasions to ask if I was okay. My guess is the Library of Congress doesn't often have a large black man sitting in the reading room crying. I called home several times to share with my wife the joy of finding the material and the sadness of the stories I read. I could almost hear the pleadings of a wife from Coffee, Georgia, begging for help in having her husband released from a plantation. I could feel the sensation of my heart pounding in my throat with the turn of each page.

I had found confirmation of the stories my grandfather had told me for years, the stories I had begun to question.

The Library of Congress Manuscript Division's Peonage Files contained thousands of letters dating from the early 1900 to the 1950's. There were cases where blacks were held as slaves all across America up until 1954. It was time to write the story after nearly eight long years. A story of this nature and magnitude should be placed initially in the Black Press, I thought. I began writing the article long before receiving responses from both major and minor black literary and news companies. I just knew the story would be snatched up as soon as an editor read the query. But eventually, each of the black news companies I queried rejected the idea. An editor of Black Enterprise Magazine told me, "Black folk don't want to hear stories about slavery; they are sick of it."

I thought: I am black and I am not tired of hearing about slavery, especially when there's new historical information. I continued trying to sell the story to the black news media but they weren't buying. Finally, as a last resort, I sent the article to the Birmingham World, my small hometown black newspaper. Once again, it was rejected.

It was impossible for me to fathom the idea that not a single black publication in the country valued my work. I gave myself the weekend to ponder whether or not to submit the query to the Washington Post. When I decided to submit it, it was accepted within a couple of hours. Two-time Pulitzer Prize winning writer Gene Weingarten was assigned as my editor.

Gene called me after reading the piece and invited me to his fifth floor office to discuss it. He was amazed and excited by the story. The piece I gave him was a bit less than half of a newspaper page in length. Gene told me to write as much as I wanted, which was nearly three newsprint pages. It took about six weeks for me to complete the story.

"I hope this is not your last piece," said Gene in a telephone conversation after I submitted the final copy. "This is a remarkable piece of work and I hope you will write a lot more."

I had spent thousands of dollars researching the story and I was not going to recoup a fraction of the money. But writing and getting published had never been about the money for me, not even when I dreamed of being published in a major newspaper. Before that first story, yes, publication was my marker of success, proof to myself that I could pursue a goal and succeed. Yet make no mistake, I loved the written word, had always loved it, even when I was a boy. I had always felt I had something to say, too, and using language, beautifully, was a wondrous way to speak to the world. Then when it was clear that I would not be able to help people heal as a priest in the Catholic Church, I knew there was another way-with words. The point of all of my efforts in writing, though, were the stories. They had to be worth telling, had to increase healing, tell an unknown story, offer another side to what we think we know.
This story started because I needed to know if my grandfather's tales were true, and it ended shedding light on an unknown history.

That Sunday morning when the story was finally printed, on Father's Day of 1996, I was visiting my in-laws in Petersburg, Virginia. I got up early to race downtown to the convenience store that carried the Washington Post. My heart filled with pride when I spotted the story on the front page of the Style Section. My brother was waiting tables in an exclusive private club in Birmingham, nearly 800 miles away, when he overheard guests discussing the article.

"My brother wrote the story," he told the guests, proudly.

When I returned to the Post on one of my rare visits, I could hardly make it into the newsroom because people stopped me along the way to comment or give me compliments about the story. I enjoyed another 15 minutes of fame accompanied by the usual television and radio appearances. At the end of one radio interview a caller asked where he could get the article and I gave him the Washington Post switchboard number. Big mistake. When I walked into the newsroom afterwards, the operator yelled, "Leeeeen! What did you do?!"

"I have never seen such a response," she said. She was a little upset with me but that didn't dampen my excitement.

Another evening I received a call from an elderly black woman who claimed to be a resident of Sumter County, Alabama. She excoriated me for writing this article. "Mr. Cooper, you should be ashamed. What you've done will only upset these white folk down here," she said.

Her delivery was calm and sweet, but still I could sense the alarm in her words. She told me I had no idea what I had done. We were both products of Alabama's Jim Crow laws. The last thing I wanted was to hurt people who had suffered more than their share.

While I did not write for money, the reality was thus far I had spent much more on research for my articles than I ever earned upon publication of the story, and this was money my family could use. The financial strain had increased now that I did not have a fulltime job, so I decided to explore other career interests. A few months after my story on extended slavery ran, I accepted a position to work as an instructor for a Virginia-based, computer-training company. I had already started spending less time writing and more time in my basement tinkering with old computers and learning to repair my own system. When the computer company hired me as an instructor, we started out on the wrong foot.

"Mr. Cooper, I hear you used to write stories for the newspaper," Paul, the owner, inquired.

"Yes I did, for a number of years," I replied.

"When did you last publish?" he asked.

"Perhaps a year or so ago I believe," I said.

"Good!" he shouted, slapping his knees. "That way you won't have to waste your time writing and you can spend more time prepping to teach more classes."

I thought he was an insensitive idiot. But I needed this job so I kept my thoughts to myself.

Anyway, I felt as though I had outgrown the Washington Post Newsroom. I didn't want to write simple articles anymore; I wanted to write long historical pieces that would be significant a hundred years from today. But the Post didn't see me as capable. So it was time to move on.

My new job required that I teach all levels of Microsoft Office Suite software. I had long ago insisted that my children be computer savvy at an early age. I also used our home circuit to teach myself the rudiments of maintaining a computer network. Our house was wired, with each family member's computer having Internet service and printers, switches and routers. At the time, most homes simply had Internet service along with one or two computers.

My early days at the training company were taxing because much of my time was spent in seclusion, cramming in preparation to teach Microsoft Word, Excel, PowerPoint, WordPerfect and other computer applications. I received high marks on my evaluations from students. After I had been on the job a year, I traveled throughout the Washington, D.C. area, teaching courses to some of the company's most loyal and important clients, work normally reserved for only the best trainers. Although the hours were long and difficult, I found pleasure in advancing my computer knowledge.

One evening I arrived home to find my wife and her best friend, Sharon, in the living room waiting for me. They were grinning and I got the sense they were up to something. Gail was all dressed up and wearing the red lipstick she knew I loved. She welcomed me with a kiss and embrace.

"Congratulations," she said.

"Congratulations for what?" I asked, while hanging my coat and hat in the hall closet.

"I got a phone call today from the National Association of Black Journalists saying you won a worldwide journalism competition for your article, "The Damned.'"

"Oh, really?" I responded, showing no interest.

Gail and Sharon glanced at each other.

""I'm neither a writer nor a journalist," I said. "Well, the National Association of Black Journalists wants you to come to Chicago to accept your prize and give a brief acceptance speech."

"You're kidding, right?" I said.

I reminded Gail and her friend that it wasn't so long ago that every black publication I submitted the article to had no interest in it and now they dared to ask me to come to Chicago to accept some stupid award.

"To hell with those Negroes!" I said.

I had no intentions of going to Chicago. As I saw it, the black news establishment had rejected both my work and me. Once the article ran in the Post, it appeared that this legitimized my writing. I wanted no part of NABJ. I didn't even know how the story ended up being submitted for the competition.

I thought this was my final word on the subject, but the question of whether or not to go kept returning to my mind over the next few days-until I found myself saying: if the Post was gracious enough to print my article and deemed it worthy to submit to the NABJ, then it was my duty to accept the award on behalf of the company.

I arrived in Chicago the day of the awards ceremony. The people at the NABJ convention had been partying and celebrating all week. I was told I had missed President Clinton, Oprah Winfrey and a few others who made perfunctory appearances. I was not impressed or phased one iota. When I arrived at the entrance to the hall, I gave my name and told the attendant I was there for the awards ceremony. The gentleman inside the booth checked his list and apologized that my name was not on it. "Sorry," he said. I was relieved.

"Please make a note that Len Cooper came by and I will be leaving for the airport," I said.

He asked me to wait as he made a telephone call. He had barely put the phone down when two beautiful women in evening gowns came out and escorted me to a roped in area. I was surprised to see journalists of all different races from all over the world. As I saw it, many of the people there seemed rather impressed with themselves. I kept my harsh critique to myself as I made my way through the crowd, rubbing shoulders with people I both detested and secretly admired. I was conflicted and it was hard to enjoy the moment with an internal debate going on inside me. I wanted so desperately to be one of them, but it seemed no matter what I did, I remained on the outside of the circle of writers and journalists.

Now those who summarily rejected it without serious consideration were celebrating my article. I can't understand it now and certainly couldn't understand it back then. I became a cauldron of unsettling emotions, not knowing whether to laugh or cry. I was so angry with these black people, my own people. But after deeper and more honest deliberation, I entertained the possibility that perhaps they weren't so bad. Through the prism of my pain and disappointments, I relived the sting of each and every rejection letter again and again. I wasn't willing to give them that "half a chance" or "the benefit of the doubt." The pain I felt for years of not quite measuring up as a writer was mine and I saw the people in that room as grand contributors to my years of rejection and nullification. Yet, I have always been quick to forgive and rarely harbor anger. And if I truly disliked the black journalists in that room that night in Chicago, I would have never agreed to come. In truth, I wanted to be there and at least for one night feel counted among them.

Still, I felt miserably out of place. For the first time, I truly enjoyed telling any journalist who approached me that I was a press operator and did not write for anybody. I suppose it was my way of saying, "See, what you do isn't so difficult."

Looking back, I realize my snide remarks actually revealed my own self-esteem issues. Nevertheless, some of the expressions I received were priceless. Once I revealed I was a lowly press operator, the conversation generally lagged and soon halted. In fairness, some people were delighted and intrigued to meet a press operator-turned-writer. But my spirit was tender after years of soaking in rejection. I was not on solid ground when it came to knowing who I was. I was teetering between who I wished I was and who I really was, which was more than enough, if only I had understood that at the time.

My inner personal conflict stopped me from seeing that wonderful night in the correct light. The truth was those people present that night probably had nothing to do with my story getting rejected from black publications.

I was talking with a friend when I heard, "Len Cooper!" and looked to the stage. I wasn't surprised I had won because I had been notified weeks in advance that my peonage story had won first place in the features category. Still, hearing my name and seeing my article on the big screen in the hall was an out of body experience. I walked toward the stage. A young woman in a long evening dressed unhooked the red velvet rope and took me by the arm to escort me. On stage, I looked out at the crowd that was cheering and applauding madly. For a moment tears welled in my eyes. Any animosity I had left me. I thanked several Post staffers for their continual support. In closing, I asked the audience one simple question: "If we don't tell our story, then who will?" A woman gave me my plaque, we posed for a photo and I left the stage, hardly having time to let the moment soak in.

More parties and festivities were scheduled for the evening, but I missed them all. I returned to my hotel, called Gail, lay on the unmade bed and watched the TV. I flew home the following morning.

I received the journalism award in June of 1997, the same summer my father-in-law was diagnosed with Alzheimer's. He and I had drawn up a preliminary plan for starting an American School in Jerusalem. Within just eight months, he had times when he didn't even know his own name. Gail's mother was having a difficult time taking care of him in their Petersburg, Virginia home. So shortly after I returned from the NABJ awards ceremony, Gail and the kids went to Petersburg to lend a hand and to give her mother some much needed rest. After they had been there for a week or so, I drove down to get the kids so they could return home and resume a reasonably normal life.

CHAPTER 21: DEATH AND DYING

I arrived on a Wednesday, the very day my mother-in-law and Gail were returning from my mother-in-law's visit to an oncologist for a consultation for a biopsy.

I took her hand to help her from the car, as I ordinarily would. "Hi Ola, how you doing?" I asked.

"Not good," she replied. "The doctor told me it's liver cancer and I have four to six months left."

I was stunned by the news and by the monotone casualness with which she delivered the news. There was no outward evidence that anything was wrong with Ola. She cooked and cleaned and got about as well as any 70-year-old. She had never complained to either of us about any discomfort. There must be a mistake, I thought.

There wasn't much talking as Ola and Gail moved about the kitchen, preparing lunches for the children to eat during the long drive back to Maryland. Ola's mood went from an intense smile one second to a darkened somber look the next. Gail and I looked on helplessly, not knowing what to say or do.

We all decided not to tell Gail's father, Ed, about Ola's diagnosis yet because there were moments he didn't know Ola and denied even being married. As planned, Gail and the kids left and I was alone to care for her parents. I stood with both my in-laws in their yard, waving vigorously as Gail and the children drove away. I loved my in-laws dearly and didn't mind staying behind to care for them. Each day, I cooked, cleaned, shaved and bathed my father-in-law. At times he was incontinent.

On my third day, a Saturday morning, Gail's mother was in bed and asked me to cook toast and ham for her and Ed. I prepared the breakfast and served them as they watched their Saturday morning shows. She took a couple of tablespoons full of Pepto-Bismol for a mild abdominal pain, but the pain steadily grew.

"I'm calling the doctor," I said.

"No Len, don't!" Ola replied. "Give me a few minutes. I'm sure it'll stop."

She turned over on her side, faced the window, stretched out her arm and began waving her hand back and forth in as slow deliberate motion.

"Len, do you see her?" she asked, while moving her hand back and forth as if to clear the mist for a better view. "This is my sister," she uttered, completely calm with a broad smile shining from ear to ear.

"No, Ola, I don't see her," I replied.

Then her pain returned. I called 911 and in a few moments sirens blared in the distance. I made a hasty call to Gail, who said she and the kids would leave immediately and arrive in a few hours.

Ola was a stately, well-educated woman from a proud Virginia family, so it must have been difficult for her to ask me to help change her under garments before the paramedics arrived, but she did. There was no time for foolish pride on my part either. As we maneuvered her clothes, I kept the blanket over her and my eyes never left hers. This small victory was monumental for her.

She continued complaining about the growing discomfort in her right side until the ambulance arrived and whisked her away to the hospital. I remained in the house with Ed. Some of Ola's friends, people Gail had known since she was a child, went to the hospital to be with Ola and wait for Gail and the kids to arrive.

Gail drove as fast as she could and was almost at her mother's hospital room, when one of Ola's friend's stopped her in the hallway to tell her that her mother had died shortly after she was admitted to the hospital. I was at the house with Ed when I received a call from Gail informing me of her mother's death.

"My mother is dead," Gail softly said. "I didn't make it in time, but her friends were there." I could hear the sadness in her voice.

"I am so sorry," I said. "Just tell me what you want me to do."

Ola and Ed thought of everything when it came to making their own funeral arrangements. After Ola died all Gail needed to do was notify the pastor. Educators throughout the Richmond, Virginia area attended the services. It broke my heart to see Ed confused, not understanding who had died.

I remained in Petersburg with him for another month. The cruel thing about Alzheimer's was there were moments when he was lucid and at those times he asked for Ola and we told him that she had passed. For a moment he wept for his love. But within a short time, the Alzheimer's swallowed without discernment all memories, both painful and joyful ones. Still, the maddening illness made Ed relive his loss every few days.

After a month, Gail and I decided to bring her father to live with us in our home in Rockville, Maryland. Gail and I gave her father our bedroom and we slept on the living room floor. Every evening just before sundown, Ed gathered his hat and coat and headed for the door. We caught pure hell trying to convince him not to leave the house. He viewed our home as a hotel or his office at the university.

Some nights we spent hours getting him ready for bed, only to find him in the bathroom a few minutes later trying to dump the dresser drawer contents into the toilet. Sometimes we laughed when we found him sitting in a chair in front of the mirror talking to his reflection, which he called "Penny." The next minute we were in near tears, watching him trying to climb stairs or open a door that was just a reflection. Most days were tolerable, as our emotions ran from finding the laughter to being melancholy about what was lost.

But one evening Ed did something he had never done before. He was conducting an imaginary board meeting at the kitchen table. My daughter Kristina, who was 14 at the time, interrupted him to ask to be excused from the meeting. Ed jumped up and before we could stop him, grabbed my daughter from behind and choked her. I had to forcibly pry his forearm from across her throat. Freed, she cried as she ran off to her room and slammed the door. It took both Gail and me to calm Ed as my son, Ariel, looked on.

I was surprised to find after this event that the kids still liked being with Ed. They understood his illness and tried to be good sports, pitching in when asked.

Later that same night, I came into the kitchen and stopped him from swallowing his wristwatch. We realized we could no longer care for this man we all loved. For his safety and the safety of my family, it was time to put Ed in a home so he could get the professional help he needed.

We found a place not far from us, an elegant old single level brick nursing home with gardens and trees surrounding it.

For nearly two years, I visited Ed daily. The staff at the nursing home made it painfully clear, that I could not show up unannounced, but had to call before each visit. I heard rumors that patients in nursing homes were mistreated and neglected by staff members and would only clean the patients or their living quarters if they were expecting visitors. I wasn't going to let this happen to Ed. The staffers at the nursing home never knew when I would show up. I figured Ed was paying $7,000 a month for this care, so I could visit whenever I felt the need, or I would find a facility that agreed to my terms. The facility continued complaining about my random visits and I continued showing up unannounced.

Meanwhile, in the midst of caring for my in-laws, I received a letter of termination from my employer at the computer training company. I was shocked. The company had cleared me to be off without pay for several months. I wasn't overly concerned. I was too busy to look for another job or contest the company's decision to fire me without notice. All of my time was spent looking after Ed and attending to his affairs.

But once Ed was settled in his new home, it was time for me to find work. I applied for a dozen jobs and was interviewed and rejected for each one. I made daily phone calls. I answered ads and pounded on doors. But months passed without any prospect of work.

Then I remembered that while I was working for the computer training company that fired me, their clients often asked me if I could work as an independent contractor and teach their staff. So I made a few calls and launched my own business--Great Linx Computer Training Company. I got plenty of business immediately, yet no matter how many hours I spent on the business,

I always made time to cut Ed's hair or nails or give him a massage.

Then late one afternoon in the fall of 1999, I was sitting in the bed at the nursing home with Ed. I held him in my arms, rocking him. The doctors had just left the room after telling me Ed was going to die soon. The hospice aide had just finished Ed's daily shave. Ed, who had retired as the dean of the business school at Virginia State University, was now just bones with little flesh.

As I rocked him, Ed grabbed my shirt and pulled me closer to him. I felt his life slipping away. Tears ran down my face.

I felt his body wrenching. I continued to rock. I pulled him closer. My tears dripped on his gown. Then after a few minutes, he was still. I pulled him away from my chest. His eyes seemed fixed on some faraway place. He thrashed once more. I held him tight until he stopped and it was quiet. Ed was still.

I had convinced Gail not to visit the nursing home during her father's final hours. She and the kids did not need to see this. I questioned God again. What lesson was to be learned from a decent and kind man dying such a horrific death? Where was God's mercy, kindness and benevolence in this moment? I didn't understand any of it.

It was September when Ed died. Once again, I needed a distraction. It was time to bury myself in work and as providence would have it, the business was going reasonably well.

In the span of two years, Gail loss both parents and several uncles and underwent major surgery herself. When life finally settled down, though we were still mourning, we worked on healing and rebuilding our family. Everyone seemed to have drifted apart during the long call of death. Together, we were in family counseling and the children saw the therapist alone, one-on-one.

Meanwhile I recognized that something in me had changed. In our first two years as a married couple, I had my doubts about my relationship with Gail. But with time I learned to love and adore her. Now I viewed her as a dear friend and not so much as a wife. Still, I tried every day to recapture that feeling that was lost.

In early December of 2000, I received an invitation to a wedding in Israel. It came in a call from my longtime friend Yafit Halevy, who at the age of seven took me, to her family's house after she found me when I left my camp site in a nearby schoolyard. Over the years, I had continued close ties with her family. Now she called, requesting me to come to Israel to participate in her wedding celebration.

I considered the troubling accounts of the crumbling peace initiative and escalating tension between Israel and Arab countries, but none of that was enough to keep me away.

"When I was little, you promised to come to my wedding," she reminded me.

"There's no way I would miss it," I assured her.

Gail agreed that I should go. I would only be away for a week, which meant that I would miss just one session with the therapist.

I arrived in Jerusalem the day before the wedding in time for the henna party, an ancient Jewish custom that is a symbol of unity. I felt honored to be included since normally only family members are invited to this event. Both the bride and groom were dressed in white clothes embroidered in golden lace. Designated women strolled about the room, placing a wad of red henna mud in the palm of each guest's hands. They then wrapped the hands with a white cloth. After 15 or 20 minutes, the wrap is removed, leaving a red round stain in the center of the palm.

The day of the wedding, I spent much of my time with the Halevy's or visiting other friends in Jerusalem. That night the ballroom was decorated in an ancient Egyptian motif with beautiful statues and columns. There was enough food to feed a small army. Yafit's mother was positioned by the door, as friends and family members handed her envelopes with a check or cash tucked inside. Kobi, the father of the bride, stood nearby, beaming with pride as he shook hands and welcomed guests. Once the music began, the dancing started and didn't stop until the wee hours of the morning. The final dance was for family members only. Kobi, insisted I join them in the middle of the dance floor. We formed a circle, locking arms around each other's shoulders as somber violin music filled the hall. We swayed side to side to the soft rhythm. Yafit's magnificent smile closed the evening, as she stood in the middle of the dance floor alone, thanking and saying goodbye to her guests.

Early the next morning, I received a call from Yafit asking me to meet her at her mother's home. At the house, she and I and the groom piled in to a small compact car and raced to his parent's home across town. Although Yafit was a newlywed, she insisted I spend most of my remaining time in Israel with her while she opened presents, visited family and counted money gifts. I gladly complied. For the rest of the trip, it seemed Yafit would not make a move unless I was with her. That seven-year-old girl who brought me home with her 18 years earlier had grown into a beautiful woman. I was extremely happy for her. But for me, the celebration was tempered by the fact that in a few hours I had to leave this land and the people I love.

The following morning I rose early with the Jerusalem sun. My flight back to the U.S. was scheduled for the afternoon, which allotted time for a final stroll through downtown, known as the Mid Rehov. Ben Yehuda Street is a popular shopping and restaurant area in Jerusalem. Since my arrival I had gone daily to King David's Treasures gift shop to have the shopkeeper show me the same piece of jewelry. I was unable to make up my mind whether or not to purchase it, a gold chain with a mezuzah. Avi, the owner of the shop, gave me his best price; still, I couldn't justify spending $363 for jewelry. Earlier, I had purchased my wife a pair of 18kt gold Yemenite earrings and many other pieces of jewelry. I browsed the store over his prayer shawls, doorpost mezuzahs, Kiddush cups and other shiny Judaica. As I was about to leave, he handed me a small package.

"Here is my card, when you get back to the States or when you come for another visit, pay me then," he said.

I was shocked. He only knew me from those few visits to his shop.

"How do you know I won't just keep it and never see you again?" I asked.

"You won't," he replied, smiling over his black-framed glasses, handing me a business card.

And it was true. I would never steal from him or anyone else. Months later, I paid Avi on my next visit to Israel. And to this day, he and I are very good friends.

Several months after I returned home, I was watching the news and saw that the same event hall dance floor where Yafit had her wedding had collapsed, killing 24 and injuring 400 Israelis attending another wedding.

Today, Yafit, the big-hearted child who saved me by bringing me home to her family, is the mother of seven children. While the stains from the henna party have long since faded from the palms of my hands, Yafit remains an indelible part of my life.

My mother loved to hear about my little adventures in Israel. There were moments when we stayed on the phone for what seemed like hours, as she listened attentively to me rattle on about the exotic foods and places I experienced regularly in Jerusalem. The thought that her son walked where Jesus walked and trotted the same paths of the prophets brought her such joy. I couldn't wait to call her and also tell her of my upcoming trip home to Alabama.

I always felt sad and empty upon my return home to Maryland, even with my beloved family waiting. In time the emptiness passes, but the longing for Jerusalem is constant.

In my home, Judaica, incenses, menorahs and more, all reminders of how much I longed to live in Jerusalem surrounded me. I was sitting at the desk in the kitchen, intoxicated by the melodic voice of Sarah Brightman playing on the computer. Gail and the kids were meandering about the house, attending to their own particular interests. I couldn't get enough of her rendition of Pie Jesu. The Latin chant emptied and refilled the room over again and again. Then the telephone rang. It was Dear. I was overjoyed. But I could hear that something was wrong. I kept quiet and allowed her to speak.

"Hey Dear, How ya doing?" I asked.

"I reckon I'm doing okay," she replied. But I heard sadness in her voice.

"The doctor told me that soreness in my stomach is cancer and nothing can be done."

She said it just like that. Succinct. Hardly a breath in between her words. Maybe she felt pressured to get it out.

I could not speak. I hoped she could not hear me gasping for air. The tears flowed from my eyes, spilling into my lap.

She continued. "They said I'd be gone in about four to six months."

A friend who was a doctor and familiar with her case later told me, "Your mother is entering into the darkest realm of her life." The disease was diagnosed as Stage IV metastatic ovarian cancer. When I consulted another doctor a couple of days later, he said, "Your mother will die a horrible death."

"Len, when I get off this phone, I need to get back to sewing those robes for the youth choir," she said.

I still could not speak. I contemplated that working toward completing her sewing brought her comfort.

"Dear, I'll be there in three days, after I take care of a few things," I said.

"I baked your favorite sweet potato pie and I'm leaving one on the table to cool, just the way you like it," she said. "I love you, Len."

"I love you too, Dear."

Then she hung up and my depression deepened and darkened over the next few hours and the remainder of the day. My children and wife watched me slowly come undone. I fought back the tears, but there was nothing I could do to stop the pain in my heart. Gail and the children needed me to be whole, so I felt as though I needed to put off my grieving for a while. Gail and the kids were already grieving and I certainly did not want them worrying about me.

Dear found peace in her church, scripture and preacher. She was a firm believer in God, but God and I had parted ways a long time ago. I had no interest or curiosity in God, the Bible, religion or any of its trappings, but I would try anything that might spare my mother the agony she was about to face. I was willing to fall down on my knees and beg Dear's God for forgiveness once more. I excused myself to the basement of our home, slamming the door shut behind me. I lay prostrate on the cold gray cement floor, begging and pleading with God to intercede. I was not reassured. I did not feel peace.

The next morning, I was up early making breakfast for the family. I had nothing to say as I went through the motions of being a good father and husband. I insisted the kids visit with their neighborhood friends, hoping to keep their lives and schedules as close to normal as possible.

"Daddy, I am so sorry to hear about Dear," my daughter said. "Grandmommy and granddaddy, now Dear. I feel bad. But I really feel sad for you."

My children had met my mother only three times in their lives. Dear came to visit us just once in our home in Maryland. Dear and Daddy stayed close to their home to help look out for her parents, who were up in age. I did take the children down to Alabama to visit on a couple of occasions. But it was a flight or a 14-hour drive. Regrettably, they were not close to my parents like they were to Gail's parents, who lived in Petersburg, Virginia, only three hours away.

Gail was supportive. "Go to Birmingham and stay as long as you need," she said.

Before I left, I spent my days in silence, unable to speak. I was broken inside.

One morning I returned to my usual place at the computer to once again listen to Pie Jesu. A few minutes passed and once again the phone interrupted my solitude. The person on the other end was barely audible. I heard an occasional word or utterance, but I recognized the voice as that of my older brother, Archie.

"Archie, is everything ok?" I asked.

There was no response, just deep breaths. I ask again.

"No, Len! No!"

I stood up from the computer.

"Archie, what's happening? Is everybody ok?"

"She's dead, Len!"

My heart dropped. The telephone crashed to the floor. I hesitated, and then picked it up again.

"Dear's dead, Len! She's dead!" My brother screamed.

I kept thinking: "How can this be?" I had just talked with her yesterday morning and she told me she was going in for her first chemo treatment today and the doctors were hopeful it would give her a couple of more months. She couldn't be dead. There had to be a mistake. Yet, I heard my father sobbing in the background.

"There's been an accident and she's dead, Len!" my brother shouted, while sobbing.

That morning, January 2, 2001, changed me forever. It seems my brother had arrived at the house to take Dear to her first cancer treatment. My sister-in-law was supposed to take her but never showed up. Archie was driving my grandmother's old 1970-something Mercury Grand Marquis. As they traversed the winding, mountainous roads of Warrior, Alabama, Dear became more and more agitated by the discomfort of the seat belt rubbing against the wound made by the biopsy incision. The moment she removed the belt, the car fishtailed and went into a spin. The passenger side door flew open and she fell out and over an embankment. She called out my brother's' name and reached for him. It was all so quick, so surreal, my brother said. The car came to rest upside down on top of her. My brother was hanging upside down in the car by his seatbelt. He managed to free himself, then climbed through the broken window and tried with all his might to free her. She reassured him she was okay, if he could move the car a bit off of her chest so she could catch her breath. But the car wouldn't budge. He climbed out of the ravine and frantically screamed for help. Witnesses stopped and offered assistance.

But it was too late. Dear was dead.

Dear and Dad's house was about five miles from the site of the accident. Archie called Dad before calling me. Dad followed the ambulance to the hospital, but could not bring himself to go into the room to view mother's lifeless body.

"When I got to the hospital, the doctors asked me if I wanted to see her," my father told me. "I wanted to, but I just wouldn't be able to stand seeing her like that," he said.

Stunned by the sudden loss of his lifelong love, Daddy drove around North Birmingham until he parked in front of the five-and-dime store where Dear worked for more than 25 years. He entered the shop where he and the owner greeted each other by first name. Daddy told the owner that he needed a battery for his watch and that Marie had been killed in an accident. The owner replied, "Marie was just in here yesterday and bought $9 worth of stockings on credit, now who is going to pay for them?"

Through his immeasurable pain and tears, Daddy told me he peeled off a ten-dollar bill and walked out of the store.

I arrived in Birmingham that Thursday, as planned. I couldn't bring myself to go to my parents' house. I checked into a hotel on the campus of the University of Alabama-Birmingham. But the thought of my father grieving alone in those backwoods weighed heavy on my mind. As night fell, I pushed my sadness aside and drove 31 miles to Hayden, Alabama, to see him. I knew he needed me to be strong.

Through barren trees, I saw the house, which sits a couple of hundred feet back off the main road. It was pitch black. Through the window, a dim, solitary light shone. I knew Dad was grieving heavily.

I sat in the car crying so hard my stomach and head throbbed. I couldn't bring myself to get out of the car and knock on his door. I thought how it is true that God's ways are not our ways, because I certainly didn't see the reasoning or logic in any of this. I must have sat on that country roadside for an hour. I was completely wrapped and entangled in my grief. Finally, I started the car and returned to my room at the university. There was no peace waiting for me in the night or in my sleep. I felt horrible leaving my father alone in those backwoods to grieve. The very next morning I showered and returned to my parent's home. This time I knocked on the door without hesitation.

I could hear my father sobbing as he fumbled with the lock on the inside, trying to open the door.

"Len!" he cried as he lunged towards me and wrapped both arms around me, burying his face and tears in my chest.

"Len. Len. Len," he said repeatedly through his uncontrollable sobbing.

I sat with my father in the living room before the large crackling gas heater. I rubbed his head, telling him that "Everything is going to be alright." I looked towards the dining room to the left and saw the pie my mother baked for me sitting under a glass-covered dish.

I slowly rose from the plastic covered white sofa and made my way to the dining room. I sat and stared at that sweet potato pie for a few minutes. One piece was missing; I assume Dear had sampled it to make certain it was perfect. It was. I didn't bother getting a knife and fork. I broke it off, bit by bit and devoured it, savoring every single morsel. My father looked at me. My face soaked with tears. He called my name, softly. "Len."

I could not imagine life without Dear. A part of me died the day she left. My wife reminded me years later in family counseling that the day I left for the funeral was the last time I touched her the way a husband touches his wife. She was probably right; I had not caressed her, kissed her, or loved her. I cried in that therapy session. I knew no matter how much time we spent with the therapist; he could not make me feel again what I could not feel. I was not bitter, just void of an emotional connection. The pain of my mother's death ran deep inside of me. When my children began acting out as teens often do, I wanted them to hurt as much as I did. Rather than responding to my daughter's teen craziness as a loving father, I threatened to put her out in the streets. My son probably was hurt the worst of all. I completely neglected him. I went for days without talking to him, unless it was yelling or screaming at him for something trivial. I became a horrible husband and an even worse father.

I thought about that day I begged God to deliver my mother from the suffering that was to come with her cancer. The very next day she was dead. Maybe this was the way God chose to answer my prayer. I thought about this many times. Normally, I am not one to question the mysterious ways of God. But I asked: Where is the grace in my brother having to witness his mother trapped under a 1,800-pound car and being helpless to do anything as she died? Where is the grace in my brother having to relive that memory over and over again?

The day of the funeral, family and friends gathered in front of Archie's home in Birmingham.

"The way she died was a gift from God," one woman said.

"Amen,"whispered another. "She didn't have to suffer."

Archie and I excused ourselves from the crowd, walking out into the yard on the side of the house. I could see that Archie was in agony. He tightly clutched the front of his shirt and doubled over in pain.

"Len they weren't there, none of them were there. I was there! I was there!" He screamed.

He cried as I helplessly looked on. My brother was still waiting for the grace that people spoke of, to experience the blessing proclaimed by people who didn't witness my mother moaning for help or reaching for my brother's unreachable hand. This is what he would have to live with all of his life. And I didn't see the grace or blessing in any of it.

Before the funeral began, I swore to myself that my last memory of my mother would not be an image of her lying cold and gray in a coffin. I explained my position to my brother and relatives prior to the funeral and at the time no one objected.

As the funeral started and relatives walked in, I patiently stood outside the vestibule while others viewed Dear's body. People peered into Dear's face and scanned her outfit. I imagined they were judging her appearance.

After the last person had viewed her body and they were about to seal the casket, relatives rushed out of the church to find me before they were going to seal the coffin forever. They insisted I pay final respects to my mother.

"Don't you want to see your momma and say bye to her?" a cousin asked.

"I have fond memories of my mother and I don't want that image of her dead body seared into my head for all eternity," I explained.

They would not accept my explanation. Two of my cousins grabbed me by both arms and pulled me to the door. A couple of female relatives stood by watching. Rather than make a scene, I agreed to go willingly. But I was angry. All I could think was, "These country-ass Negroes. I walked pass my mother's casket, paused momentarily, trying my best not to see Dear although my eyes were wide open. One cousin placed her heavy arms around me and said, "Go on, it's okay to cry."

I had no intentions of crying. I was cried out. Of all the places on the planet, this was the last place I wanted to be. I took my seat on the front row with my father and my brother.

Well-intentioned family members believed that forcing me to look upon my dead mother was best for me. Now all my thoughts and memories of Dear are tied to what I saw, looking down at her lifeless, cold body in that white casket. My middle brother, Alfred, came to the church, but refused to come inside. He headed home to Texas, before the service concluded or any of us had a chance to speak with him.

In some southern black congregations, a funeral is not complete and the preacher has not done his job unless a few sisters shout and fall out in the aisles. Dear's place of worship was one of those churches. My brother and I had already discussed that we did not want any of that at Dear's funeral. I discreetly passed our wishes on to the preacher before the ceremony. During the service whenever I thought the good reverend was heading down that path, I stared him down while shaking my head.

I was ready to stop the service if it meant sparing my father one second less of unnecessary anguish. He had already confided in me that parts of his body had been numb since the day of the accident.

"I hope the preacher will be brief and not get everybody worked up," he said.

I was going to make certain he got his wishes. Nevertheless, others in the congregation egged on the pastor, shouting, "Amen!' and standing and waving their arms.

The ride to the cemetery took about 20 minutes. My brother and I, along with close cousins, served as pallbearers. The graveside service was short but far from painless. I know that friends and relatives saw me as cold and void of emotions.

"You are very composed for someone who knows he will never see his mother again," one relative said.

I didn't care what they thought. I was focused on one person, my father. I had to remain strong or pretend to be strong for him.

Finally, the crowd dispersed and I, my father and brother, and several other stragglers were left alone in the quiet. It was a beautiful sunny day. Elmwood is the most popular cemetery in all of Birmingham, with beautiful flowers and well-kept evergreens. While my father and brother said goodbye and thanked the people, I found three medium size red stones on the mound of earth near Dear's final resting place. I placed each one in a line on the white casket. Then, slowly, the coffin was lowered into the ground.

I watched, swearing to myself, "I will never return to this grave."

For the next few days, I remained on the farm with my father. At night I heard him crying in the room next to mine. I found comfort sleeping in Dear's sewing room, by her hairbrush filled with strands of her hair, engulfed by air that still smelled like her perfume; where the clothes remained as if she had just walked away, some still hanging on the line and others in the dryer. There was no escaping the memories and I did not want to. The memories comforted me, but for my father they were reminders of the reality that the woman he came to cherish was gone forever.

The morning following the funeral, I decided to visit the accident site. I drove up the winding country road and parked the car about 100 yards from where the accident took place. I stood there, looking down in the ravine. I don't know what I expected to see, but what I saw was my mother's knitted shawl she made, one black loafer, and a few small pieces of paper that possibly fell from her purse. I could not move. Standing there, I wept. I can't remember how long I stood there. I became aware of my phone ringing. At first it sounded like it was in the distance, then louder, my pants pocket vibrating. I answered. It was my best friend, Juan.

"I've been looking for you. Where are you?" he asked.

"I am looking at Dear's stuff in the hole where she died."

"Listen to me Len! Leave that place right now!" Juan screamed. "Do you understand? Turn and walk away. You don't need to be there!"

For that surreal moment, Juan's voice was a beacon of light. I was marooned on the darkened shores of despair. His instructions were a lifeline, reeling me in from the depths of my sorrow.

I made my way to my car. As I left, I added to my new list one more place on this earth that I would never visit again.

I returned to my father's and found him sitting alone on the porch outside. January in Alabama is usually brutal, but during this time the weather was warm like a spring day. I joined my father as we sat quietly. Soon, a black mid-size automobile drove up the dirt and gravel drive. A rather burly white fellow dressed in jeans emerged and politely greeted us.

"Good morning. How ya'll doing?" he said in a rich southern drawl.

"We are well," I replied. "And you are?"

"I knew Mrs. Cooper,..." he said, as I stopped him mid-sentence.

"Please come sit with us," I replied, clearing a chair for him. He climbed the few wooden steps and sat.

We made small talk about the agreeable weather for a few minutes. There was a little light-hearted laughter between he and I, as my father sat silent with his eyes focused towards the floor. I observed the man trying to be inconspicuous as he scanned the property and made an occasional entry in a small notebook. He was particularly interested in the doublewide trailer parked next to the house as his eyes lingered. Dear bought that trailer for my grandmother to live in after my grandfather passed, but it was never used.

"Now tell me, how do you know my mother?" I asked.

The man grinned and said, "I talked with your mother a few times every now..."

"Wait a minute," I angrily replied. "You've never met my mother and you don't know her. What is your interest in that trailer? I see you keep staring at it and writing something in that friggin' notebook!"

I paused as I remembered something from a conversation with my Father.

"Wait a second! You're the repo man and you're here to look at my father's property in case you have to repossess that damn trailer!" I shouted.

I stood up, my father, hearing the anger in my voice, grabbed me by the arm.

"I think you'd better leave and leave quickly!" I shouted with my fist clinched. "I swear to you before God I will not ask you again!"

The man jumped up from the porch and ran down the wooden stairs and into his car.

"I'm just doing my job!" he shouted as he drove away.

My father held my arm even tighter. And it's good he did because the car stopped at the end of the drive and the man removed a small camera, snapping a few pictures. I could have easily thrown stones at him to chase him off the grounds.

A few days later, it was time for me to return to my life in Maryland. I kissed my father goodbye as tears fell down both our cheeks.

"I love you Daddy and I will call you and come back as soon as I can," I said.

He just shook his head in agreement. There was no need for words. We knew we suffered from the same loss, only from different perspectives. For me, leaving him there in the woods alone was one of the most painful moments of my life.

My little computer training enterprise required all of my attention. My customer list included the National Endowment for the Arts, National Labor Relations Board, law and accounting firms, and the D.C. Housing Authority. The National Endowment was my largest customer, paying nearly $1,000 a day for my instructions in Microsoft Office software programs. I paid my instructors $400 a day to teach classes. I never had a problem getting contractors to instruct courses.

I was teaching one class at the National Endowment when a uniformed building security guard entered the class and interrupted the course.

"Please gather your things and leave the building immediately," he said, while pointing towards the door. "What's going on? What's happening," an Endowment employee asked. "Please do not ask any questions, just leave the building immediately," he said, again hurrying us to get out. As we walked towards the stairs, a crowd was lingering by the window facing the Pentagon. Smoke was bellowing from the building in the distance.

"A plane flew into the side of the Pentagon and the World Trade Center in New York," someone said. We rushed down the stairs to leave the building. It was September 11, 2001, the day of the terrorist attack.

After that day, the majority of my clients no longer saw computer training as a priority, so the contracts were not renewed. I was told all training was placed on hold until further notice. This left me with no business and no source of income.

A month later, I was sitting in front of my house lamenting over the downturn in the business when my 13-year-old son, who was sitting with me, said, "Dad, why don't we make signs saying that you fix computers."

He and I rushed off to Home Depot to buy white board, spray paint and stencils. Once we finished making the signs, we placed them in strategic areas throughout the neighborhood. The selling point was that all work was guaranteed the same day and if the customer was not satisfied with all aspects of the job, there was no charge. Shortly after the signs went up, I had new clients and a new business.

One of the benefits of running my own computer business was that I acquired computers, printers and monitors that were in pretty fair condition. I had clients who wanted me to dispose of new systems simply because they didn't think a computer was fast enough or because a friend recommended a different one. As part of the business, I found underprivileged children and families, and gave them these used computer systems.

Business was going reasonably well and I was burned out from late nights spent worrying about keeping the family and the business financially afloat. The business alone did not provide enough revenue to sustain us. Thank goodness Gail still had her job with the government. Together, we managed to maintain a near normal lifestyle.

Gail must have seen changes in me that I was completely oblivious of. To get me out of the house, she gave me a voucher to attend an evening continuing education class for A+ and Microsoft Certified Systems Engineer (MCSE), offered through Howard University. I had no interest in taking a class of any kind.

"Well, if you don't find the course agreeable, you can quit after one meeting,' Gail said.

I went reluctantly. But I enjoyed the first class so much that I never missed a session for the next seven months. And in the following years, I studied and passed my A+, which certified me to work on computers and I passed the MCSE exams, which qualified me to work on larger computer networks.

Once I received the certification, Gail encouraged me to apply for other positions, each having more to offer than the previous. Gail always gave me great support and encouragement, and she seemed to know exactly what I needed to take the next step forward. For the next few years, because of my training and certifications, instead of applying for positions, recruiters contacted me.

I believe Gail saw potential in me long before I did. She was an integral part of jump-starting my career rehabilitation. What is sad is that as she helped me with my career, our marriage fell apart. It was as if something inside of Gail broke. She stopped cleaning our house, even if she was home all day. She lost her job and didn't bother looking for another. She got out of bed and didn't bother to dress. She went to bed looking exactly the same way she looked when she woke up. I knew my wife was having a difficult time dealing with the deaths of her parents and she had her own health issues in dealing with the effects of multiple fibroid tumors. She seemed able to help others, but not able to help herself. Her heart may have been broken, but she was still able to love. In her darkest hour, she helped me and I'll always love her for it. I tried to return the love by suggesting new career goals, including her in all aspects of my writings and new business ventures, but she wasn't interested.

Death had changed us both and therefore had altered our relationship. I knew a part of me died when Dear died and I did not know how to revive it. But I believed Gail could help me, as she always did. Her methods of healing me had worked before. At night, she shared stories with me from a book she was reading, or from articles about some unique findings by inventors or scientists. I loved her for this, for her constant thirst for answers. There was no one who could hold my attention as she did.

But this time I had put an unfair burden on her. I expected her to save me when she was suffering too.

Before the death of her parents, our house was always clean and in order. I could clean the house from top to bottom in just two hours. After her parents died, the house became cluttered. I so desperately wanted things back the way they were, so I cleaned and cleaned. But things kept coming undone, a little every day.

We both saw it happening, yet we couldn't stop it. It frightened both of us. The only time I remember ever having a serious discussion with Gail regarding the schism between us was in the presence of the therapist. The family was already in weekly counseling, trying to cope with the death of our parents and relatives. The therapist was also a trained marriage counselor so Gail and I continued the sessions. I felt my love for Gail draining from my heart and I didn't know why.

We were in counseling for nearly five years. During one session I broke down in tears and rather than console me or try to make sense of what I was feeling, Gail asked me later, "Why are you so puny in the sessions?' Even now, years later, I remember that remark and it still hurts. To me, she was questioning my manhood and my ability to be the head of the household. I deduced that she had no respect for me.

Over the next few years, the quality of our marriage worsened. For nearly five years there was no intimacy between us. We went out to movies and dinners and visited friends. But our relationship was like that of close friends, not lovers.

I kept trying. One day I called Gail from work and said, "I want you to be ready when I got home, so I can treat you to a romantic evening, starting with dinner." I remember standing in the hall of our home wearing my blue suit, white shirt with cuff links, burgundy shoes with a high gloss shine and a fresh haircut. Gail came from the back yelling, "I'm ready!"

She came out with a colorful scarf tied around her head to keep her hair in place. She wore loose fitting sweat pants and a sweatshirt covered by an oversized burgundy coat. This is hardly what I had in mind for a romantic evening. My teenage daughter looked at her mother with a disappointing gaze, then turned her eyes towards me.

"Daddy is going to leave you one of these days if you keep looking like that," she said.

"Be quiet and stop being disrespectful towards your mother!" I yelled.

We made it to dinner that night and saw a late film, but something was missing. I just wanted to go home and Gail had very little to say during the evening.

My son was in his final year of high school and my daughter was living between the university and home. In addition to doing my computer repairs in the evening, I began working for the Transportation Security Administration in Northern Virginia. I spent long hours at work and when I was home I spent hours mopping, doing laundry and cleaning well into the night.

Then one evening in the fall of 2004, I made a comment to Gail that I still wish I could take back. "Gail you don't do anything; just merely exist," I said.

I was frustrated. But seeing Gail standing before me hurt and dejected, made me see myself as an insensitive, heartless jerk at that moment. I left the room, returning to the kitchen to attend to other matters. Gail removed the top mattress from the bed where we slept and placed it in the bedroom across the hall from her.

She didn't need to tell me what this meant. For whatever time we remained together, she and I would never share a bed again. I slept in the adjacent bedroom. I planned to remain in the house and with Gail for a few more months, until our son graduated from high school. Gail and I discussed the plan and while she wasn't happy about it, she agreed that it was best. Just before Christmas I reminded her of my intentions to leave in the spring.

"You don't expect to stay in this house until then, do you?" she asked in a quiet gentle manner.

I found a two-bedroom apartment in Northwest Washington, D.C and moved out before the end of the week. The thought sickened me of having to walk out on my family, but as I saw it, I had no choice. Even so, I felt as though I was abandoning them.

It was not my initial plan to permanently leave Gail and the children. I tried courting her once I moved out, but the problems that existed between us grew worse. On the couple of occasions when I stopped by to repair the computer, the house was a mess. Gail refused to throw away junk mail and expired coupons and she became angry if anyone else tried to discard them. I even took out a monthly membership to the gym for her. She went once and stopped going. Month after month I paid the bill. I told her over and over again I would cancel the membership if she didn't use it. She became furious with me. Finally, after six months of paying the fee and her never using the membership, I cancelled it without consulting her. For her birthday, I bought tickets to an Isaac Hayes concert. We agreed to meet in the parking lot of the subway near the house. When I arrived, she wasn't there. After waiting for nearly a half hour, I called her. She said she wasn't dressed and she hadn't had a shower.

"What have you been doing all day to cause you to run so late?" I asked.

"I've been home all day, not doing much of anything," she replied.

I was furious. I also realized there was no way we could make it to the show in time, so I returned to my tiny D.C. apartment. I concluded that she wasn't interested in seeing the show or me. After Gail canceled several other dinners and appointments, I just settled into my new life of being alone.

I didn't bother divorcing Gail. I knew how important good health insurance was to her and as long as we were married, she was covered. I had no interest in remarrying so the question of divorce was never an issue. We just stopped communicating with one another. As time passed, if I received any news about Gail, it was through our children. Ariel and Kristina came to visit me in my apartment in Northwest Washington. They ate dinner with me and occasionally I prepared a special dish I knew they enjoyed. On the surface, our relationship appeared normal. We laughed and joked around, but deep down inside, I knew both of them were hurting.

I remember the first time Ariel came to visit. When it was time for him to leave, we walked out the building and I stood there watching him walk away. That moment tore me apart inside. I felt as though I had abandoned all of them, but especially Ariel, who was still in high school. The life they knew, which brought them comfort, security and normality, was gone because of me.

After Ariel graduated from high school, I realized with my children grown I could turn my attention to my own dreams, those hopes I packed away to happily provide for a family. I knew that whatever great adventure unfolded for me next, it would be without Gail at my side. Yet I owed sincere appreciation to her and the experiences we shared; all of that prepared me to have the courage to follow my heart.

Even today, I often think of Gail's loving encouragement and the deep experiences with her family, especially the bond I had with her father. And I cannot separate Gail from our two wonderful children, who came through her and to whom she devoted herself. Not a day passes without me reflecting on how my leaving may have adversely affected them. Ariel was always respectful, but I noticed he was becoming more and more distant. It was like he didn't need me in his life at times. It seemed my daughter and Gail couldn't agree on the simplest things and they fought almost daily.

For years following Dear's death, there were moments when my sadness and anguish overflowed. One morning in particular, I was driving to work while listening to the radio when a song came on that I knew my mother would love. I scribbled down a reminder to share it later with Dear. Then it dawned on me that my mother was dead and I'd never share anything with her again. Ever.

I pulled the car over to the roadside, rested my head against the steering wheel and cried until my eyes hurt and it was difficult to breathe. Friends and comforters reminded me time and time again, "You will come to terms with your mother's death one day."

Five years passed. I waited. I hid my tears, believing I should be further along in my grieving. I did not want my children or wife to see me come undone as I often did.

Maybe this story would have had a different conclusion if Gail and I had not retreated inside ourselves and left the other to deal with their own pain. Thinking back, it would have been healthy and possibly healing for my children to see their father's vulnerability and grief. Instead, I suffered in silence. Gail and I did not discuss what the other was feeling. And now I know pain and grief can cloud one's judgment.

As I saw it at the time, the children needed their father and my wife needed her husband to be strong, resilient, and self-assured. During this time, I was none of the above. For years I mimed masterfully being a good father and husband. In reality, I just wanted to be left alone and become invisible. Maybe my hidden grief just exacerbated the already existing problem, causing my anger to turn into unbridled emotions and hostility. Maybe I took out this anger on my children and the brooding resentment out on my wife. But this is all in retrospect. In that moment, I thought I was doing what was best for my family.

CHAPTER 22: THE SECRET

Archie Lee Cooper, Sr. is the only man I will ever call "my father."

A year before Dad's call to tell me he was dying, my brother Archie called on Skype while I was working on the computer at my home in Naples, Italy where I had moved years earlier (after accepting a permanent position following a brief assignment as a contractor in Europe). Archie and I often shared early morning face-to-face chats. I always looked forward to talking to him. Sometimes he called at three and four o'clock in the morning, waking me from a deep sleep. I didn't mind at all. I love him very much and told him that regularly. On this morning there was something noticeably strange and different about him. Archie wasn't one to mince words or engage in foolish bantering, but on this day he filled our conversation with small talk. While we were chatting, his eyes stared downward toward his computer keyboard. To me, he looked as if he was searching for the right words to say something. I didn't press him. My respect for him was near reverential. I sat quietly and patiently, eyes focused on the bright computer screen.

"I've been waiting for the right time to tell you something," he said, while still focusing elsewhere. "I am not sure this is the right time, but I think you should know."

I wasn't excited or eagerly anticipating hearing whatever words had taken refuge in his mouth and did not allow him to look me in the eyes. I just wasn't sure what to think, so I remained neutral.

Archie sighed. "Ok, here goes: Daddy is not your real father."

I was speechless. Archie was silent too. Archie must have braced himself for the floodgate to fly open and a sea of emotions and questions to come gushing from my mouth. I didn't say a word.

"We, I mean I, think that your real father was a football player from Detroit and he and Dear had their moment at some point." I knew that what he meant by "moment" was that Dear had been in an affair early in her marriage to Daddy.

I said nothing. I was not upset or nervous. I felt the same as I had felt before Archie called. Maybe subconsciously I suspected this to be true way before he told me. After all, when I was much younger, Daddy never missed a chance to tell me I was not his child. Now, I didn't care. My only concern was to continue standing guard over whatever fleeting moments of peace my father might enjoy. At this point, the doctors told him his cancer had returned and he needed to start aggressive treatment immediately if he was going to stand a chance. My father refused the treatment. This man I loved so much and hated so much was the only father I'd ever known. Archie's disclosure, though well intended, had zero effect on me and how I felt about Daddy.

Maybe the thought of having another man's son under his roof as a result of Dear's infidelity was too much for my father. Was this the reason he beat Dear and treated me so badly?

Archie's words gave meaning to who I am *not*, but said nothing about who I am. I had no questions for him. He tilted his head to the side, raised his eyes and looked at me for the first time. He looked perplexed.

"Archie, please don't share this information with anyone else," I said.

I definitely didn't want Daddy to know I was aware of this. His pain and anguish already kept him company day and night. The realization that I discovered he was not my real father would only bring him more sadness.

It was nearly a half year later, shortly after spring planting, before seedlings had barely taken root, when Daddy called me to say, "I don't think I'm gonna make it," he said, as his words filtered through a laboriously strained whisper of a voice.

Daddy was tired of living. I knew this from discussions we'd shared. My grandmother (Dear's mother) had departed peacefully in her sleep in the guest room in her house six years after Dear died. Daddy was the only remaining elder in the Cooper family. Archie lived in my grandmother's house, after returning from Houston years prior. My dear brother Archie had assumed the unlikely role as our family's gatekeeper between this life and whatever lies in the hereafter. He had cared for and buried Dear and Muh. And now it was Daddy's turn to leave.

Archie had been calling me regularly the past few days to ask my opinion on what type of coffin to purchase or which minister should preside at Daddy's funeral.

"I trust whatever decisions you make,' I told him.

Daddy knew his time was drawing near and he was ready.

"Everybody's gone," my father said. "Marie, my momma, my daddy, my sister and every last one of my friends. I'm the only one left. It's time for me to go, too."

When Daddy called to say this to me, a wave of calm rushed over me. It was the end of March, 2012. I listened intensely to each word that parted his lips. As he spoke, I walked about my living room, flicking off one light after the other. I still don't know why. Maybe under the cloak of darkness, I could hide the pain I did not or could not feel. I had already shed enough tears over the years for my mother to wash away much of the sadness I thought I had reserved for Daddy. But Daddy got to say he was ready to die. Who was I to try to make him stay?

"I know Daddy, I know," I said.

CHAPTER 23: O' BLESS ME FATHER

Daddy had cried daily for nearly 13 years, since the day of Dear's accident. He cried until he died. Shortly after Dear's death, I recall helplessly watching the veins bulge on his trembling hands as he struggled to remove the white plastic lid from the little orange tube containing his anti-depressants. But those pills never seemed to release him from his torment. I remember 10 years after the accident seeing my father sitting in his old rusty metal garden chair on his front porch, with tears streaming down his lineless face.

"Len, what am I supposed to do?" he cried. "What am I supposed to do, Len?"

My heart broke into a million pieces and fell through the cracks of that gray wooden deck.

Now, I traveled to Alabama to anchor myself by my father's bedside.

I pulled up to the house and Archie greeted me in the front yard with a warm embrace. We stood under this monstrous oak tree whose branches spread clear across the top of the house onto the backyard, a tree my grandfather had planted when I was a child.

Inside, Archie said, "Daddy has lost a lot of weight and he is quite frail. Sometimes it's hard to hear him when he speaks, but he is in good spirits."

We headed down the hall towards Daddy's room.

He was exactly as Archie described him. He reached out for my hand and gently pulled me towards him. Daddy's knuckles, wrists and elbows all looked like swollen knots on a tree branch. His eyes sunk deep into the recesses of their sockets. Where his jaws once stood were two deep depressions on either side of his face.

"Hey Len, how you doing?" he whispered, while stroking my hand and dawning a clear smile that stretched the width of his tiny face. He sat up in the hospital bed that hospice had provided. "Len look at me," he said, holding up both hands, twisting them back and forth, exposing the palms, then the back of the hands, over and over again. He had wasted away to a thin layer of skin wrapped around bone.

I noticed his grooming accessories on the chair across the room. My father sat up with the head of the bed elevated as I lathered and shaved him, then I trimmed his hair. I didn't bother asking him and he didn't object. He slept through the entire procedure.

"It's almost over," he whispered with his eyes closed.

"Are you scared?" I asked, pausing from my haircutting chore.

"No" he replied in a calm tone. "I wish I could be in my own house, but what can I do? I'm not hurting. I'm alright."

Daddy had stomach surgery as part of his cancer treatment shortly after Dear's death. I came home from Washington, D.C. just to take him fishing, his first true love. I had to pick him up and place him in the small aluminum boat. I was hoping I could grant him this joy one last time, but he was too weak.

"Make sure that boy, Marilyn's boy, keeps the grass cut at the house for me," said Daddy, while looking out the large window next to his bed. His eyes were focused as if he was looking beyond anything outside that old window.

I am my father's son. At that moment, I loved him so much more than I had ever hated him. Like Dear, after she received news that she would be dead in a matter of months from cancer, Daddy assumed an honorable demeanor as he walked in the shadows of death. He had no fear and thought only of us and our well-being. Daddy was leaving this world with class and on his terms. My admiration for him grew each passing day.

"I don't want you all worrying about me. I am fine," he whispered in a raspy voice. "I have a little something in the bank for you. Your name is on it and you can do as you please with it."

In all of our conversations that afternoon, he never once asked me about ministers, prayers, God or anything that had to do with religion. I suppose the afterlife was of little concern to him.

I recalled a previous trip to visit Daddy, when he had asked me if I believed in God?

"Daddy, you know there are millions of people who swear by it," I replied.

"No Len," he followed. "I want to know if *you* believe in God and heaven and if there is a hell?"

Daddy and I had always been candid without reservation, without hesitation. This time was no different.

"No Daddy, I don't," I said. "I am 100% certain we got most of that wrong."

Surprisingly, he returned to reading the paper and chomping down on that pipe with no further questions.

In the morning, I rose when the dew was still on the grass and returned to Daddy's bedside. Alfred, my middle brother, drove 10 hours from Houston, Texas to spend a couple of hours with Daddy before turning around the same day and driving back. This was the first time the three of us brothers had been together in more than 20 years. Alfred had relocated to Houston more than 30 years before, to raise his family and open a car repair shop.

The three of us sat on Alfred's old car, surrounded by some of my nieces and nephews. There, Alfred, Archie and I exchanged tales of our childhood that fascinated the young ones. This went on until Alfred had to leave.

All the while I was with my father, there were relatively few calls and almost no visitors. I had witnessed him giving money to needy relatives and friends. Where were they? Some people called and offered to pray for him, but they didn't come in person. Daddy never complained about the lack of visitors, so I reckon it bothered me a lot more than it bothered him.

"It would be nice if they offered to sit with him or bring by a bucket of chicken so no one would have to cook," my brother said. "I guess they feel they have fulfilled their religious and moral obligation by just offering to pray for him."

I couldn't spend too much time second-guessing the motives of those who were supposed to be close to Dear and Daddy. Each day, I returned to my father's bedside and remained there until he fell asleep. When he asked me to get him an order of shrimp from the nearby restaurant, I did. He ate half of one shrimp and said, 'That's enough."

While he was dying, Daddy and I covered every topic from the Middle East crisis to U.S. politics. He was animated and engaging, although his voice was raw and sounded like his throat was filled with gravel. As we sat talking one afternoon, in the middle of a sentence he became silent. His eyes were partially closed. There was nothing. No breathing. He did not move. I had seen this before with Gail's father the day before he died. After about 10 seconds or so, Daddy's eyes refocused as his head sank deeper into the white cotton pillow.

I returned to my parents' home. I lay atop Dear's quilts for what seemed like hours, reflecting on all that Dear had to endure in this life. My pillow caught the tears that rolled off my chin. When the sadness was too much, I rolled over and wrapped myself in one of my mother's patchwork blankets, trying to recall the feel of Dear's embrace.

Archie and I spent much of one day at the funeral home, making the final selection for the coffin and taking care of other details. I wanted no part of any of this, but knew Archie shouldn't have to make the preparations alone. I appreciated the time with him while wishing simultaneously that it were under different circumstances. That night, after hours of tossing and turning, I slipped into a deep rest.

Around eight o'clock the following morning, the house phone rang. I knew who it was.

"Daddy passed away this morning," Archie said, calmly. "If you want to see him before they take him away, you should come quickly."

"I prefer you take care of that before I come," I said.

I had decided long ago that once my parents drew their final breath, I would not lay eyes on them again. I never wanted my memory of them associated with the visual of their dead bodies in a casket. My wishes had been dismissed by well-intentioned but misguided relatives at my mother's funeral. But on this day, I was able to avoid the image of my father lying cold and lifeless.

I wanted so badly to cry during the drive to Archie's, but the tears wouldn't come. I arrived at the house around the same time as the coroner. I got out the car, but when I saw two men walk up the steps and into the house with a stretcher, I turned away. Leaning against the car, I drew indistinguishable figures in the gravel with the tip of my shoe. I needed to be distracted. Again, I did not want the last image of my beloved father to be one related to death rather than life. I needed this moment to myself, free of meaningless chatter, just me alone with my thoughts and despair. By all accounts, it was a glorious day for Daddy to die.

My mother's death had left me damaged and broken. Some pieces of my life would never fit again after Dear left. My grief for Daddy was different. Even as I mourned my father, deep inside I felt in time I would be okay. With my mother I never felt that reassurance. The pain of her loss seemed to be a permanent part of me, like walking or breathing. There was never a second in Dear's life when I did not love her. I had to learn to love my father after hating him for so long. I knew that Daddy was going to die and I was well prepared for it. Dear was taken suddenly, tragically and her death turned my world upside down.

I stood at the window, unable to move. As a little boy, I spent hours in that window waiting for Dear to come get my brothers and me after a long tiring day of working at the ladies clothing store. In my mind, I could still see Daddy Yo sitting on the front porch in one of those cheap nylon folding lawn chairs he bought from Sears Roebuck. He dug his hands deep into the pockets of his blue denim Liberty overalls, searching for his brown and white ivory handled pocketknife. I remembered how he removed his top denture and used the tip of that knife to flick out whatever was trapped between his false teeth. I remembered looking out to see Muh bent over at the waist with spade in hand, turning the earth surrounding her Begonias and rose bushes while humming an unfamiliar tune.

This was the same window where Muh placed her blue and white plastic candelabra during the Christmas season; the same window where I stood, watching for the return of the summer sun after a mighty downpour; the same window where as a child I prayed my grandfather would put a single bullet in my father. Now I stood at that window crying uncontrollably for my father, the man who brought my family torment for so many years.

I did not know it yet, but as agonizing as my grief was for Daddy's death, it was to be short lived compared to the length of the grief I felt for Dear. Dear, in all her imperfections was everything to me and in many ways I realize even today that this is still true. I see no end to my mourning for my mother.

My Father died the morning of April 4, 2012 and his funeral followed three days after. We buried him next to my mother. There was no repeat of what happened at Dear's funeral, no zealous relatives imposing their wishes on me, no viewing of my father's remains, no graveside singing or prayers. And I kept my promise to myself to never visit Dear's gravesite. The morning of my father's burial, I wished my brother well as I headed to the airport.

EPILOGUE

I've exhausted way too much energy searching for God, then hating Him and denying Him, only to discover that I am no closer to understanding Him now than I was when I was a boy in my mother's church. A colored boy in Birmingham in the 1950s needed God. He certainly couldn't depend on the fellow human beings he knew, especially not on white people, who did evil things like set a bomb in a church that killed four little girls. So I explored the depths of my being, trying to make sense of God's purpose and how I fit into His plan. Yet for me, God has been and I suppose will forever remain an elusive dream.

None of it matters much to me now, anyway. And it hasn't mattered for a very long time. This may have been coincidental but my life became meaningful and peaceful once I released religion and all that it encompasses. Prayer and scriptures have been absent from my life for decades.

It isn't necessary for me to look to ancient scripts or lore as a guide for living a good and correct life. Dear raised me to be good. If I follow her example of love, my life will naturally be a constant, never ending mantra for goodness, an echo of her melodic rhythms of kindness and grace. When I step out of my own way I am drawn towards experiences that are enriching and enlightening to my life. The hermits of St. George's Monastery near Jerusalem once told me, "Your spirit knows the truth when it hears it."

The feelings of being detached from God and life, set apart, not quite fitting in, are all still very much a part of me and dwells just beneath the surface, as it does with the 'knee baby.' Other than being a constant reminder of the road I've traveled throughout my life, these feelings no longer play a part in determining my future as they did before.

In the height of my despair, when I first moved to Washington D.C, I truly had to hit rock bottom before I looked up and took note of just how far I had fallen. It was then that my spirit taught me the true meaning of giving through selfless acts of sharing, as well as receiving graciously. On the streets, I learned that when we give, we should give freely to all who ask in sincerity. Give to strangers, friends and foe alike. When you are down to your last, this is when you should give the most. Character is tested when you hold true to your values under the worse possible conditions. Expect nothing in return, no blessing, no rewards no accolades. Give anonymously and joyfully. If you have no money to give then share your abilities and your availability.

People often tell me, "God has blessed you beyond measure." I am in no position to argue that point. One thing is for certain, I have benefited equally in my relationships with the saved and those judged as sinners; with the clean and unclean, the righteous and the transgressors. At one point, I traveled halfway around the world, trying to connect with God, camping out under the heavens in the Judean desert and seeking the wisdom of the desert fathers. I didn't find God, but I found a place that felt like home. And I realized that it felt like home because I found unconditional love from strangers, people with whom I did not share a language or customs. I had to suffer and then return to Alabama with new eyes and a contrite heart to forgive the pedophile pastor who baptized me and introduced me to Jesus. There was no burning bush moment when I realized I could *forgive*.

I did not have to inherit the God of the Baptist or Catholic Church or the God of a racist white Christian who would ask a poor grieving man to pay the bill of his newly deceased wife. But I had to learn to forgive them all. Once I learned to forgive all of my transgressors, I had to learn the most difficult lesson of all: To forgive myself.

As a Black man, I have grown up in a country that hated me and insisted that I give respect to a God created in the image and likeness of the white men who hated me. This is asking too much! I can fashion God into who or what I want Him to be. I can accept the teachings, which are good, fair and just from all the worlds' religions, and I can discard the rest. Love should be the mortar, which binds the entire community together. For me there is no God that requires of me praise and thanksgiving without ceasing or finds long suffering to be noble. I chose to follow one simple rule: To love everybody and all of creation over and above all things.

I long for my mother's calming caress on the back of my neck and ears. I miss the smell of her Dixie Peach pressing oil that filled the air when she styled her hair. The pain of losing Dear and a never-ending longing for Jerusalem are my constant companions.

Today, I call the chaotic majestic city of Naples, Italy home. My peaceful slumber is gently awakened by the fiery sunrise blazing the slopes of Mount Vesuvius. Shallow mist caresses the deep blue waters as the bay's glittering waves dance below licking the rocky shores. In the fall of my years, sadness lingers on my stage. Yet, with the dawning of each day, I am granted another opportunity to make the day better than the one before. I live in great expectation of what tomorrow may bring. I try to savor the sweetness of life; squeezing it for the last drop, like I squeezed nectar from the Alabama honey suckle outside my mother's door. More often than not, the balance of happiness tilts in my favor. Even without my Dear, my heart and soul are filled with gratitude and joy, unspeakable joy, as I continue reaching towards an upward call.

50523147R00220

Made in the USA
Columbia, SC
08 February 2019